"The Transfiguring Sword"

STUDIES IN RHETORIC AND COMMUNICATION
General Editors:
E. Culpepper Clark
Raymie E. McKerrow
David Zarefsky

Cheryl R. Jorgensen-Earp

"The Transfiguring Sword"
The Just War of the Women's Social and Political Union

The University of Alabama Press   Tuscaloosa and London

Copyright © 1997
The University of Alabama Press
Tuscaloosa, Alabama 34587–0380
All rights reserved
Manufactured in the United States of America

∞

The paper on which this book is printed meets the minimum requirements of
American National Standard for Information Science–Permanence of Paper for
Printed Library Materials, ANSI Z39.48–1984.

Library of Congress Cataloging-in-Publication Data

Jorgensen-Earp, Cheryl R., 1952–
     The transfiguring sword : the just war of the women's social and
political union / Cheryl R. Jorgensen-Earp.
        p.   cm. — (Studies in rhetoric and communication)
     Includes bibliographical references and index.
     ISBN 0–8173–0870–9 (cloth : alk. paper)
     1. Women's Social and Political Union (Great Britain)—History.
2. Suffragists—Great Britain—History. 3. Women—Suffrage—Great
Britain—History. 4. Political violence—Great Britain—History.
I. Title   II. Series.
JN976.J67   1997
324.6'23'0941—dc20   96–34736

British Library Cataloguing-in-Publication Data available

For Mama
Born seventeen days after women
achieved the franchise in this country.
With her humor, cleverness, and resolve,
she would have made a wonderful suffragette.

Contents

Acknowledgments

Books only come into being through a collaborative effort, and I am deeply grateful to all who contributed to this book's completion. In attempting to acknowledge at least some of these efforts, I must begin where this project started—in the Speech Communication Department at the University of Washington. I want to thank Haig Bosmajian for his willingness to share his expertise and his ability both to challenge and support. Many thanks are due to Barbara Warnick, not simply for her excellent critique of this project but for her continuing encouragement in so many ways. My special thanks go to John Campbell, now at the University of Memphis. John was largely responsible for my early interest in the suffragettes, and he guided this project with his typical insight and care. I only wish that everyone in academics could have such a generous mentor and friend. I would like to thank Nicole Mitchell of the University of Alabama Press and the reviewers who gave such excellent advice on the revisions. I would particularly like to thank Karlyn Kohrs Campbell for her very helpful guidance. I also want to thank such supportive friends as Ann Staton, Katie Heintz-Knowles, Paula Wilson, and all of my colleagues in the Communication Studies Department at Lynchburg College.

I have always relied upon the kindness of librarians. It has been my good fortune to have the help of the librarians of Knight-Capron Library at Lynchburg College. I have yet to have a question they could not answer or a problem they could not solve, and their continuing good humor is always appreciated. My thanks, also, to the librarians of Fintel Library at Roanoke College, who were so helpful in the early stages of this project.

The WSPU cartoons reproduced in this volume were originally published in *Votes for Women* and *The Suffragette*. They appear here by permission of The British Library. I would like to thank Sue Tryon for her excellent work in reproducing the illustrations. Financial support for the inclusion of these cartoons was provided by the Faculty Research and Development Committee at Lynchburg College. The "Verbatim report of Mrs. Pankhurst's speech, delivered Nov. 13, 1913 at Parson's Theatre, Hartford, Connecticut" first appeared in pamphlet form published by the Connecticut Women's Suffrage Association. Quotations from this speech appear in this book by permission of the General Research Division, The New York Public Library, Astor, Lenox and Tilden Foundations.

Finally, and most importantly, I want to thank my family. Like Emmeline Pankhurst, I have "drawn prizes in the lucky bag of life, in the shape of [a] good father, [a] good husband," and a good son. My father would have "gotten a kick" out of seeing this book published, and my one regret is that he is not here to be handed a copy. My love and thanks go to my husband, Darwin, who has no fear of "strong-minded" women. Without his love, patience, and very practical support, this book would have never been finished. And my love also goes to my son, Ethan, who has patiently shared his mother with women of another era. He is a constant reminder of that better world for which the suffragettes risked so much.

"The Transfiguring Sword"

Introduction

In the opening days of 1913, English militant suffragette Mary Richardson, accompanied by another young woman now believed to have been Lilian Lenton, made a quickly arranged journey to Birmingham. Traveling under the names Polly Dick and Lilian Mitchell, they spent the night at the home of a sympathizer who had herself arranged to be out of town on the pretext of visiting an ailing sister in London. In the absence of their hostess, the two women were entertained at dinner by the sympathizer's husband, a businessman completely unaware of the women's suffragette ties or the true purpose of their visit. After dinner, the two women retired to the library for tea and, at ten o'clock, to their room for a few hours of sleep. Richardson was awakened by her companion with the news that "Black Jennie," a homemade bomb in a marmalade pot, was "spluttering" in its hiding place in the wardrobe. As Richardson later recounted, the two women dressed quickly:

We were soon ready. Lilian opened the wardrobe door. "You carry Jennie," she said casually.

I looked at Jennie in alarm. She was certainly spluttering and hissing. I felt that my last moment had come, and the thing would explode the moment I touched it. To pick up that black bag with the home-made time bomb inside terrified me. I took the strings of the bag carefully in my fingers and lifted. The splutterings increased.

"Don't drop her, whatever you do," Lilian said. She led the way.[1]

The two women slipped out of the house and traveled on foot along the dark edges of fields to the newly constructed railway station. Climbing through an uncompleted section of roof, they left "Jennie" inside the station. Richardson and Lenton then retraced their steps to the house and tiptoed to their room. Reaching there undetected, they climbed into bed after taking double doses of aspirin to ensure that they would sleep through the noise of the explosion. Over breakfast the next morning, the two women responded with innocent surprise as their host angrily read the morning paper and railed against "those blasted women" who had blown up the new railway station.[2]

The destruction of isolated railway stations was only one of a series of violent acts perpetrated by the Women's Social and Political Union (WSPU), the militant branch of the English women's suffrage movement. During the final two and a half years of its active involvement in the suffrage campaign, the WSPU turned to arson, bombing, and widespread property destruction as strategies to acquire the franchise for women. The guerrilla militancy of the final years of the WSPU campaign was limited only by restrictions against physically harming anyone (except themselves). The catchphrase used in the union to describe (and, indeed, extend) this prohibition was that "not even a cat or canary must be harmed."[3] Despite this prohibition, the WSPU strategies culminated in thirty-three months of what is properly called a terrorist campaign. Because of its rarity, terrorist violence by reform movements, and the rhetoric that frames and justifies it, has seldom been examined. Such terrorism seeks only limited change and is often directed at government policies on very specific issues. Occasionally it may be inspired by anger at a particular public official or used to punish an organization for taking some specific action. Generally, such terrorism is limited to attacks upon property. Examples of such attacks include Welsh nationalist protests that resulted in more than eighty arson attacks during a seven-year period (1979–86) against summer cottages belonging to English urbanites.[4] Examples closer to home include the modern anti-abortion movement, which went from pressuring the government for reform and picketing abortion clinics to physically barricading, bombing, and torching these clinics. In the same movement there was a growing tendency to terrorize "abortionist" doctors with threats against their families and property. Of course, with the advent of actual murders of doctors performing abortions, the level of violence in the anti-abortion movement escalated beyond that of reformist terrorism. The animal-rights movement has also escalated its tactics from picketing of science labs using animals for research to bombing and torching such labs. "Raids" are conducted against the labs, and sometimes diseased animals are set free. Some animal-rights groups have physically threatened (or attacked the private property of) scientists who conduct research using laboratory animals.

The escalation of militant strategies in reform groups is triggered by the need to make the movement visible and to place movement concerns high on the current political agenda. Reform movements quickly learn that the ability to force others to attend to their message requires a certain degree of power.[5] If movement members already possessed conventional power, they would work through "the system" to have their needs addressed and, quite probably, would never mobilize into a reform movement. In lieu of such power, movements attempt to force a crisis, a breach of social norms that will redefine their invisible and powerless movement as a potent entity to be ignored only at the peril of the status quo. The rhetoric of violence becomes a means to create reality, to guarantee that movement issues become salient.[6] Reformers as well as revolutionaries learn the lesson that their concerns will be addressed only when they are made equally salient for those in power. Such salience may come naturally from the issue itself, but, if necessary, it may be artificially produced by forcing a crisis of confrontation or strategic violence.

Political actors with inadequate resources need to find novel activities to promote their political agendas. For many social movements, this need for innovation leads to an escalation into violent strategies and, ultimately, into terrorism.[7] The relationship between violence and persuasion is never simple. Like many nonverbal acts, violence is a "clumsy and ambiguous mode of communication."[8] Terrorism is a "communication strategy" in which the process of communication is "activated and amplified by violence."[9] That the terrorist act is *political* violence means that "it is theoretically and practically rhetorical." Furthermore, terrorists see themselves as engaged in a conversation with the power structure and often describe their actions as responses to the violence that exists in the system itself. They characterize *their* acts of violence as answers in an ongoing dialogue, "a response that *communicates*," and, through this conversation of violence, they attempt to change attitudes and behavior in the larger society.[10] However, terrorism is a rejection of *conventional* communication. Bombing may thus become a "form of language" designed to gain access when other forms of communication are blocked.[11] Through violence, terrorists hope to break through perceived impediments to communication, end their isolation, and give their ideas value in the larger community.[12] The resort to violence is an indication that more conventional discourse and compromise have failed.[13]

The audience-centered emphasis of terrorism allows researchers in the field of communication to speak of a rhetoric of terrorism. But if there is a general consensus among rhetoricians that violence speaks, there is little acknowledgment that its voice may be a female one. Recognition that women have utilized violence in their own cause is not common even in feminist scholarship. Our societal problem with the very concept of women and violent behavior is particularly evident when the female terrorist is considered. According to Maxwell Taylor, "The woman terrorist seems to offer a challenge to the contemporary stereotype of the woman as caregiver and protector and the notion of the violent woman seems to give rise to both horror and fantasy for Western man. It also seems to offer an unusual reflection on the notion of 'equality' of opportunity, and clearly reflects upon our most deep seated prejudices about gender appropriate behavior, especially with respect to fighting and aggression."[14] Interestingly, one of the loudest voices raised to divorce women from acts of terrorist violence comes from feminist critic Robin Morgan. Viewing the terrorist as "the logical incarnation of patriarchal politics in a technological world," Morgan states quite accurately that "the majority of terrorists—and those against whom they are rebelling—are men." Women, along with children, are caught in the middle of terrorist violence, usually as the victim, or, as Morgan quotes the Vietnamese proverb, women are "the grass that gets trampled when the elephants fight." Although statistically Morgan may be correct that "history is a record of most women *acting peaceably*, and of most men *acting belligerently*" (emphasis in original), this view is largely responsible for a misreading of women's capacity for terrorist violence in general and the WSPU's use of such violence in particular.[15] In his book *Crusaders, Criminals, and Crazies*, Frederick Hacker states that "no violent terroristic act has been performed specifically to advertise or further the cause of women's liberation."[16] Morgan makes the same point when she writes that "women as a group do not mobilize for our own rights through violent means."[17] I would disagree with both statements and point to the WSPU as proof that women have used terrorism specifically to obtain their rights.[18]

Do the violent actions of the WSPU "fit" with current definitions of terrorism? Chalmers Johnson provides as criteria "the employment of destructive violence, its use against political targets, and the sporadic and clandestine nature of the acts. The latter element [is] felt to be necessary to exclude terrorism, planned or unplanned, which is intrinsic or incidental to 'an ongoing movement of armed revolution.' "[19] Certainly, the suffragettes employed "destructive violence," and these were not minor acts but involved arson, bombing, and destruction of public artwork and private property. Their target was ultimately political; for, even though one hallmark of violent militancy was the attack on private property, the suffragettes made it very clear that their primary target was the government. The whole purpose for striking at private property was to force the public to pressure the government to yield to union demands. And the WSPU at this phase operated in the "guerrilla" fashion through clandestine operations and an avoidance of arrest whenever possible. Perhaps the best indication of the terrorist nature of the WSPU acts is Lisa Tickner's brief assessment: "No longer interested in converting the public, they [the suffragettes] set out to astound and appal it."[20]

Also, in their final phase of militancy (following a massive breaking of store windows on November 21, 1911) the WSPU entered into the "fundamental triangular relationship" that Robin Gerrits calls the distinguishing feature of the terrorist strategy.[21] In terrorism there is generally a split between the target of terrorist action (the victim) and the *actual* target of the action, the person or persons intended to be influenced by the violence. This audience component is vital to Schmid and de Graaf: "Violence, to become terroristic, requires witnesses." When the suffragettes attacked private property rather than official property belonging to (or symbolic of) the government, they moved to a third-party strategy that sought to pressure the "guilty" (the Liberal government) through attacks upon the "innocent" (the British public). The British public thus became "merely instrumental, the skin on a drum beaten to achieve a calculated impact on a wider audience."[22]

Why is it important to see WSPU violence in terms of terrorism? It is not to prove that women are as, or more, violent than men but to see the suffragettes as they saw themselves and to characterize properly the nature and extent of their militancy. There is a tendency to read suffragette actions in the way most conducive to the particular political point the writer is seeking. For example, Robin Morgan, in seeking to show terrorist violence as a problem with the patriarchy, describes WSPU violence in the following manner: "I read about the Pankhurst women in the British suffrage movement. Careful acts of select damage only ever against property. No harm to life. Mass demonstrations. Humor (red-pepper 'bombs' thrown at the king in procession). Hunger strikes while in prison. Militance without a lust for death."[23] The reader who turns from this description (or from George Dangerfield's description of "small bands of women" with their bedraggled "little purple banerettes") to actual accounts of suffragette violence will be deeply surprised.[24] Although many of the suffragette attacks were imaginative, the continuous destruction of letter boxes and resulting loss of important mail, the nearly daily window-breaking raids on private businesses, the destruction of telegraph lines (particularly the severing of the connections between London and Glasgow), and the destruction of valuable museum artwork must have seemed more than a humorous nuisance. The slashing of Velasquez's *Rokeby Venus,* the bombing of Chancellor of the Exchequer Lloyd George's new home, and the vandalizing of the Kew Garden Orchid House (destroying some flowers that had taken ten years to cultivate) were acts that rival the property destruction of any number of terrorist groups. Life under threat of suffragette violence took on a different feel: fifty caddies guarded night and day the golf links at Walton Heath where Lloyd George played, guards were posted at corner letter boxes, and "children played the 'Suffragette Game,' placing homemade bombs on neighbours' doorsteps, and parading with handwritten sandwich boards threatening 'Votes or Boms.' " The press (earlier so silent on constitutional suffrage efforts) kept the public constantly apprised of the danger: " 'Bombs have been found in St. Paul's Cathedral and elsewhere,' said the Press. 'London is "locked up," and very great nervousness prevails.' "[25] It is only when the destructive nature of WSPU reformist terrorism is fully acknowledged that we can appreciate the strategic nature of both the acts of violence themselves and the rhetoric that accompanied and justified those acts.

One problem with past studies of the Women's Social and Political Union has been their failure to examine the union's turn to terrorism from a rhetorical perspective. Very quickly the question always turns to whether WSPU terrorism was an *effective* tactic in support of their reformist cause. The effectiveness of WSPU violence is (and always must be) difficult to assess, largely because of the intervention of World War I and the resulting time lapse between the end of violent militancy and the granting of the franchise. Although the specific pro and con arguments over suffrage militancy have been put forward extensively, what has been lacking is a broader perspective that views the adoption of violent tactics as a question of rhetorical invention. The WSPU provides a case study of two important aspects of reformist violence hitherto underexplored. First, it is the pressure of changing rhetorical exigencies that leads many reform groups to escalate their tactics to the level of terrorism. Second, there are inventional resources that skilled rhetors can use to frame acts of reformist terrorism in ways that make them intelligible to the general public. Through an examination of the rhetoric of the WSPU, this study will show the power of rhetoric to justify actions that on their face seem unjustifiable.

To say that skilled rhetorical invention can justify violence by a group of women reformers is not to say that the task is easy. Clearly, the burden of rhetorical justification falls more heavily upon women adopting what has always been perceived as an option granted only to men. Women, if only by cultural fiat, cannot adopt a strategy of

Two lessons from this case study

violence without appearing to violate the philosophy of care considered vital to feminine nature and a feminine style of discourse. Arguments are still made, as they commonly were during the Victorian and Edwardian periods, for the "existence of women's special skills in regard to children, health care, education and domestic morality."[26] The concept of woman that has changed least over time is her role as nurturer. The modern version of the nurturing role can be seen in the "caretaker" image currently addressed by feminist writers.[27] In general, women still carry the primary burden of caregiving for the young, the ill, and the elderly. Expressing impatience, demanding political change, and taking violent action are the antithesis of the patience, self-renunciation, and unconditional love that we expect from the caretakers of society.

true!

true

Strategic violence also violates a feminine style of discourse, for it is both authoritarian and confrontational.[28] Rather than allowing the public to draw its own conclusions from the discourse presented by the agent of change, the use of violence presumes that the agent has already decided what is right. This decision is then urged on the public in a forceful manner. Women who utilize violence must justify their acts to a greater extent than men, for whom aggression is seen as a more natural and acceptable trait. Even if the double standard for the use of political violence has lessened today in the wake of the Weathermen, it was certainly in place during the time of the suffrage campaign. G. K. Chesterton wrote disapprovingly about the use of militant tactics in a 1910 *Illustrated London News* article: "The tactics were bad because they were not female and did not use the natural weapons. A woman putting up her fists at a man is a woman putting herself in the one position which does not frighten him."[29] Many women refused to take part in even nominal militancy, not because the actions were wrong in themselves but because they were wrong for women.

In moving to violent tactics, reformers also face justificatory pressures not shared by their revolutionary counterparts. It is the difference between the revolutionary goal and the goal of the reformer that would appear to preclude the use of strategic violence by the latter. The reformer does not seek the overthrow of the current system but the "change or repair of particular laws, customs, or practices." Reformers seek their rightful place within the system as well as the power to correct the flaws within that system as it currently stands. Yet, as years turn into decades in the pursuit of a particular reform goal, even movements that desire to maintain the purity of classic reform methods find it difficult to do so. The influx of a new generation seeking an old reform may revitalize a movement but may also lead the movement to question the patient strategies of the past. It is not only internal pressures that may force a change in reformist tactics. If the desired changes appear no closer to being obtained as a reform movement ages, and the routes of protest become increasingly overburdened, there may seem to be little choice but to escalate into militancy or violence.[30]

Although a movement may adopt new actions that are efficacious from a practical standpoint, these actions may carry a heavy burden of rhetorical justification. At such times the action of a movement "runs ahead" of the rhetoric in place to justify movement strategies. The movement is left with the distinctly rhetorical problem of justifying new and controversial tactics within an old framework of discourse that is not always adequate to the task. The movement must either find space for the new actions within the old rhetorical framework or must develop a "line of talk" that will provide new justifications for the new strategies. These rhetorical pressures are only exacerbated when the new action undertaken by the movement involves terrorist violence. One problem faced by movement rhetors is managing both the violence and the perceptions of violence as it occurs. In his study of the Chartist movement, James Andrews claims that the problem of the Chartists, "who never, after all, advocated the outright overthrow of existing institutions, but, rather, their radical amendment, was when and under what circumstances to encourage violence, or at least threaten it, and how to control violence so that the whole repressive weight of government was not brought to bear to destroy the movement."[31] A reform movement must rhetorically control the way its violence is perceived by those outside the movement. The reformers must strike a balance between encouraging sufficient terrorist action to be taken seriously as a threat and promoting the restraint necessary to maintain their legitimacy as agents of reform rather than revolution. Even after the movement ends its use of violence or once the reform is achieved, there is a need to persuade the larger structure to accept the reformers "back into the fold." Because they do not seek an overthrow of the system, reformers will be dealing in the postreform future with the very people whom they now vilify and whose property and livelihood they now physically attack. Although reformist terrorists are aware that they are breaking the law at the time of protest, I see little in their rhetoric that indicates a belief that, in the shining future wrought by their successful reform, they will continue to be treated as outlaws.

In these reform groups, too, there is a rhetorical tension between the extradiscursive rhetoric of the terrorist act and the reformist values held by movement members. Reformers are generally led into the desire for reform by their highly developed sense of what is morally right. Jerome Skolnick claims that for some reformers, "the ethical posture of nonviolence is no less important than the cause for which they may be agitating." Therefore, the rhetoric of the reformist terrorist must justify movement violence not only to the dual external audiences of the target of reform (usually the government) and the general public (which can bring pressure on the target of reform), but also to the internal audience of movement members who must carry out the violence. Movement members must also be inspired to take part in the new activities. Because, as Skolnick puts it, the "cultural fear of violence is psychologically damaging and may be politically inhibiting," the use of violence must be negotiated both outside and inside the reform movement.[32] For the benefit of both the external and internal audience, then, there is a need for the extradiscursive rhetoric of the terrorist act to be mediated by an accompanying discursive rhetoric.

The increased need to justify violent tactics faced by both women and reformers resulted in a double justificatory burden for the WSPU. The experience of the Women's Social and Political Union in its move to violence reveals the rhetorical tensions that result when practical necessity grates against a movement's own sense of ethical superiority. The union members felt compelled by practical necessity to go outside of convention for effective methods to attain their political goals. Yet their reformist allegiance to the basic values and conventions of British society never gave way to revolutionary desires for total societal revision. Rhetorically, the WSPU faced what Eugene Garver calls a "problem for stable innovation"; that is, they needed to "invent in fact, in actual event and institutions, the stable structures for changing events."[33]

A recurrent difficulty faced by rhetors seeking change involves the need to make their goals and methods comprehensible to a conservative or even a reactionary audience. As John Campbell poses the question, "If an intellectual change is truly fundamental, how can it be socially intelligible?" Nominal change is easily understood, but we often lack a vocabulary to describe and comprehend true change. It is vital, if a movement seeks an ultimate, general acceptance of its cause, that its arguments be socially grounded and resonant at some level with tradition. Revolutionaries are less bound by—although not wholly exempt from—this requirement, for they seek the total overthrow of a corrupt system. The reformer needs, however, to "exploit the resources of the tradition for persuasive advantage."[34]

I have argued elsewhere that Emmeline Pankhurst, the leader of the WSPU, was the past mistress of utilizing conservative discourse to advance a radical cause.[35] In the earlier, nonviolent phase of union activity, she salted her speeches in support of women's suffrage with appeals to an essentially Victorian view of women. Pankhurst sought to show that voting was resonant with the "separate spheres" tradition, where men had mastery over the public domain while women were tenders of the private sphere of the home. Utilizing images from the Victorian cult of "True Womanhood," she showed how the vote could enhance the positive role of the pious and domestic Perfect Lady (the "Angel of the House"). Pankhurst also showed how the vote would help to alleviate societal problems wrought by the two negative incarnations of woman, the prostitute (the Fallen Woman) and the spinster (the Redundant Woman). By working within the separate spheres tradition, Pankhurst portrayed voting as part of a neotraditional view.

I would argue that, in justifying the step to strategic violence, Pankhurst exercised a similar rhetorical tactic. Even more vital than grounding new images in an understandable and conservative discourse, new protest strategies must be justified in terms that are socially intelligible. The WSPU sought to ground a specific innovation—women utilizing violence to advance their own cause—in the stable and specific traditions of English society. Prior tradition became an inventional resource for union rhetors and one that allowed them "to situate radical action in the context of conservative allegiances."[36] Thus, in seeking a rationale for violence, the suffragettes turned to the common conservative tradition they shared with British men for explanation and justification of their acts.

This study argues that the Women's Social and Political Union presented a rationale for limited terrorism that was essentially two-pronged. First, the union claimed that violent militancy was a practical strategy designed to force a national crisis of sufficient magnitude that the government would yield to union demands. Second, the WSPU justified this strategy of forcing the crisis by arguing that its violence was part of a "just war," undertaken only under extreme provocation and waged by legitimate agents and through legitimate means. There were four component arguments of the union's just-war rationale: first, suffragette violence was a defensive response to a culpable opponent; second, the suffragettes had legitimate authority to take violent action; third, suffragette violence was an effective and valuable tool of reform; and fourth, any evil inherent in violent means was far outweighed by the positive ends that would result.

In justifying their use of reformist terrorism to force a government crisis, union rhetors went far beyond Taylor's description of the usual "rhetoric of the terrorist, which frequently seeks justification for acts of violence in terms of the logic of warfare."[37] Rather than consisting of the simple use of military metaphors, union rhetoric provided a complex and consistent argument in a variety of rhetorical forms. From Western tradition they appropriated the philosophical rationale behind the *justum bellum* (the "just war" or "justified war"), a concept that has developed over time as the primary organizer of "Western Christian thinking about the problem of war" and violence.[38] The modern concept of the just war comes down to us from the late middle ages in a bifurcated form. Just-war doctrine is divided between the *jus ad bellum*, criteria determining when it is just to enter into war, and the *jus in bello*, criteria determining proper conduct in the waging of a war.[39] The *jus ad bellum* found its basis in church writings from St. Augustine through Thomas Aquinas and in canon law. The *jus in bello*, on the other hand, had a secular basis, and elements of its development have been traced to Roman law, the code of chivalry, and the *jus gentium* (customary agreements and "community practice").[40] The code of chivalry lent to this aspect of just-war doctrine a concern over the treatment of the innocent and a desire that noncombatants be protected. The *jus gentium*, a secular conception of "the common body of agreements binding all men together in mutual relationships," increasingly came to determine what was acceptable common practice during the actual conduct of wars.[41]

The same inherent ethical tension over the use of violence for a worthy cause that led the Christian church to develop the concept of the just war led the suffragettes to use that concept in their own defense. In making this claim, I am not necessarily arguing that this pattern of argument was a conscious decision made by union leaders and members. In occasional editorials, particularly ones by Christabel Pankhurst, questions of whether the "women's war" was justified were directly addressed in terms identical to the ones found in other situations where the just-war doctrine had been utilized. Generally, though, suffragette use of just-war rhetoric was less explicit. Union rhetors turned to just-war concepts simply as a series of natural arguments that have evolved over time in Western culture to explain and justify the use of violence. The concept of a "just war" is as surely a part of Western woman's rhetorical tradition as it is a part of Western man's, although it is an argument women have generally approached from a noncombatant position. Pankhurst and other union rhetors would have absorbed this pattern of argument from its use in justifying such violence in the national interest as the promotion a few years earlier of the Boer War. What is unusual in suffragette rhetoric is the application of the concept of the just war to violence utilized *by* women for the sake *of* women. The justificatory rhetoric of the suffragettes was wound tightly around the same questions that are raised in the just-war tradition: Was there just cause for the use of violence? Do the combatants have the legitimate authority to use violence? Are the violent acts conducted with an ethical concern for the rights of noncombatants? Does the good to be gained from violence outweigh the evil inherent in violence?[42] The suffragettes attempted through their rhetoric to answer in the affirmative these primary questions raised by their use of violence in a reformist cause.

In examining WSPU rhetoric, this study first identifies the unique conditions that led to an escalation of suffragette militancy: the police attacks on union members during their constitutional efforts, the exorbitant sentences meted out by the courts for nominal militancy, and the government's refusal to grant women their bona fides as reformers rather than criminals. Second, this study examines how, through a skilled rhetorical invention, union rhetors used these conditions as the basis of their justification for violence. I will detail the general rationale presented by the WSPU for a strategy of terrorism as well as the four-part union argument portraying its actions as constitutive of a just war. Finally, this study will argue that the rhetoric of violence (whether expressed in terrorism or dissent) is not the sole prerogative of men. There exists a preconception that femininity and violent action are incommensurate, that women employing violence must destroy their credibility as women. Yet this idea ignores conditions that create inventional resources and the ability of skilled rhetors to make situational justifications. The Women's Social and Political Union, as a reform movement utilizing terrorist violence for the benefit of women, faced its double rhetorical burden with a discursive defense of unusual power and consistency.

Understanding the rhetorical burden faced by these women reformers who used violence in their own cause answers many of the unresolved questions about suffragette violence: How could the leaders of a movement whose object was reform justify, to themselves and others, the adoption of essentially revolutionary methods? How could intelligent women from the social class and historical period of the suffragettes support the use of violence, however worthy the cause? The answer to these questions lies neither in an exclusive study of the acts of violence nor in an examination of the psyche of their perpetrators. Rather, it is important to understand how suffragette rhetoric domesticated the use of violence through just-war appeals. Jean Bethke Elshtain has described the "just warrior" as "a complex construction, an amalgam of Old Testament, chivalric, and civic republican traditions. He is a character we recognize in all the statues on all those commons and greens of small New England towns: the citizen-warrior who died to preserve the union and to free the slaves." Rather than fulfilling the complementary feminine role of the "beautiful soul . . . the long tradition of women as weepers, occasions for war, and keepers of the flame of non-warlike values," the suffragettes took upon themselves the mantle of the Just Warrior.[43] The concept of justice feminized the masculine strategy of violence by returning to it the philosophy of care for others. The rhetoric of terrorist violence was itself, thus, rhetorically "managed" by the essentially conservative discursive rhetoric that accompanied WSPU terrorist activity.[44] Reformist terrorism was made palatable to the suffragettes and their supporters by a rhetoric that positioned violence as acceptable, even as traditional, within the context of a just war.

1

A Rhetorical Path to Terrorism

Understanding the militancy of the English suffragettes has been problematic for scholars since the time of the movement. The most well known of contemporaneous explanations came from Sir Almroth Wright, M.D., who blamed women's participation in militancy upon the "physiological conditions" faced by the excess number of women in England. In a 1912 letter to the *Times*, he stated that, since there were more women of marriageable age than there were men to accommodate them, these "surplus" women faced "severe sexual restrictions" and were, therefore, "sexually embittered." This condition led to a "mental disorder" that expressed itself in the violence of militancy.[1]

Other psychological explanations have included Samuel Hynes's reference to suffrage militancy as "mindless acts of aggression and protest" and his description of the movement's "passionate and irrational revengefulness." Hynes made the sweeping (and unsupported) claim that the "movement offered manhaters an outlet and form of expression." He provided the punch line by suggesting that England, in order to escape the suffragettes, "went to war in 1914 with apparent relief, as a husband might leave a nagging wife."[2] For George Dangerfield, the movement was an attempt by women to regain their masculine nature; the militants were merely puppets jerked hither and yon by autocratic leaders teetering on the edge of insanity; further, the militant campaign was an expression of "pre-war lesbianism."[3] Andrew Rosen searches in obscure places for sexual symbolism, apparently intent upon the same equation of sexual frustration and militancy first claimed by Sir Almroth Wright. When, during one protest, Christabel Pankhurst tells union members to seize the mace if they are fortunate enough to enter the House of Commons, Rosen speculates that, "perhaps, to Christabel, the mace, symbol of the authority of the House, embodied the concept of masculinity itself." He searches the words of the suffragette martyr, Emily Wilding Davison, for such terms as "ejaculates" (used, as was common at the time, in a nonsexual context to refer to sudden verbal declarations) to prove that Davison "found a quasi-sexual fulfillment in the contemplation of self-destruction."[4] Underlying all these views is the apparent opinion that normal, mentally healthy women are never violent.

One major problem with most earlier analyses has been the tendency to see union militancy all of a piece. References are made to WSPU violence without any acknowledgment that militancy *evolved* into violence. One reason, too, that so many researchers have viewed the suffragettes as hysterical and their militant acts as irrational has been the tendency to view particular acts quite apart from the rhetorical exigencies that prompted them. The union escalated its protest tactics as a rhetorically motivated response to a specific series of contingencies. Beginning with purely constitutional methods, union members turned to militancy only when it became clear that the constitutional approach would remain as ineffective in their hands as it had in the hands of earlier suffragists. Similarly, the level of WSPU militancy escalated only when new conditions imposed by the suffragettes' opponents threatened to halt union progress. Militancy under the WSPU, therefore, was not a single tactic but a path forged through new territory whenever more established routes appeared blocked.

The First Act: Nominal Militancy

When Emmeline Goulden Pankhurst invited a group of women to her Manchester home on October 10, 1903, to form a new political movement, the drive for female suffrage was undergoing a revitalization. The decade prior to the founding of the Women's Social and Political Union proved to be a time of hopeful signs marred by great losses in the movement for women's suffrage. Suffrage was granted to women in New Zealand in 1893 and in South Australia in 1894. Then, in 1897, the wonderfully named Mr. Faithfull Begg introduced an English women's suffrage bill that reached its second reading and passed with a majority of seventy-one but was then "killed" before the committee stage. As the new century came in, suffrage work continued and petitions were still being signed, but the press treated the issue of women's suffrage as an extended joke and subjected serious news of suffrage efforts to a press blackout. Because of the ongoing Boer War, opponents claimed that any agitation that distracted the government while "our lads" were fighting was unpatriotic.[5] The war against the Dutch farmers in South Africa was deeply divisive at home, fueled by inflammatory speeches against the war by David Lloyd George. When Lloyd George spoke against the war in Birmingham, native home of Colonial Secretary Joseph Chamberlain, a riot ensued that caused the death of one man and injury to ninety-seven police. Women were not peripheral to this controversial war. Displaced Boer women and children were placed in overcrowded "concentration camps" (a term devised for the occasion), and 20,000 of the 117,000 camp residents died. When concerned women in England sent Emily Hobhouse in 1901 to inspect the camps, she was detained in Capetown for deportation upon her return from the camps. The news that Hobhouse had physically resisted her guards electrified the opposition to the war and presaged the more physical tactics women would soon employ for their own political rights.[6]

The close of this divisive war in 1902 finally left the public free to realize fully the excitement of a new century and a new monarch. For suffragists this excitement brought renewed hope that the moribund women's suffrage cause could be resurrected. The Women's Social and Political Union was established in Manchester in such an atmosphere of hope and confidence. Because of her late husband's work with the Independent Labour Party (ILP), and because of her recent work with the Manchester Labour men, Emmeline Pankhurst initially thought of founding a women's branch of the ILP, much as already existed in the Liberal Party. She had a change of heart when she discovered that women were not allowed to join the branch of the ILP that met in Pankhurst Hall, the building named for her late husband.[7] Instead, Pankhurst founded a new organization named the Women's Social and Political Union. Open only to women, it was not affiliated with any party. Whereas women suffragists of the past had accepted reassurance of support by politicians who took no action on their behalf, the WSPU adopted the motto "Deeds Not Words."[8]

The new union did not lack for social and political models in choosing the militant path that would later escalate into violence against property. As Sandra Holton has argued, "The militant was more than a victim of her own temper or psychology, more than a vehicle for forces beyond herself, or for processes in which she had become locked."[9] The suffragette leaders had gleaned two basic political lessons from the political agitations of the preceding century: first, violence had been instrumental in gaining additional political rights for men (and denying political rights to women); and second, constitutional efforts had been ineffective in remedying this situation. Violent agitation in 1832 had culminated in the passing of the Electoral Reform Bill and in a radical change in the political status of women. Until that time most men and women shared equally in whatever few political rights they had. The lack of a female franchise was less apparent when the majority of men also could not vote. The Reform Bill of 1832 was worded with reference only to "male persons"; the result was that women were denied any voting rights at the very time that a male, middle-class franchise was created.[10] When the new Electoral Reform Bill came before Parliament in 1866, some saw it as an opportunity to correct this injustice. Dr. Richard Marsden Pankhurst, a Manchester solicitor, helped John Stuart Mill draft an amendment to the Reform Bill of 1867 to enfranchise women on an equal basis with men. Massive petitions were put forward on the amendment's behalf, but the amendment did not survive the debate.[11]

After Richard Pankhurst and Emmeline Goulden married, in 1879, they worked together to seek a redress of women's political inequality until Dr. Pankhurst's death, in 1898.[12] One particular event in the early years of Emmeline Pankhurst's political life may have predisposed her to view a crisis as politically expedient. When the Liberals did not include women in the Franchise Reform Act of 1884, the Pankhursts founded the Women's Franchise League.[13] In 1894 they made a final break with the Liberals, and Dr. Pankhurst became a driving force in the Independent Labour Party in Manchester.[14] During the first years of the Pankhursts' work for the ILP in Manchester, the party faced considerable repression. Often unable to acquire halls in which to speak, the ILP took to organizing outdoor meetings, often at the popular city park of Boggart Hole Clough. On May 17, 1896, Labour speaker John Harker was issued a summons for holding a meeting in the park. More summonses followed as speakers persisted, and imprisonments began as the speakers refused to pay their fines. On Sunday, June 21, Emmeline Pankhurst spoke in the Clough, declaring her willingness to face imprisonment. When the authorities did not prosecute her, she vowed to continue speaking, claiming, "As long as I have my personal freedom, I shall go Sunday by Sunday to Boggart Hole Clough." The controversy brought large crowds to the Clough; the city council passed a bylaw forbidding any meeting in the Clough without consent of the Parks Department. On Sunday, August 16, a massive protest was held in the Clough. This sign of public support and the increase in Labour votes at an election held at the same time encouraged the home secretary to refuse approval of the bylaw.[15] The crisis brought about by civil disobedience and the willingness to face imprisonment had forced the public officials to back down.

Such early political lessons may have been responsible for Emmeline Pankhurst's view of "human progress as having advanced through the tumultuous acts of the oppressed." Reportedly, she was also influenced by her revolutionary paternal grandfather and by a girlhood friend who descended from a French communard. As a girl, Pankhurst had often indicated her pleasure that her birthday fell on Bastille Day.[16] Whatever her early influences, clearly Pankhurst did not view a crisis as a negative event but as an opportunity to drive a wedge into the existing political structure and thus create a space for new political participation.

Until 1905, most WSPU activity was confined to organizing in and around Manchester. When the new session of Parliament opened on February 13, 1905, Emmeline Pankhurst and her daughter Sylvia journeyed to London. Sylvia, a woman of considerable artistic talent and social conscience, would later lead the suffrage campaign in the East End of London. The two women spent eight days lobbying Parliament members who had previously pledged suffrage support. They finally convinced Bamford Slack, who was fortunate enough to have drawn a place on the ballot, to introduce their bill.[17] The bill was a simple one that stated that all words referring to the masculine gender in the voting qualifications should be held to include women. This bill was to be introduced on May 12, 1905. It was the second bill of the day; the first bill was one requiring that lights be placed on the back of a cart when in traffic.[18]

On May 12, the lobbies of the Parliament were filled with women: Lancashire textile workers, National Union of Women's Suffrage Societies (NUWSS) representatives, and WSPU members among them. They were treated to the spectacle of Parliament members stringing out the "debate" on the Roadway Lighting Bill with stories and jokes. In jovial collusion, the other members egged them on with laughter and applause. In this way, the suffrage bill was "talked out."[19] The constitutionalist NUWSS, accustomed to such offhand treatment, politely withdrew. This was, however, the first real taste of frustration and betrayal for the WSPU members, and they were unwilling to yield easily. Mrs. Pankhurst and a small group of women held an impromptu demonstration at the door of Parliament. Elizabeth Wolstenholm-Elmy, a famous elderly suffragist and reformer still adorned with the ringlet curls—now grey—of an earlier age, attempted to speak. The women were hustled away, first to the statue of Richard the Lion-Hearted and then to the Broad Sanctuary. A brief, indignant meeting ensued. No arrests were made, although the police took down the names of the women.[20] Thus, peacefully, the first militant act of the WSPU took place.

Exigence One: Breaking Through the Blackout

The escalation from this only nominally militant act to actual violence was many years in coming. The first situation that early militancy was designed to meet was the continued refusal by the press to print any news about women's suffrage. On October 13, 1905, a pre-election meeting was held at the Free Trade Hall in Manchester. The candidate was Winston Churchill, newly swung to the Liberal ranks, and the speech in his support was by Sir Edward Grey. Mrs. Pankhurst's oldest daughter, Christabel, attended the meeting. Considered by her mother to be a natural politician and soon to receive her LL.B., Christabel would become the primary strategist for the movement. She was accompanied to the meeting by Annie Kenney, a Lancashire factory worker of great intelligence and loyalty to the Pankhursts. In the middle of the meeting Annie Kenney rose and asked "Will the Liberal Government give votes to women?" as Christabel unfurled a "Votes for Women" banner. When Sir Edward Grey refused to answer, even upon the requested submission of the question in writing, the two women again interrupted the meeting. They were manhandled outside and restrained as they tried to speak in the streets. Deciding to force arrest, Christabel made a dry-spitting motion at a police officer. Both women were arrested; Christabel Pankhurst was sentenced to one week's imprisonment and Annie Kenney to three days'. As Christabel intended, news of their imprisonment finally broke the long silence by the newspapers on the suffrage issue.[21] The press engaged in considerable hand-wringing over the "wickedness" of the two women and the deleterious effects their actions would have on the suffrage cause. Even such negative editorials were preferable to the usual silence on suffrage. The response to this one act made it clear that a "wonderful new weapon, the weapon of publicity and advertisement, was put into the hands of the Women's Social and Political Union, and the leaders at once saw its value."[22] This breaking through of the press blackout also confirmed that a crisis could be manufactured in order to bring attention and action to bear on a political issue.

Far from discouraging women from joining the union, news of the incident attracted many Manchester women to the suffrage ranks. Among them was Flora Drummond, a short, stocky woman of considerable tenacity. Her bulldog features and nature, combined with her organizational talents, made her a mainstay of the union and inspired the nickname "The General." Of even greater importance to the future of the union was the decision of Emmeline Pethick-Lawrence to join following the relocation of the WSPU to London in January 1906. Emmeline Pethick, who was born in prosperous circumstances, had spent a number of years in the East End involved with mission work among young women. In 1901 she married Frederick Lawrence, and it is an indication of their strong partnership that they both chose to hyphenate their last names. Once Emmeline Pethick-Lawrence had joined the union as treasurer, her husband worked closely with the suffrage women, devoting his time and money to the cause. He was truly, as one author called him, "the Prince Consort of militancy."[23] In October 1907 the Pethick-Lawrences started the newspaper *Votes for Women*, which would serve as a major propaganda tool for the movement.

Exigence Two: Stone-Throwing to Force Arrest

If the need to break through the press blackout led the union to provide a newsworthy minor crisis for its initial move into militancy, the next step in militancy came as the result of the suffragettes' experience during legal protests. Early "militancy" for the WSPU had generally consisted of heckling government speakers, making speeches in occasionally inconvenient places, and attempting to deliver resolutions to the House of Commons. Although the heckling of speakers (and especially the asking of embarrassing questions) is a standard procedure in British politics, the union women found that such actions would result in their arrest and imprisonment. The suffragettes were also arrested and given outrageous sentences for making speeches of their own. Mass arrests and prison sentences were the result, too, when the WSPU passed resolutions and sent deputations with the intent of delivering these resolutions to Parliament. Well aware that English law could prohibit large meetings within the one-mile radius of Parliament, the union always sent a smaller, legal deputation to carry the resolution to the House of Commons. Supporters would follow behind, generally in small groups and at a discreet distance from the initial deputation. The women were invariably met by police—mounted and on foot—who would block their path. The women would attempt to continue forward; they would undergo a period of serious buffeting by the police; and they would then be arrested. It is interesting to note that the women would then be charged with "obstructing the police," tried in the police courts, and imprisoned in the second division, which was usually reserved for common criminals rather than political offenders.[24]

The experience of the suffragettes during these deputations provided a second situational exigency, one that would lead to stone-throwing, the first major escalation in union militancy. Early stone-throwing had a symbolic aspect because the missiles were aimed at government property, but generally the impetus for the act was the purely practical desire to force an early, less wearing arrest. "Buffeting," where arrest was delayed while the suffragettes were pushed and pummeled by the police and angry male crowds, was a major problem throughout the suffrage movement. Most stone-throwing and simple assaults on police (such as spitting) were initially undertaken to avoid as much buffeting as possible by achieving an early arrest. Despite its basis in practical necessity, many union members were apparently conflicted over taking such action. They wrapped the stones in heavy paper (containing appropriate messages), and some even tied long strings from the stone to their wrist to avoid accidental injury to bystanders. In reporting these precautions, historian Constance Rover remarked, "It is difficult to imagine anyone but a middle-class Englishwoman resorting to such a procedure!"[25]

But, in 1910, stone-throwing was unable to prevent one of the worst instances of the police and crowd attacks. This event, known in suffragette circles as Black Friday, would serve as a strong symbolic impetus to the later adoption of reformist terrorism. Black Friday would be pointed to during the period of violent militancy as proof, not only of government treachery and the failure of constitutional efforts, but also of the need for suffragette violence in their own defense. Black Friday followed the failure of the First Conciliation Bill, a women's suffrage bill composed by parliamentary suffragists across party lines. The bill would give the parliamentary vote to all women householders (i.e., women owning a house, part of a house, or even a room) and to women occupying business premises who paid £10 or more a year in rent. Marriage could not disqualify women, although men and women could not use the same property as qualification.[26] Despite the bill passing its second reading by a considerable margin, the government suddenly refused to consider the bill further.

In response to this governmental chicanery, a deputation of twelve, including Mrs. Pankhurst, Dr. Elizabeth Garrett Anderson (qualified to practice medicine in 1865 and the first female mayor in England, still active in women's rights in her seventies), and Mrs. Hertha Ayrton (a scientist who later developed an invention to protect against poison gas effects in World War I), led the way to the House of Commons despite a little difficulty.[27] Such was not the case for the some 450 women who followed. Moving in small groups, they carried clever banners reading "Where There's a Bill There's a Way" and "Women's Will Beats Asquith's Won't." These banners were ripped from their hands and shredded by the police.[28] It became quickly apparent that these were not the usual Westminster police but police brought in from the East End—men accustomed to dealing with prostitutes and rowdy drunks. It is difficult to know if their orders were to intimidate the women physically into retreat, but arrest was delayed for five to six hours while the usual "buffeting" was replaced with actual beating.[29] Emmeline Pankhurst described the police action: "Then they laid hands on the women and literally threw them from one man to another. Some of the police used their fists, striking the women in their faces, their breasts, their shoulders. One woman I saw thrown down with violence three or four times in rapid succession, until at last she lay only half conscious against the curb, and in a serious condition was carried away by kindly strangers."[30]

Reports of what appears to have been a "police riot" (to use modern terminology) are borne out by the few photographs allowed to appear and by anecdotal accounts. Some of the worst reports were generalized as "Acts of Indecency" at the time—usually meaning the women were seized by the breasts and in the genital area. According to Sylvia Pankhurst, "Some were dragged down dark streets and indecently assaulted"; the actual form of the assault—in true Edwardian fashion—was never elaborated upon.[31] Black Friday ended finally with the arrest of 115 women and 4 men. Home Secretary Winston Churchill ordered their release the next morning—perhaps as pre-election clemency, but more likely so that the reports of police violence would not be aired in a public trial.[32]

Even before Black Friday, supporters realized that stone-throwing and early arrest could not protect union members from physical abuse during legal deputations. Also, apparently the courts were willing to cripple the movement by giving union members extraordinary sentences in the second division. By being denied first-division status, the suffragettes lost considerable privileges, including the use of reading and writing material and the right to wear their own clothes rather than prison garb. Symbolically, consignment to the second division identified suffragette protests as crimes rather than political acts. To meet this third particular exigency and force an earlier release, the union turned to self-directed violence in 1909.

Exigence Three: The Hunger Strike to Force Release

Wallace Dunlop was the first suffragette to adopt the hunger strike to protest the court's refusal to grant her status as a political prisoner. This new tactic forced her release after a ninety-one-hour fast, and as

Emmeline Pethick-Lawrence put it, "Never again were Suffragettes to suffer the insult of being treated as criminals without making this protest of the hunger-strike."[33] This new union policy put extraordinary pressure on the government. There would be a tremendous public outcry in the case of the death of a hunger-striking prisoner of the class and gender of the suffragettes. Yet the government refused to yield by giving the suffragettes the first-division status common to political prisoners. The government moved to resolve this dilemma in September 1909. Partially at the instigation of the king, the government at this time determined to retain the suffragette prisoners for the length of their sentences. Rather than releasing the women, the prison officials began a program of forcibly feeding the hunger-striking prisoners. Briefly, forcible feeding involved forcing a tube down the prisoner's nose or throat and pouring some form of nourishing liquid directly into the stomach. Although this procedure was an old practice in insane asylums, the suffragettes were not cooperative with this attempt to thwart their hunger strikes. The prisoner would be forcibly restrained by wardresses, and wedges would be used to pry open her clenched jaws. The chipping and breaking of teeth was not uncommon, nor was it all that uncommon for the tube to cause injury in transit (or even to reach the lungs rather than the stomach). A good portion of the time, the patient would vomit continuously throughout the process.[34]

Therefore, for two years prior to the final escalation of militancy, both the union and the government had established patterns of protest and response. It was suffragette policy to throw stones (of limited number and seeking limited damage) at targets symbolic of the government. The suffragettes did not seek to avoid arrest for their actions. Arrests also continued as the result of legal deputations to the House of Commons, on the general charge that the suffragettes "obstructed" the police who blocked their path. Following arrest and subsequent police court trial, suffragette prisoners would seek status in prison as political offenders and adopt the hunger strike to protest their consignment to second-division criminal status. The government had also settled into its policy of seeking considerable sentences against the suffragettes, treating them as common criminals rather than political prisoners, forcibly feeding them as a response to hunger strikes, and releasing them when their health deteriorated.

Exigence Four: Reformist Terrorism to Force a Crisis

This tactical policy might have continued unchanged had the treacherous defeat of the Second Conciliation Bill not provided the final exigency for the escalation to violence. The Second Conciliation

Bill, an amendable version of the earlier bill but without the £10 occupancy fee, was debated May 5, 1911, and carried by the impressive majority of 255 to 88. Chancellor of the Exchequer Lloyd George told the Commons that, although there would not be an opportunity in the 1911 session, the Conciliation Bill would be granted a second reading in 1912.[35] However, in November, Prime Minister Asquith announced his intention to introduce an unsought manhood suffrage bill in the next session of Parliament. Lloyd George happily declared that the Conciliation Bill was "torpedoed" but that this new reform bill could be amended to include women. The WSPU well knew that such an amendment, with the prime minister opposed to women's suffrage and without the support of the Liberal government, would never take place.[36]

Frustration over government betrayal of the Conciliation Bill and a simmering anger over Black Friday and the policy of forcible feeding caused the suffragettes to rethink their strategy. Earlier lessons over the efficacy of "forcing a crisis" for the government argued for an escalation in militancy. The union had seen clearly that the arrests and imprisonments of suffragettes for asking questions in political meetings had broken the press boycott and given the suffrage cause a place on the government agenda. The early militancy had been designed "to break the stalemate caused by public apathy and press indifference, and to force the hand of a Liberal Party sympathetic in principle but dilatory in practice." In many ways, restrained militancy had been successful, but slowly the rank and file of the movement chafed under that restraint. Now, in 1911, with the failure of the Second Conciliation Bill, early techniques to cause a crisis appeared "played out" to the union leadership. Pankhurst came increasingly to believe that they "had exhausted argument. Therefore, either we had to give up our agitation altogether, as the suffragists of the early eighties virtually had done, or else we must act, and go on acting, until the selfishness and obstinacy of the government was broken down, or the government themselves destroyed."[37]

On November 21, 1911, Emmeline Pethick-Lawrence (in the absence of Emmeline Pankhurst, who was fund-raising in America) led a deputation in protest from Caxton Hall to Parliament Square. Police blocked all ways to Parliament Square.[38] A group of suffragettes met at 7 P.M. at 156 Charing Cross Road; carrying bags of stones and small hammers, they set out to break windows not only at government offices but also at business premises. Andrew Rosen provides a list of the damages of the evening: "Windows were smashed at the Home Office, Local Government Board, Treasury, Scottish Educational Office, Somerset House, National Liberal Federation, Guards' Club, two hotels, the *Daily Mail* and *Daily News,* Swan and Edgar's, Lyon's and Dunn's Hat Shop, as well as at a chemist's, a tailor's, a bakery, and other small businesses. Two hundred and twenty women and three men were arrested."[39] Previously the targets of stone-throwing had always been directly connected with the government or with the Liberal Party. This was the first instance of an attack upon private property to protest the government's policy on women's suffrage, and it inaugurated a new policy of militancy in the WSPU.

After November 9, 1912, damaging of letter boxes became widespread. Corrosive liquid (or inflammatory liquid and a lighted rag) would be poured into the box to destroy the letters within. Following an encouragement of stronger militancy during a series of appearances by Emmeline Pankhurst in February 1913, arson became a major tool of militancy. On February 12, 1913, a Regent's Park refreshment kiosk was burned. Also burned during the arson campaign of 1913–14 were houses, mansions, and the Ayr racecourse stand. Bombing began with explosions in empty railway carriages, station houses, and unoccupied summer homes; bombs were also discovered in churches. Golf greens and parks were damaged by having "Votes for Women" carved across them in large letters.[40] Art galleries were attacked, with the most famous incident being the slashing of the *Rokeby Venus* by Mary Richardson in 1914. According to Sylvia Pankhurst:

Petty injuries and annoyances continu[ed] side by side with large-scale damage. Street lamps were broken, "Votes for Women" was painted on the seats at Hampstead Heath, keyholes were stopped up with lead pellets, house numbers were painted out, chairs flung in the Serpentine, cushions of railway carriages slashed. . . . A mother and daughter, bearing an ancient name, spent much of their time travelling in trains in order to drop pebbles between the sashes of carriage windows, hoping the glass would smash on being raised. Old ladies applied for gun licences to terrify the authorities. Bogus telephone messages were sent calling up the Army Reserves and Territorials. Telegraph and telephone wires were severed with long-handled clippers; fuse boxes were blown up, communication between London and Glasgow being cut off for some hours.[41]

Several personal attacks on cabinet ministers occurred; a hatchet was tossed into Asquith's carriage when he visited Dover in June of 1912, and a bag of flour was thrown at him upon his return to Chester. The union sent envelopes of red pepper and snuff to each cabinet minister—successfully in each case, according to reports.[42] The following listing by Antonia Raeburn of a typical week of attacks on property in 1913 will give some sense of the serious nature of the movement's actions:

April 3   Four houses are fired at Hampstead Garden Suburb. Three women damage the glass of thirteen pictures in the

Manchester Art Gallery. An empty railway carriage is wrecked by a bomb explosion at Stockport.

April 4   A mansion near Chorley Wood is completely destroyed by fire. A bomb explodes at Oxted station.

April 5   The burning of Ayr racecourse stand causes an estimated three thousand pounds' damage. An attempt to destroy Kelso racecourse grandstand is discovered.

April 6   A house at Potters Bar is fired. A mansion is destroyed at Norwich.

April 7   An attempt to fire stands on Cardiff racecourse is discovered. Fire breaks out in another house in Hampstead Garden Suburb. In the ruins of Dudley Castle the Suffragettes charge one of the ancient cannons and cause a shattering explosion.

April 8   "Release Mrs. Pankhurst," cut in the turf at Duthie Park, Aberdeen. The word "release" is twelve feet long.

April 9   A haystack worth a hundred pounds is destroyed near Nottingham.[43]

A Mrs. Cohen came from Leeds to London and, not being inclined toward window-breaking, chose instead to travel to the Crown Jewels exhibit at the Tower of London. Using a bar from an iron grate, she broke the case containing the Regalia of the Orders of Merit. Such incidents led to the closing of the royal houses at Kensington Palace, Kew Palace, Hampton Court, and Holyrood to members of the public.[44] On February 19, 1913, the militants managed their most famous exploit, the bombing of Lloyd George's unfinished house in the Surrey countryside.[45] Reportedly, the bomber was a suffragette named Emily Wilding Davison, who escaped while leaving suffrage literature behind her. Emmeline Pankhurst immediately claimed responsibility for the action, telling a public meeting in Cardiff, "We have blown up the Chancellor's house!"[46]

Clearly, even this simple overview shows how different the late militancy of the WSPU was compared to the symbolic militancy of its early years. I doubt whether the union member of 1903 could ever have imagined herself planting bombs or planning arson raids in 1913. However, the series of four major exigencies detailed above encouraged the union to seek new rhetorical responses. Previous analyses that ignore the gradual escalation of militancy and that divorce union decisions from the situations prompting them cannot help but misinterpret suffragette motivations, the mental state of those who took the step into reformist terrorism, and the rhetorical nature of escalating violence.

To borrow from Edward Gude, in the case of the suffragettes "it seems a more difficult task to explain why violence did not occur" sooner than it did than to explain why it occurred at all.[47] Increasing militancy was designed to meet very specific needs of the union, and political violence was becoming a proven element in Edwardian politics. The final element encouraging increased violence by the militants was a number of very personal sacrifices resulting from the rigors of the early militant campaign. Mary Clarke, Emmeline Pankhurst's sister, died on Christmas Day from a cerebral hemorrhage. She had been released on December 21 following her month-long imprisonment for participation in the Black Friday demonstration, during which she was reportedly injured. Barely a week later, Henria Williams, another one of the suffragettes injured during Black Friday, died of heart failure.[48] Other instances, such as the paralyzing stroke suffered by Lady Constance Lytton following her forcible feeding, also reveal the personal cost borne by union members for the violence directed against them. As with other social movements that proceed to violent tactics, the union sought through its militancy to shift the price of change—long borne by movement members—to those outside of the movement.

In many of the early studies of the WSPU there is a troubling assumption that the union lacked a coherent rationale for its actions. Even in more recent studies, I often find a false dichotomy established between reason and emotion, when WSPU strategies were actually grounded in both. It may well be that loudly proclaiming reformist terrorism as irrational is a form of whistling past the graveyard. The purpose may be to make an undesirable tactic unpalatable to reformers by labeling it as devoid of reason. Yet, a careful appraisal of WSPU rhetoric reveals that it was a reasoned passion that inspired union members. It allowed them to seize the conditions imposed upon them and use those conditions not only to inspire new tactics but also to justify their adoption.

The move to reformist terrorism was a strategic choice made by union leaders, and union members who remained and entered into actions of reformist terrorism made a conscious personal decision to do so. I believe that the strategic violence of the Women's Social and Political Union was not an aberration but an inventional response to the constraints faced by a reform movement that had exhausted peaceful methods. Faced with tactical adaptation or failure, the suffragettes seized upon limited terrorism as a practical tool to accomplish their reform ends and faced the resulting criticism with a series of justificatory arguments remarkable for their thematic consistency.

Although the decision to use violence was tactically driven, the defense of that decision raised the militant suffragettes to a new appreciation of the principles underlying their actions. Particularly for many of the rank and file in the movement, defending the use of violence took precedence over the strategic value of the act itself. Soon the emphasis upon this controversial strategy and the need to justify acts of violence began to co-opt union rhetoric. Arguments justifying the principles behind the use of violent means for a worthy end far outweighed practical arguments in support of the vote. As Roberta Kay Carson perceptively put it, the union "moved from justification for women's suffrage to justification for militancy."[49]

As Chaim Perelman points out, justificatory rhetoric "only concerns what is disputable and disputed." Justification in this view consists either of refuting a particular criticism or showing that the act undertaken possessed such positive aspects in its favor as to be "above criticism."[50] By presenting justifications to refute criticisms of their violence, the suffragettes accomplished two goals. First, their justificatory arguments met the practical rhetorical needs of holding their membership together for further action and rationalizing their actions to the electorate/government who could yield to their demands. Second, the very act of offering justificatory arguments mitigated the union's use of violence. According to Perelman and Olbrechts-Tyteca, justification is itself a moderating act—a step away from violence and toward "the establishment of a community of minds" that will exclude further violence.[51] As the following chapters will show, by offering justifications for their acts based on traditional norms and values, the union leadership took the initial step to restore their standing in the larger community.

2

The Strategy of Forcing the Crisis

As a first step in their move to reformist terrorism, the WSPU leadership needed to establish their willingness and capacity for strategic violence. Therefore, the union's initial rhetorical task was to make a highly specific call to action. In this aspect of their justification, union rhetors approached the move to violence as a practical issue, attempting to show how such a policy could be successfully implemented by a small group of middle-class women. In this chapter I describe, first, the strategic reasoning behind a reform movement's use of violence to force a national crisis and the practical rationale presented by the WSPU for its policy of reformist terrorism. Second, I discuss the union's need to prove that such violence could be a *successful* reform tool in the hands of women. Finally, I examine the union's attempts to portray political violence as consonant with English tradition and with a traditional view of women.

Eugene Garver speaks of those who would achieve new political authority as employing a rhetoric "making activities the fundamental locus of value." In such a rhetoric the invention process is grounded in "a prudence connected with deeds beyond words."[1] The tendency, strong in the union from its inception, was to hallow active intervention, to make action the ultimate value. The motto of the suffragettes, "Deeds Not Words," was originally directed at politicians as a demand that they "put up or shut up" on the issue of the female franchise. Increasingly, this motto became the benchmark by which a suffragist's commitment to fighting the evils of society was measured. In this emphasis on action, the reformist violence of the suffragettes found its strongest link with the violence of revolutionary terrorists, because "the rhetoric of terrorism routinely ranks all ideas by how they relate to 'action.' "[2] In the nineteenth century, anarchist Peter Kropotkin penned an ode to action: "Sometimes tragic, sometimes humorous, but always daring; sometimes collective, sometimes purely individual, this policy of action will neglect none of the means at hand, no event of public life, in order to keep the spirit alive, to propagate and find expression for dissatisfaction, to excite hatred against exploiters, to ridicule the government and expose its weakness, and above all and always, by actual example to awaken courage and fan the spirit of revolt."[3] Like revolutionary terrorists, the WSPU had practical and philosophical reasons for glorifying action. In terms of strategy, the use of violence against property was chosen to force a crisis for the public and the government. Obviously, therefore, the movement audience had to be induced to participate in these actions, and the constant references to the superiority of deeds to words was a form of exhortation. Emmeline Pethick-Lawrence admonished those who worked in the cause of suffrage to "beware of emotion that finds no vent in action . . . translate every emotion, every feeling into deed, and act."[4] As a philosophical argument directed to those outside the movement, the need for action became a justification for violent militancy. Valuing action was not a repudiation of traditional values but "transform[ed] values from being eternal objects waiting to be exemplified into *agenda,* things that need to be done."[5] The union liked to quote Walt Whitman's "How beggarly appear arguments before a defiant deed" as proof that the time for words was limited and must yield to the time for action.[6]

The chief practical problem faced by the Women's Social and Political Union was gaining a place on the political agenda and in the public mind during a rancorous age. The competition among movements to see which could create the most discomfort and thereby achieve a redress of grievances was very great during this reform-minded era. The industrial crisis and the unrest in Ireland were prime competitors and were supported by men who could bring pressure through the franchise.[7] The main obstacle faced by a movement to obtain the franchise was the lack of an effective yet constitutional tool to pressure the government. Emmeline Pethick-Lawrence viewed the lack of an effective tool as the prime reason that women's and children's issues inspired laughter rather than action in Parliament: "Supposing you were a general, and supposing that on every side of you were enemies who were challenging your very existence. Supposing your life depended upon your breaking out of that ring; at what point would you choose to break out? Well, you need not be a great diplomatist to answer. You would rush the place where the ring is weakest. . . . It is the women of the country who have no voice, who cannot take political vengeance, who cannot politically defend themselves; that is where the ring is weakest."[8] To strengthen the ring against the assaults of politicians required actions "aggressive enough to command their attention and respect."[9] The suffragettes felt that reform would be achieved not by relying on "the favour and good will of Governments, but by the relentless pressure of political force."[10] On her third major speaking tour in America, in 1913 (and the only tour during the policy of violent militancy), Emmeline Pankhurst complained to a New York City audience that something of "a volcanic nature . . . something very nearly approaching a revolution" was needed because "the whole machinery of government in England may almost be said to be an elaborate arrangement for not doing anything."[11] To overcome the government's inertia, the union settled on a two-pronged strategy to pressure the government through a crisis wrought by acts of strategic violence against the electorate.

As the years passed and early techniques failed to win reform, the suffragettes also came to the conclusion, as have so many other reformers, that the public attention span is lamentably short. Reformers must overcome public inattention by endowing their causes with "a *presence* that prevents them from being neglected."[12] "Presence" is the ability of an orator to use style to create a sense of immediacy.[13] Perelman speaks of various verbal methods (e.g., repetition, anaphora, amplification) used by speakers to affect the audience members' sensibilities and thus bring the topic closer to the audience "in space and time."[14] For a social movement, presence is often achieved nonverbally. Reformers seek new and exciting protest tactics that will keep the movement before the public eye. Over time the novelty and spectacle of early protest techniques pale, and movements find that their processions, demonstrations, and "raids" no longer draw public and press attention. It is at this point that strategic violence presents itself as an attractive alternative.

Reformers must convince the power structure that the movement is "serious" and a force to be ignored at the system's peril. Terrorist acts (whether revolutionary or reformist) serve a dual purpose of provoking an immediate crisis and previewing the retaliation to come if the government does not comply with movement demands. The very act of using violence against the power structure cannot help but produce a crisis (whether large or small) for the status quo. The simple existence of violence is a challenge to the system and questions whether that system has the legitimate right to make and enforce the rules.[15]

Until the advent of window-breaking aimed at private establishments, the militant policy of the WSPU harmed only the women involved in the protests. The new policy of guerrilla actions was predicated on the idea that, to be effective, militancy needed to "at the very least, produce intense inconvenience and even a certain alarm to the Government."[16] The union leaders came to believe that if an event sufficiently "urgent and so pressing that it has become politically dangerous for the government to neglect that question any longer" were to occur, women would find their cause attended to in quick order. Emmeline Pankhurst favored an extended and homey analogy whose use was shared by other suffragette speakers, such as Annie Kenney. In Hartford, Connecticut, Pankhurst described the following hypothetical situation:

You have two babies very hungry and wanting to be fed. One baby is a patient baby, and waits indefinitely until its mother is ready to feed it. The other baby is an impatient baby and cries lustily, screams and kicks and makes everybody unpleasant until it is fed. Well, we know perfectly well which baby is attended to first. That is the whole history of politics. Putting sentiment aside, people who really want reforms learn that lesson very quickly. It is only the people who are quite content to go on advocating them indefinitely who play the part of the patient baby in politics.[17]

Pankhurst specialized in this type of "home-truth," easily grasped by any audience and resonant with her own ethos as a mother. Suffragette demands were presented as natural, not selfish, and disruptive behavior became the only way an innocent and neglected creature had of obtaining the sustenance it needed. In order to accept strategic violence, movement members must adopt the mindset that Pankhurst presented here with such cagey common sense: movement rhetoric must turn the "virtue" of patience into the "vice" of passivity.

But forcing a crisis for the government requires the indirect pressure that can be wielded only by the electorate. In the eyes of the Pankhursts, one major problem in pressuring the government for reform was the tendency of the British public to observe the suffrage struggle "with too much equanimity."[18] Argument, the suffragettes claimed, may convert the British public, but it will not stir them into action: "It requires a strike, or a Titanic tragedy, or some other upheaval to galvanise the placid British public (which for practical purposes means the enfranchised men) into action." The sinking of the *Titanic* in April 1912 served as an arguing point in both suffrage and antisuffrage rhetoric. Christabel Pankhurst used the disaster as an example of the self-absorption of the average man. She pointed to the deaths of numerous seamen caused by Lloyd George's raising of the Plimsoll line, which was a load line marked on the sides of merchant vessels indicating the level above which the ship could not be safely and lawfully submerged. Despite an increase in seamen's deaths, "since the average man is not a seaman, and is not likely to become one, the average man does not excite himself about these deaths." Yet the *Titanic* stirred the public to deep concern over maritime safety because "they had friends or relatives whose lives were lost, and in addition many of them feared that in the event of another such calamity they themselves might lose their lives."[19] This was Pankhurst's acknowledgment of the issue of salience. Salience existed naturally in the case of the *Titanic*, because the average male citizen could identify his concerns with maritime safety and pressure the government for reform.

Such salience is not always natural to reform issues. Therefore, the crisis created by reformers must link movement concerns with those having the power to bring about change. Strikes, boycotts, and various forms of terrorism provide what could be called "artificial salience" because they are often imposed in situations where reform issues could otherwise be ignored. Christabel Pankhurst used the example of a recent coal strike as the model of this method: "The miners have shown us the way. By announcing a strike which would bring loss and suffering to the entire community, they have drawn forcible attention to their grievance. The public, whose own interests are at stake, have insisted that something be done to prevent the national calamity involved by a coal strike. The Government are thus compelled to take measures to bring the strike to an end."[20] In other words, the public forced the government to pay the "price of escape" because the average citizen refused to be made a party to the difficulty.[21] The union believed that its cause had "to be carried by storm . . . a difficulty from which all concerned are eager to escape."[22]

Unlike terrorist groups that leave doubts about the rationale for their attack or the specific grievances they hope to alleviate, the WSPU made explicit the ways in which its actions would create a crisis for the British government. Emmeline Pankhurst explained that the object of violence against property was to make difficulties for key groups of the franchised, which would then put pressure upon the government to end the attacks:

Your stockbroker, whose communication with Glasgow was cut off for several hours during very important business hours, does not want that to be a weekly occurrence. Your business man who sends important communications through the post does not want his communications to be interfered with as a regular and permanent institution. . . . Your business man, whose customers mostly are women, does not like the idea that in the interval of buying hats, his customers may be breaking his shop windows; and your insurance companies won't like to have the drain upon their resources and their profits cut down by having to make good these insurance policies. It is an impossible situation.[23]

The reader should notice the not-very-veiled threat in these words, which not only commented on what had already happened but also pointed to the possibility of a "weekly occurrence" of attacks and violence made "regular and permanent." A pamphlet entitled "Window Breaking: To One Who Has Suffered" was created and presumably left behind following attacks upon shopwindows. Signed by "A SYMPATHISER," the pamphlet began: "Dear Sir, You, a prosperous shopkeeper, have had your windows broken and your business interfered with, you are very angry about it, and no wonder." One section of this short pamphlet is worth quoting at length, for it shows how the union urged a response to its violence in favor of acquiescence to its demands:

> Put a stop to window breaking, and put a stop to the sufferings and sacrifices of the women, by telling the Liberal Government that you will *stand no more of it and that women must have the Vote.*
> Believe me, the women will never give in, and you would think the less of them if they did. It is the politicians who must give in, and you and your fellow electors can make them do it.[24]

This was the way the strategy should work in principle, but Emmeline Pankhurst also provided audiences with examples of how the strategy should work (and was working) in actual life. In Hartford, she described her stay at a small house on a golf links where she had gone to have a weekend break from her work. Although the links had not been damaged (spared, Pankhurst assumed, because prominent suffragettes were members of the club), once Pankhurst's presence was known, the members became anxious:

> Well, then that morning I was rung up over and over again by excited gentlemen who begged that those golf links should be spared, saying: "I don't know whether your followers know that we are all suffragists, on our committee, we are entirely in favor of woman suffrage." And I said, "Well, don't you think you had better tell Mr. Asquith so, because if you are suffragists and do nothing, naturally you will only add to the indignation of the women. If you really want your golf links spared you had better intimate to Mr. Asquith that you think it is high time he put his principles into practice and gave the women the vote."[25]

This little story modeled the response desired by the guerrilla militants and simultaneously made the claim that the strategy of violence was working in ways hidden from the public eye.

Once the basic policy of forcing the crisis was established, the union had to convince the enfranchised public and the government that it "meant business." Suffragette rhetors needed to put forward three basic arguments proving that women could be determined and capable terrorists. Because, as women, their ability to terrorize might be taken lightly, union rhetors had, first, to heighten the threat of their new strategy and prove that the union was strong enough to carry it out. Second, the suffragettes had to give those movement members who were asked to carry out such a difficult policy every assurance of the strategy's ultimate success. Finally, the WSPU had to portray the use of violence both as a common tradition of English politics and as resonant with traditional roles of women.

Heightening the Threat

Just like revolutionary terrorists, reformist terrorists need to advertise their "movement's strength and capacity for destruction."[26] The confronter faces a dilemma: power may be sought through threat, but that power will only be granted if the threat is taken seriously. The union resolved this dilemma by emphasizing the serious nature of its attacks and attempting to convince the public that its militancy was not merely "pinpricks." After the union adopted guerrilla action, *The Suffragette* dedicated a central two-page spread to the week's acts of militancy. These pages were filled with accounts of arson, bombings, and other damage, generally described dispassionately and often reported using the accounts from local and national newspapers. The headlines from these papers trumpeted the dire effects of suffragette actions:

> "Militancy—A Spreading Fire. Outbreaks All Over the Country."
> "Militancy Must Prevail—The Government Frightened"
> "Guerilla Warfare—Militant Outbreaks Throughout Great Britain"
> "Militancy Increases. More Damage to Property. Fire and Bombs!"
> "The Women's Revolution—A Reign of Terror—Fire and Bombs!"
> "No Peace Anywhere in the Kingdom"[27]

These stories blended an air of defiance with a tone occasionally so objective that it appeared to bemoan the union's own actions. The union hoped to show a determined militancy that could not easily be dissuaded. For example, the October 31, 1913, headline was "The Withering of Militancy," and a smaller heading read, " 'I am very glad to see Militancy is withering.'—Mr. Lloyd George at Swindon, Oct. 22nd, 1913." These headlines were followed by stories of a mansion ruined by fire, two country houses gutted, three railways fired, and a Bristol pavilion destroyed.[28] It was vital to the terrorist function that their deeds appear serious and widespread. Even the objective tone of some of the headlines ("Facts of the Week as Recorded in the Press") and articles conveyed a feeling that these were deeds of serious consequence. Oddly effective were the headlines ("The Militant Problem") that viewed the destruction with alarm and joined in the general consternation over an effective solution. These "Police Are Baffled" reports played up fears of a guerrilla group capable of striking effectively and avoiding arrest. With limited strategic violence, it became important that each deed achieve the maximum effect, that the deeds appear as widespread and uncontrollable as possible, and that the police be portrayed as powerless to stop the acts.

As women, WSPU members were more likely to have their violence, regardless of its actual level, characterized as inconsequential, and this problem was magnified by the small numbers taking part in the actual attacks on property. They experienced the difficulty of needing to "find a means of making their protest not only visible but also plausible."[29] Emmeline Pankhurst attempted to do this in Hartford when she compared the suffragettes' successful severing of "the telegraphic and telephonic communication between Glasgow and London" to the siege of Adrianople in the Balkan States when telegraphic communication was maintained even during the course of the shelling. "I am not going to tell you," Pankhurst told her audience, "how the women got to the mains and cut the wires; but it was done. It was done, and it was proved to the authorities that weak women, suffrage women, as we are supposed to be, had enough ingenuity to create a situation of that kind."[30] Pankhurst presented the suffragettes as reliant on their wits to achieve the most damage with the minimum amount of physical force. This allowed the union to maximize the reports of damages without making inordinate claims about its own physical resources or the size of its forces.

One way the union gave its acts legitimacy as violence was by pointing—sometimes humorously, sometimes seriously—to the fear triggered in the government by them. Emmeline Pankhurst could not resist a little humorous irony in making this point during the 1912 Conspiracy Trial of the suffragette leaders when she questioned a Detective-Sergeant Seale:

Have you been one of the gentlemen allotted to go into the country for the protection of Cabinet Ministers? —I don't follow.

When a Cabinet Minister has been going to speak in the provinces, has it been part of your duty to accompany him—to go in the same train? —No.

But you said that is done? —Yes, I know it is done.

Can you give me any idea from what Cabinet Ministers need protection? —No, madam, I could not.

You could not say whether they were to be protected from violence, say, on my part? (Laughter.) —I could not say.

Would it be the duty of the officer to prevent women saying, "When is the Liberal Government going to give women the vote?"—Possibly.[31]

Despite Pankhurst's light touch in the questioning, it is clearly the point of this interrogative that cabinet ministers do not take detective-sergeants along for protection unless they feel that a threat is very real. Annie Kenney, during a speech at the London Pavilion, addressed her opening remarks to "any Scotland Yard men who may be present—any who belong to us, you know, for they had to create a special department in Scotland Yard to deal with the Suffragettes."[32] Again, this was a "where there's smoke, there's fire" argument through which Kenney was underlining the threat by pointing to the forces mobilized to counter it.

In her 1913 Hartford, Connecticut, speech, Emmeline Pankhurst attempted to heighten the threat by increasing uncertainty about its source. In an industrial strike, Pankhurst suggested, it is easy to "locate the difficulty" and know where violence will occur and who is likely to perpetrate that violence. In the case of the suffragettes' "war against the Government," however, knowing from which source violence would come was difficult. Pankhurst indicated herself and Mrs. Hepburn, the American woman who introduced her to the audience, and asked, "How could you tell that Mrs. Hepburn is a non-militant and that I am a militant?" Even more disturbing, Pankhurst intimated, was the hypothetical plight of any father in the audience if he lived in England: "He couldn't tell whether some of his daughters were militants or non-militants. When his daughters went out to post a letter, he couldn't tell if they went harmlessly out to make a tennis engagement at that pillar-box by posting a letter, or whether they went to put some corrosive matter in that would burn all the letters up inside of that box. We wear no mark."[33] The inability to distinguish those guilty of perpetrating violence from the innocent is a hallmark of terrorism. And if the guilty cannot be identified in advance, how can those in power protect against the terrorists?

The union played upon these concerns and added the intriguing argument that men were particularly "afraid of women's blows." This fear was ascribed by union rhetors not merely to the fact that "men do not like to be hurt" but also to men's "superstitious terror of woman in revolt." According to Christabel Pankhurst, men had a particular fear of women, with their "unknown stores of force, moral, spiritual, and physical, with incalculable motives and mysterious springs of action, who have remained silent and patient and submissive for centuries and now are divinely discontented, divinely impatient, and divinely brave." This argument could be dismissed as poetic hyperbole were it not for later feminist discussions of the special qualities of revolt when it happens within the closed society of the home. The strong reaction to feminism, much like the intense reaction to the early civil rights movement, has been partially fostered by the uncertainty both movements introduced into the home environment. A man could hold forth at the dinner table against women's rights or racial and class disturbances and receive the silent acquiescence of his wife and servants. But what did they really think, and would they secretly act against him? Christabel Pankhurst strongly advanced this fear of the "viper in the bosom." She pointed to the severe repression by the government against the suffragettes as indication that "the fear of women is at last entering into the heart of the Government" and as a proof that "women are in very truth becoming terrible as an army with banners." The union portrayed the police as attempting at all costs to avoid a battle with Emmeline Pankhurst's female bodyguard. Christabel Pankhurst reported that the police acted when her mother's bodyguard was not with her and even fortified Victoria Station with police should the bodyguard "spring up . . . to rescue her." "Who will say now," Christabel asked rhetorically, "that women cannot terrorise?"[34]

Viability of the Militant Strategy

The union pointed consistently to an increase in militancy as the only tool adequate to force the crisis, and argued for its effectiveness on two primary grounds: first, milder forms of militancy had worked for the union in the past; and second, governmental response to women's increasing militancy proved the strategy to be working. It was only by the pressure brought to bear through militancy, the union claimed, that votes for women had become "a living question."[35] The many years of work without success by the National Union of Women's Suffrage Societies (NUWSS) had long been a major theme of the Women's Social and Political Union. The constitutionalists of the NUWSS were often shown as allowing politicians to declare their sympathies with suffrage at the same time that they expended no energy or political capital to pass a suffrage bill. Yet, within a short time after the advent of mild WSPU militancy, serious women's suffrage bills were being debated in Parliament. Union member Mrs. Israel (Edith) Zangwill, speaking at the London Pavilion, used Jesus' words to the scribes and Pharisees to show the comparative effectiveness of militancy: "It has just occurred to me why people swallow camels and strain at gnats. The government for nearly half a century swallowed the camel of the National Union without the slightest discomfort, but from the first tiny inception of the

WSPU, the government strained at that gnat! The explanation is, that gnats bite."[36] This comparison also allowed the WSPU to make the point that the size of the larger NUWSS was no indication of effectiveness. The cause would be won by those possessing the ability and readiness to take stinging action.

Suffragettes did not need to intimidate every person in England, Christabel Pankhurst claimed, but merely to achieve "the effective intimidation of twenty-one persons—in other words . . . the intimidation of the British Cabinet."[37] Suffragettes took great delight in showing that this intimidation was effective by using comical examples of cabinet members cringing from a "run-in" with union forces. In a speech in Edinburgh, "General" Drummond told the following tale: "I was passing along Parliament Street the other day and saw another pitiable sight. I saw the First Lord of the Admiralty crawl along in the shadow of the Board of Trade offices, keeping his weather eye open. I stepped off the bus on the chance that I might have a word with him, but I found that he had many escorts who were there to look after him. That brave man in the Admiralty afraid of women asking him a question!"[38] Such images reduced the cabinet ministers to cringing cowards scared of women who simply wished to deal with them directly and honestly. One editorial cartoon made the same point visually by showing a small group of cabinet ministers huddled together in a doorway arch while a policeman checks to see if the coast in clear. The caption read: "Time—Midnight, Policeman (in a hoarse whisper): 'All clear, gentlemen! If you run, you'll get home safe.' (General stampede of Cabinet Ministers.)" The headline in bold type over the cartoon was particularly mocking: "The Statesman Homeward Wends"[39] (Figure 1). Christabel Pankhurst reiterated this point in a later editorial when she spoke of "the sheer panic betrayed by Cabinet Ministers and witnessed by their frightened huddling behind ranks and rows of police."[40] The doggerel of "A Suffragette Alphabet," which was published on August 2, 1912, by *Votes for Women*, reinforced the image of the terrified cabinet minister. Among the other letters were the following:

> **D** is for Downing, a street full of police,
>   Each Cabinet Minister has a thousand apiece.
> **N** for the Nervous breakdowns that they get
>   If they meet unexpectedly one Suffragette.
> **X** for the 'Xtra Police force required
>   When a Cabinet Minister's being admired.[41]

Christabel Pankhurst developed this same theme when she claimed that announcement of the formation of a female bodyguard caused the government to "turn purple, white, and green [the union colors]

(*The Speaker of the House of Commons, in distributing prizes at Framlingham College, is said to have quoted the following lines from Crabbe, saying that they reminded him of the attitude of the modern politician towards the Suffragette:—"Women and men he strove alike to shun, And hurried homeward when his work was done."*)

TIME—MIDNIGHT

Policeman (in a hoarse whisper): "All clear, gentlemen! If you run, you'll get home safe." (General stampede of Cabinet Ministers.)

Figure 1. "The Statesman Homeward Wends," *Votes for Women*, August 2, 1912 (All illustrations by permission of the British Library)

with terror."[42] This image of the frightened cabinet minister used irony to support, rather than attack, established norms.[43] It played off of expectations that men are brave and have a considerable physical advantage over women. The union winked at its audience and shared the joke of dignified, grown men hiding like frightened rabbits from those who were physically much smaller and who had, as a child might put it, "promised not to hurt them." It was a turn on the old joke of the elephant frightened by the mouse.

All of these jokes at the expense of cabinet ministers functioned to diminish them. In many of the editorial cartoons, particularly the excellent ones by Alfred Pearce, published under the pseudonym "A Patriot," the cabinet ministers are shown as little boys.[44] The editorial cartoon for the July 12, 1912, *Votes for Women* portrayed the cabinet as a group of frightened little boys in bathing suits standing on a rowboat in a sea of "Equal Franchise for Men and Women" (Figure 2). They are approached by a tall, lovely woman in bathing clothes who wades through the water toward them. The caption reads: "W.S.P.U. Swimming Mistress: 'You'd better take the plunge now, my little fellows, or I'll come and push you in!' "[45] The cabinet was reduced to little boys gently but firmly guided in the proper direction by their

40 / The Strategy of Forcing the Crisis

THE PLUNGE

"Let us once be clear that this question must and will be settled in the only way that plain Justice admits, and we shall not hesitate to take the plunge now rather than later."—*The Daily News and Leader.*
W.S.P.U. SWIMMING MISTRESS : You'd better take the plunge now, my little fellows, or I'll come and push you in!

Figure 2. "The Plunge," *Votes for Women*, July 12, 1912

nanny or schoolteacher. Although far more visual humor was directed *at* the suffragettes, jokes based on the frightened man or the naughty little boy dragged by the ear into compliance were points where gender stereotypes played in the union's favor.[46] This humor, whether delivered through a written, oral, or pictorial medium, clearly met Freud's definition of a tendentious joke. Although Freud saw the tendentious joke as a substitute for hostile deeds (which the union employed as well), he claimed that "by making our enemy small, inferior, despicable or comic, we achieve in a roundabout way the enjoyment of overcoming him."[47] Particularly in visual representations, the comparative stature of the female reformers juxtaposed to "enfant terrible" cabinet ministers provided a counterpoint to the antisuffragist portrayals of thin, shrieking harridans and dignified statesmen.[48]

The Assurance of Success

The problem confronting small reformist and revolutionary groups (or small and ill-equipped standard armies, for that matter) is legitimizing their authority to call for violent action in the face of belief that they cannot succeed.[49] To place one's own forces in danger and to call down the destruction inherent to violence when one has little hope of ultimate success is considered both unjust and irresponsible. The women of the WSPU faced this problem to a greater extent because of their gender. As Emmeline Pankhurst told her Hartford, Connecticut, audience:

After all the most practical criticism of our militancy coming from men has been the argument that it could not succeed. They would say, "We would be with you if you could succeed but it is absurd for women who are the weaker sex, for women who have not got the control of any large interests, for women who have got very little money, who have peculiar duties as women, which handicaps them extremely—for example, the duty of caring for children—it is absurd for women to think they can ever win their rights by fighting: you had far better give it up and submit because there it is, you have always been subject and you always will be."[50]

Pankhurst refuted the accuracy of these perceptions and included the probability of success as one of two criteria she used in determining union policy: "When you adopt the methods of revolution there are two justifications which I feel are necessary or to be desired. The first is, that you have good cause for adopting your methods in the beginning, and secondly that you have adopted methods which when pursued with sufficient courage and determination are bound, in the long run, to win."[51] Although the vote was not yet won, Christabel Pankhurst pointed to the fact that the female franchise was now a serious issue as one measure of success. Such women's issues were previously greeted in Parliament with laughter and off-color comments, but now "the grin has been struck from the face of the low-minded among the politicians, and the ribald jest has been thrust down their throat."[52] Success was shown as inevitable because government coercion would break down and the government would find that their "torture" of the suffragettes was ineffective. The WSPU felt that it had placed the government in a wholly untenable position: "driven to choose between votes for women or death for women."[53] George Bernard Shaw summed this belief up by presenting a classic ethical dilemma: "If persons with a grievance against you lie down to die on your doorstep, you let them die if you are in the right; if not, you admit that your conscience or public opinion, or both, are against you. Well, the women have lain down to die on the Government doorstep."[54] Success, and the legitimation for their actions that success brings, would be attained for the suffragettes by their courage and their refusal to yield.

Not only did union rhetors show that the violence of guerrilla militancy was effective, but violence also served a purpose in answering a key argument advanced by the antisuffrage forces. Antisuffragists claimed that government ultimately rested upon physical force. In other words, laws (or international relations) were only as good as the lawmakers' ability to physically enforce them if the need arose.[55] This form of social Darwinism excluded women from making or enforcing laws, owing to their presumed physical weakness.[56] In mockery of this theory, Lord Hugh Cecil asked, in the Commons on July 11, 1910: "The honourable and learned gentleman, the Member for the Walton division of Liverpool, would not therefore, I suppose propose that I should be disenfranchised and that Eugene Sandow [the 'strong man'] should become a plural voter on a great scale?"[57] When the *Times* of June 15, 1908, said that only the male voter could "argue out his views for his country's good on equal terms with his fellow, and in the last resort can knock him down if he chance to be the better man," the *Westminster Gazette* remarked, "It is an assumption, we cannot help saying, which has in recent years been somewhat frowned upon by the police."[58] Despite the ease with which the physical force argument could be satirized, it held such sway in antisuffragist circles that Brian Harrison called it the "jewel in their apologia."[59] Suffrage violence met this argument directly by showing that women could exercise strategic force and best the efforts of men to capture and punish them. Emmeline Pankhurst pointed to the inability of the police to discover the perpetrators of suffragette violence: "You see two women walking along the street. How are you to know which of those women is a Suffragette? How are you to know which of them has destroyed letters in pillar-boxes, or broken windows, or fired the orchid houses, or blown up Mr. Lloyd George's house? If you read your papers they say, 'Clues to the perpetrators of the outrage to Mr. Lloyd George's house!' A galosh! Two hatpins without heads! Two hairpins! and they are still searching."[60] The success of union violence was a graphic illustration that physical force could be exercised through cleverness and planning, not simply by muscle.

Playfulness, a publicizing of cleverness and resourcefulness—both generally undervalued as female traits—appeared in WSPU political cartoons. In a cartoon for *The Suffragette*, Prime Minister Asquith—dressed as a female cook—sits beside a big, empty kettle worriedly reading a recipe book. Recipes (for dealing with the suffragettes) are flying around that read: "Flogging," "Transportation," "Forcible Feeding," "Shave Their Heads," "Strangle 'em all," "Boil in oil," "Give Them Votes." In the background, a hare labeled "Suffragette" is racing quickly away past a letter box. The caption was presumably

Figure 3. "First, Catch Your Hare," *The Suffragette*, December 13, 1912

taken from the first line of the recipe for "jugged hare" in the popular *Mrs. Glasse's Cookery*,[61] which read, "First Catch Your Hare"[62] (Figure 3).

The suffragettes argued that law was not based on physical force at all but rather on the consent of the governed. Pankhurst attempted to show that power in the government came from the bottom up, that the government "cannot govern us if we refuse to be governed. . . . Your police force, your police magistrates, your judges, your army, the navy if you like, all the forces of civilisation, cannot govern one woman if she refuses to be governed. Government rests upon force, you say. Not at all: it rests upon consent, ladies and gentlemen, and women are withdrawing their consent."[63] Increasingly, the suffragettes refused to obey laws in which they had had no say, particularly those concerning treatment of prisoners. The union often pointed out that the women were tried in courts before a jury of men, sentenced by a male judge, and made to serve time in prisons administered by men. Suffragettes refused to cooperate with prison regulations that treated them as criminal rather than political prisoners. By the final year of the militant movement, many women would disrupt court proceedings against them by continuous chanting, hurling objects at the judge and prosecutor, and physically resisting court officers.[64] Further proof of the failure of coercion was embodied in suffragette leaders who would escape from police waiting to arrest them and appear dramatically onstage to address a meeting. Annie Kenney became the master of such sudden and theatrical appearances, once even passing the police lines and being delivered onstage in a wardrobe basket borrowed from an actress.[65] That the government often appeared flummoxed over how to "handle" the suffragettes led Emmeline Pankhurst to claim that "the weakest woman, the very poorest woman, if she withholds her consent cannot be governed."[66]

Political Violence as Common Tradition

Finally, union rhetors supported a generic use of political violence based not on the issue of women's suffrage but on justifications provided by common tradition. In doing so, they found their own innovative answer to Garver's question of how to defend new forms of action as rational according to current practice. New actions become politically feasible only when they are understood in the light of commonly accepted standards.[67] One place for WSPU rhetoric to begin was with the oft-used touchstone of male actions. The union took the stance that "if it is justifiable to fight for common ordinary equal justice" for men, then women "have greater justification for revolution and rebellion than ever men have had in the whole history of the human race."[68] The union made use of male examples of justified rebellion throughout history. Frederick Pethick-Lawrence pointed to such men as John Hampden, who failed to make his point in court and turned to force of arms.[69] Emmeline Pankhurst made the analogy between Cromwell fighting against the divine right of kings and the suffragettes fighting against the "divine right of the man voter." And, she added wryly to one audience, "it takes a great deal more courage, ladies and gentlemen, to fight against eight million divine rulers than it did to fight against one."[70] Pankhurst pointed to the violence that preceded each extension of the franchise to the men in England: "In 1832, you know we were on the edge of a civil war and on the edge of revolution, and it was at the point of the sword—no, not at the point of the sword—it was after the practice of arson on so large a scale that half the city of Bristol was burned down in a single night, it was allowed to pass into law."[71] Pankhurst made it clear that the weapon of attack (arson) utilized by the suffragettes and so often criticized as irrational and hysterical was the precise weapon chosen by men in their franchise efforts. She pointed to the Reform Act of 1867 and the riots in its support when the Hyde Park railings were pulled down. Finally, she examined the efforts of the agricultural laborers in 1884 when the simple threat of violence by men was enough to guarantee them the franchise. In comparison, Pankhurst presented the efforts, in the 1880s, of women who presented larger petitions than men seeking the vote, held bigger meetings than the men in support of women's suffrage, and passed more resolutions through "great corporations, great town councils, and city councils" urging the female franchise. Yet, "men got the vote because they were and would be violent. The women did not get it because they were constitutional and law-abiding. Why, isn't it evident to everyone that people who are patient where government is concerned may go on being patient? Why should anyone trouble to help them?"[72] Through these historical examples the union directly tied its methods to the violence deemed acceptable for male reformers in the past. In this way union rhetors fulfilled Garver's recommendation that reformers use a rhetoric of stable innovation "not to erase the old from memory but to join it in argument."[73]

More recent history also supported the union view of the right of violent rebellion in certain cases. To give further proof of militancy as a viable strategy, the union directed observers to militancy recently employed by men in reform efforts. Two major issues—Irish home rule and industrial agitation—competed with women's suffrage for a place in both the public mind and in parliamentary legislation. Both movements had turned increasingly to violence and the threat of violence. In the 1910 parliamentary election the Liberal Party was forced to form a Coalition government with the eighty-two Irish nationalists under John Redmond. Despite the earlier failure of home-rule bills under Gladstone in 1886 and 1893, the 1910 coalition made the introduction of a home-rule bill inevitable. The Home Rule Bill, introduced in 1912 by the Asquith government, was opposed by the Conservatives, who felt so strongly on the issue that they had long used an alternate name, Unionists. Protestant Ulster, unwilling to be ruled by Catholic southern Ireland, led the opposition to the bill with a renewal of the 1886 slogan, "Ulster will fight and Ulster will be right." Ulster leader Sir Edward Carson led 471,444 men and women in signing "The Covenant,"[74] a document that in its different versions pledged the signatory to use "all means which may be found necessary to defeat the setting up of a Home Rule Parliament in Ireland."[75] This undercurrent of violent threat became more unsettling with the knowledge that Catholics and Protestants were both smuggling guns into the country. Concern grew in March 1914 during the "Curragh Mutiny," when a number of Conservative army officers resigned rather than follow orders to move north to counter possible violence.[76]

Labor agitation during the Edwardian period also based its gains on violence or the threat thereof. Labor lost faith in parliamentary solutions for low wages and dangerous working conditions, and the concept of syndicalism gained increasing favor. Syndicalism, imported from France, counseled a combative approach by which trade unions would seize control of production through a series of small strikes culminating in one general strike.[77] The growing popularity of this tactic may be seen not only in major agitations—the Great English Transport Stoppages of 1911 and 1912 and the Great Coal Strike of 1912—but in the sheer number of grievances, strikes, and settlements. Nineteen thirteen was particularly contentious, with at least 1,497 separate disputes of varying importance.[78] The danger of strike violence came from multiple quarters—railway men, coal miners, and port employees—and provided leverage in the negotiating process. Suffrage workers could see clearly both the power the franchise granted to working-class men and the even greater power wielded through the threat of violence.

I believe the WSPU learned from Ulster and industrial agitation the lesson that political violence was efficacious. Lloyd George had made the statement against women's militancy that "its practitioners seem to think that they can terrorise and pinprick Parliament into giving them the Vote. . . . Until they learn something of the people they are dealing with, their whole agitation, as far as the House of Commons is concerned, is simply and utterly damned." Christabel Pankhurst was quick to assure Lloyd George that the union had learned from Parliament's response to men's violence: "The men terrorised Parliament into giving them the Vote. The Catholics terrorised Parliament into giving them emancipation. The nationalists (by their votes in the House of Commons) are terrorising Parliament into proceeding with the Home Rule Bill."[79] The example of Ulster was a primary proof that violence, or the threat of violence, could wring concessions from the government. Pankhurst claimed that "government's capitulation to Ulster's force—or, rather, threats of force—is the greatest encouragement and the greatest incitement ever offered to women of the militant movement." Like the WSPU, Sir Edward Carson and his volunteer army in Ulster could not overcome the greater forces of the English army. What they *could* do was make the suppression of their violence so costly and protracted "as to be unpalatable to the Government."[80] This method worked in Ulster, and it worked so well for the miners that Emmeline Pankhurst declared, "Cabinet Ministers have gone cap in hand to the Miners' Federation to persuade them to come to terms with their industrial opponents."[81] From such events Christabel Pankhurst extracted the political lesson that not only could Parliament be terrorized but also "that Parliament never grants reform unless it *is* terrorised. . . . Terrorism is, in fact, the only argument that Parliament understands!"[82] Past government concessions put the lie to claims that "Englishmen will never surrender to force, and they will never surrender to threats."[83] Lloyd George was viewed as one politician who knew well the falsity of such statements, because he had a history of legally questionable actions in support of reform goals and had himself stated, "The kingdom of politics is like the Kingdom of Heaven: it suffereth violence, and the violent take it by force."[84] The suffragettes were more than happy to quote his own words back to him. Christabel Pankhurst turned to the words of a 1914 speech by Winston Churchill in Bradford, where he described the circumstances that would justify revolt and revolution: "They are he says, firstly, *real and unbearable oppression*, and secondly, the *lack of any other remedy save militancy*" (emphasis in original).[85] The Pankhursts thus used the very members of the cabinet who attacked suffragette violence to show that, under certain conditions, violence was an acceptable and even a traditional part of English politics.

To show that political violence was an acceptable part of English tradition was only the first step, because all the available examples referred to male reformers. Extending that tradition to women could not be accomplished by referencing actual events. The single exception was Boadicea, the British queen of the Iceni, who led a revolt in A.D. 60 against Roman rule. Following the death of her husband in that year, Boadicea was betrayed by the Roman rulers, who plundered her family wealth and annexed the kingdom. She led a rebellion in East Anglia during which seventy thousand Romans and their supporters were killed and the Ninth Legion was greatly diminished. Although the Roman forces were ultimately triumphant and Boadicea committed suicide in defeat on the battlefield, this was one instance in British tradition of a female warrior opposing an unjust government.[86] Boadicea appears for the suffrage cause in a cartoon that depicts a haphazard knight riding an ass labeled "Liberal Government." The knight, armed with the jousting pole of "prison regulations," the sword of "forcible feeding," the mace of "Government brutality," and the shield of "official lies," among other weapons, pauses to speak to the statue of Boadicea near Parliament. The conversation was recorded, as follows: "BRAVE MCK.NNA [McKenna] OF THE HOME OFFICE: 'Hail, Boadicea! I hie me in hot haste to His Majesty's Gaols to exterminate therein thine unwomanly descendants!' BOADICEA: 'My poor little official, give it up! You can't fight the Spirit with weapons like yours!' (He has been giving it up ever since.)"[87] Through Boadicea's approval, the suffragettes tied the spirit of the new English-woman to that of British history and presented the militant woman as the fulfillment rather than the renunciation of her heritage.

The union also linked the spirit of the suffragettes to the uncon-querable spirit of English*men*. Emmeline Pethick-Lawrence explained, "We sometimes speak of the dogged tenacity of the men who have conquered land and sea for our country's glory. There is an undaunted spirit in the mothers of the race also, or it would not be made mani-fest in the land; there is a bit of the bull-dog breed in the women of our country as well as in the men."[88] This spirit, according to Em-meline Pankhurst, allowed women to say, "I would rather be a rebel than a slave."[89] Flora Drummond took this same view of the spirit of women and claimed that "women are made of the same John Bull that men think so much about."[90] The continuing theme of the WSPU was that men should see themselves—their heritage of revolt, their pride, their tenacity—in the rebellion of militant women. It was important in carrying out reformist terrorism to have women within the movement identify with male revolutionaries and the actions men took to gain liberty in the past. However, the union also sought to have men in the external audience identify with these new female revolutionaries by showing them that the English fighting spirit tran-scended gender.

To justify the general use of violence by women, the union usu-ally mined common tradition for images that would permit such vio-lence. Moving metaphorically, the WSPU expanded in detail on the most obvious image of violence permitted to women—that of a mother protecting her children. "Children" in this case was also a figurative notion because it was tied to a union concept Emmeline Pethick-Lawrence referred to as "a new sense of race motherhood."[91] The concept of race motherhood preceded the move to guerrilla mili-tancy and was common to both the British and U.S. movements in their constitutionalist and militant forms. This concept of militant women as the mothers of the race was exceedingly clever for a num-ber of reasons. First, it tapped into the one unquestioned role granted women and the role in which they had some personal, if not any legal, power. Even a woman's position as wife was often personally power-less and treated with disdain, but a grown man was considered to owe fidelity and a certain level of obedience to his mother—if only out of respect for the life she purchased him through the dangers of child-birth. Second, the concept of race motherhood put forward the idea that militant women were not acting selfishly in their own interests but in the interests of their "children," that is, in the interests of the race. Third, race motherhood challenged the prevalent stereotype of the embittered spinster suffragette by making all of the militant women into mothers in the figurative sense. Speaking of motherhood in its figurative rather than its literal meaning opened up the concept to rhetorical use by the married and the unmarried alike.

In expressing their concern for "the race," the suffragettes co-opted one of the major issues of the Edwardian period for use in their justificatory arguments for violence. Samuel Hynes traces much of the Edwardian concern over the deterioration of the race to anxiety aroused by change. The advent of the twentieth century, the death of the "Old Queen," and the quagmire of the Boer War all contributed to a loss of certainty in the nation. The popularity of Gibbon's *The Decline and Fall of the Roman Empire* soon became a focus upon "The Decline and Fall of the British Empire" (as reflected in Elliott Mills's 1905 pamphlet by that name). Hynes sees in these largely Tory concerns an "assumption that all change is decline" and a belief that a golden age "when Englishmen were agrarian, seafaring, frugal, and pious" was now over. Worries over the physical deterioration of Englishmen were heightened by the citation in *Contemporary Review* (January 1902) that 60 percent of Englishmen were unfit for military service, and by the 1908 report of a Royal Commission that there was a tremendous increase in national "feeble-mindedness." All of these concerns found their focus in a concern over national defense and spawned a rash of invasion literature, particularly between 1906 and 1909, in which England was invaded (usually by Germany). Although these tales in their early form ended with England's triumph, they grew progressively more pessimistic as the Edwardian period continued.[92]

The women of the WSPU made shrewd use of these common concerns of their countrymen. Christabel Pankhurst complained in one editorial that "Englishmen are falling behind in the race. Even in sport they do not hold their own. We learn of the 'Waterloo of British Boxing' and their pre-eminence on the plane even of physical strength." Women, it was generally believed in "the older traditions of Evangelicalism," shared "a special moral and spiritual responsibility . . . in the regeneration of the race."[93] Christabel Pankhurst made this claim for women, declaring that "it is the daughters of the nation . . . who now have the greater share of that strength which is needed for the salvation of the race!"[94] Because the race as a whole was in danger, and because men, owing to their moral and physical degeneration, could not grasp the reins of leadership, women were legitimized in calling for revolutionary means in order to save the race.

The government's attack against the suffragettes was portrayed as an attack on the ability of women to protect the race. Emmeline Pethick-Lawrence turned this concept into a powerful metaphor that justified women's violence as the defensive posture of the mother animal protecting its young:

My friends, the government have driven women to the wall; they have hunted the women of this country until at last, in despair, they have turned to give battle with all the courage of the mother creature at bay. (Applause.) Yes! that is the secret of this movement . . . it is that a new consciousness of race motherhood has been evolved in the hearts of the mothers of the country. We have always possessed the deep instincts and the consciousness of individual motherhood, and always loved and cared for our own children, but within the last few years a new sense has arisen that individual motherhood is not enough, that race motherhood is wanted, too. . . . I want you to see this womanhood of the future that they are driving against the wall, turning in defence of this idea of race motherhood, turning at bay to do battle. . . . Are we going to side with the hunted, or are we going to side with the hunter?[95]

Suffragette arguments based on race motherhood and the need to guard the purity of the nation bought for the union the right to a certain degree of belligerency. Even ardent traditionalists recognized the clichéd right of the mother tigress to protect her cubs. There was considerably expanded leeway granted to the methods used by a mother to guard the purity of her children (particularly her daughters). Violence under such conditions still might not be acceptable, but it was at least understandable.

In the name of race motherhood, the union became involved in the purity campaign, one of the most misunderstood parts of the militant movement. Through the campaign against venereal disease, the union fastened upon a mainstream Edwardian concern that tapped into the indignation of the righteous, and argued for the cleansing fire of violent militancy. Violence would, in this estimation, cauterize the festering sore of male impurity. Christabel Pankhurst's book on "the social evil," *The Great Scourge and How to End It*, has been much maligned by earlier historians studying the WSPU. According to Roger Fulford, Pankhurst's "arguments and facts fortunately need not detain the reader."[96] Andrew Rosen could not understand why, in the light of Pankhurst's exaggerated estimation of the extent of male venereal disease, the members of the union continued to follow her leadership.[97] Susan Kingsley Kent has corrected these early views of union worries over venereal disease and their combined call for "Votes for Women and Chastity for Men." As Kent points out, Pankhurst's statistics of the incidence of venereal disease were those widely accepted by the medical community, and her concerns over the devastating impact of such illnesses upon the larger society were shared by physicians and social reformers.[98] Pankhurst and the WSPU utilized this aspect of the Edwardian concern over decline, decadence, and the effects of immorality on national strength and security to strategic advantage. The Edwardian period also saw the founding of the National Social Purity Crusade by the National Vigilance Association. In what has been called the "Galahad Concept," moral strength was equated with martial strength, and there were serious concerns that immorality by men would weaken the ability of England to defend itself.[99]

The euphemism preferred by Emmeline Pankhurst for infection by venereal disease was the term "poison," and it appeared to need no translation for audiences. She asked one audience to consider the feelings of mothers when "thousands upon thousands of little children are born, who are tainted with the most horrible human poison before they are born."[100] It is the individual mother and child who suffer when "the very fount of life is being poisoned," but the duty of women extends past the home.[101] "Men and women with a sense of responsibility towards the race" know that the country is in danger, for when "you have love polluted, you have the home desecrated by this horrible poison which is destroying the race."[102] The vilification of men in these statements is relatively covert because the dual moral standard of the time made the bringing of venereal disease into the home a presumably male transgression. Pankhurst could then declare unity with "the best of men" who were disease-free and in favor of the female franchise (and imply that the two were synonymous).[103] Such unity could not be achieved with the members of the government who were already guilty of collusion in the spread of the poison:

So we have this moral cancer which is destroying the race, which is eating at the heart of the race itself. I want to say to men that from a Parliament elected by men we shall not get laws reforming it. I want to say to you—Is it not very like asking the wolf to protect the lamb? Because even a Government which is responsible for carrying through such legislation has not clean hands in this matter. What about the state of poor women in India or wherever our troops are stationed? What about those women who are looked upon as necessary victims for the British Army and Navy?[104]

The implication was clear that members of Parliament (the cabinet in particular) were little more than pimps, unwilling to act against a disease that they probably had themselves. Emmeline Pankhurst declared, "We are going to have a clean House of Commons, elected by clean men and women; and when we have got that, we will have clean legislation; and when we have got clean laws, we shall have clean legislators."[105] Again, the forecast of future and conditional cleanliness implied clearly Pankhurst's opinion of the current purity of the parliamentary body. The government had partners in its collusion with the forces of impurity, as was depicted in a political cartoon

THE FORCES OF EVIL DENOUNCING
THE BEARERS OF LIGHT.

Figure 4. "The Forces of Evil Denouncing the Bearers of Light," *The Suffragette*, October 17, 1913

in the October 17, 1913, issue of *The Suffragette*. In this cartoon, a woman stands in battle garb, wearing a WSPU sash, holding a sword, and carrying a shield of "Purity." She faces a large dragon which wears the collar "Indecency." A man carrying the banner "The Press" urges the dragon toward the woman dressed in armor, and men's hands reach into the scene to propel the dragon forward. The caption described the scene as "The Forces of Evil Denouncing the Bearers of Light"[106] (Figure 4). In this Manichaean image, the suffragettes in their purity and vision faced a diverse but organized foe that preferred the status quo in all of its darkness and disease to the new world of light and health.

There were two ways in which the concept of race motherhood (and the accompanying purity campaign) authorized militant violence directly. First, according to Christabel Pankhurst, women were justified in adopting window-breaking as a means to force arrest and avoid physical injury: "It was felt that if any other method of protest were available as an alternative to having their bodies injured, women, if only because of their race responsibility, ought to adopt that alternative. A window can be replaced; a woman's body cannot."[107] Of more importance, Pankhurst described suffrage militancy in its violent form as the "moral purge" that would lead to "sweetness and cleanness, respect and trust, perfect equality and justice."[108] So important was the use of militancy to resolving the problem of moral impurity that one union editorial called it "a sign of national decadence" that any British man or woman considered militancy as morally wrong.[109] The union vision was of a stronger, tempered race created out of the holocaust of militancy. In the fires of suffragette arson, the taint of disease and deception would be burned away and a new world created where men and women could meet as equal partners joined in their devotion to the health of the race.

Through historic and current examples of acceptable political violence and by appeals to national concerns, WSPU rhetors put their own spin on British standards of appropriate political behavior. As this chapter has shown, the suffragette move to guerrilla militancy against private property was not a simple and inevitable escalation to the next level of violence. Rather, it was a clear strategic choice made by the union leadership and fully understood by the rank and file who chose to remain and carry out the new policy. Union rhetoric clearly pointed to awareness on the part of WSPU members that they were taking a grave step. Theirs was the same decision that has been made by other terrorist groups. The WSPU reluctantly concluded that the only way to reform lay in creating for the government a crisis that could no longer be ignored. Because the suffragettes stopped short of lethal violence (and because violence by women was considered an incongruous joke rather than a serious threat), union rhetoric needed to heighten the impact of each act of arson or window-breaking. Only by making the threat of violence real to the British public could the WSPU make the women's franchise salient to the average enfranchised male. With that salience would come pressure on the government to end the crisis and restore peace. Historic example and traditional image could support the general use of political violence, but it remained for the WSPU to convince the public that violence was justified in the specific case of the suffragette cause. It was vital that peace should be purchased through government acquiescence on the suffrage issue and not through further repression of those who sought the reform. The union thus turned to a rhetoric that would justify this violence both to the British public and to the individual suffragette who was the agent of the new policy. In the following chapters, I explore the suffragettes' four primary justifications that defined their reformist terrorism as legitimate within the tradition of the just war.

3

The Defensive Response to a Culpable Opponent

Once the new policy of strategic violence was actually put into practice, it prompted resounding criticism from multiple quarters. The government, the antisuffragists, and the property owners who faced the first attacks were not alone in their angry response. The union also faced opposition to the use of violence from within the militant suffragette ranks. Even those who were definite supporters of both women's suffrage and the earlier militancy were forced to decide whether they were willing to take this additional step. In October of 1912, nearly one year into implementation of the new strategy, Emmeline and Frederick Pethick-Lawrence were asked by the Pankhursts to sever their ties with the union. This news was staggering to the average union member, because the Pethick-Lawrences had been considered co-leaders of the union along with the Pankhursts ever since the early years of the WSPU's campaign in London. They were responsible for the founding of the paper, *Votes for Women*, served as the editors of the paper, and provided much of the union's financial backing. In the summer of 1912, the Pethick-Lawrences had privately questioned the Pankhursts about the wisdom of moving farther into violent militancy. The Pankhursts, believing that the leaders of the union must present a completely united front, ousted the Pethick-Lawrences from the union against their will. Following the split in the union leadership, *Votes for Women* remained in the control of Frederick and Emmeline Pethick-Lawrence. The WSPU started another paper, *The Suffragette,* on October 18, 1912.[1] Movement members were forced to choose between nonviolent militancy championed by the Pethick-Lawrences and the increasingly covert and violent militancy of the union. Although no longer personally taking part in the guerrilla militancy of the WSPU, the Pethick-Lawrences continued as apologists for the WSPU's use of violence against property.

The tension within the movement following the split between the Pankhursts and the Pethick-Lawrences was best characterized by the cartoon that appeared in *Punch.* It showed two young women in earnest conversation, with one asking the other, "Are you a Peth or a Pank?"[2] The use of strategic violence was a change in tactics, but it also forced a change in women's self-concept. It would now be more difficult to portray women as morally above the violence and rancor that had characterized men's political pursuits. As Chaim Perelman has pointed out, only change requires justification, and to make that justification in a given societal context we turn to acts, agents, values, and beliefs that a society currently approves.[3] These already approved acts, norms, and values are used to make the argument that the criticized behavior should also be approved on the same basis. The suffragettes used as the basis of their own justification the generally accepted concept that war (or violence) was in certain instances justified. In equating their militant movement with a just war, union rhetors turned first to the just-war criterion that violent action should only be undertaken as a defensive measure.

In Robert Tucker's view, warfare is justified by its being either "in self-defense or in collective defense against armed attack," and the WSPU made its arguments on both these fronts.[4] The women's war, the union maintained, was forced on the suffragettes both as the only means to defend themselves and as the only means to make a collective defense of the women of England. Perhaps the cause for violence most readily grasped in Western culture is that of self-defense. Any child, when taken to task for apparently aggressive behavior, will be quick to report who "started it" in order to frame his or her own act as a defensive one. Nations, even when they are not behaving like small children, often frame "the enemy's action . . . as 'voluntary' and 'initial' and contrasted with a reaction that was 'involuntary' and 'defensive.' "[5] In answering the question of whether waging war was always a sin, St. Thomas Aquinas replied that "a just cause is required, namely that those who are attacked, should be attacked because they deserve it, on account of some fault."[6] Thus Robert Ivie describes a view of warfare and violence as "a necessary evil forced upon a reluctant nation by the aggressive acts of an enemy bent upon the alienation of humankind from their liberties."[7] In characterizing one's own violence as a part of a "just war," one must portray the enemy as striking first and without just provocation. What Ivie calls the "claim of reluctant belligerence"[8] is not, of course, limited to warfare between nations, but it is important, according to Frederick Hacker, in the justifying of political violence and terrorism. From the terrorist's viewpoint, "One's own violence is always experienced as counterviolence, as aggressive antiaggression. It is always the others who have started or could have started; it is they who are wrong and therefore carry all the responsibility for their terrorism and for one's own terroristic antiterrorism."[9] The claim of reluctant belligerence was also made by the Women's Social and Political Union; and, as it has in other contexts, it "serve[d] as a crucial premise in the overall justification" of the union's acts.[10] Proof of the suffragettes' reluctance lay in the defensive nature of union violence, in the immorality of their opponent, and in their refusal to take up violence except as a last resort.

Reformers who would resort to terrorism face a problem based on their claim of acting in the best interests of the oppressed. Accommodating their stated belief in the value of the individual with the strategy of striking *at* the innocent individual through violence against private property is difficult. Maxwell Taylor describes two general approaches the terrorist takes to lessen this problem: "either by denigrating the qualities of the victim, or by locating responsibility for any injury on another agency."[11] As I will discuss in a later chapter, the WSPU used the first of these approaches when justifying specific acts of violence. In justifying the use of violence in general, the WSPU clearly took the second of these options, placing the responsibility for its guerrilla militancy squarely on the Liberal government.

As a part of their rationale for defensive violence, WSPU members rehearsed their grievances against the government, the press, the courts, and the prisons. Continually, the history of violence perpetrated against the suffragettes was brought before the eyes of movement members. Just as the strategy of violence lent presence to the movement as a whole, union rhetoric sought to give presence to events of the early movement when peaceful suffragettes were on the receiving end of violent measures. Tales of such events as Black Friday were part of the movement canon and served as a goad to indignation and action for movement members. Combined with this repeated litany of personal affronts experienced by the WSPU was an even longer list of general grievances held by the women and children of England. These stories of married women denied the right to raise their families, violated and neglected children, and women forced into prostitution provided much of the dramatic tension in suffragette rhetoric.

Taking all of the injuries and attacks on women and children in sum, the WSPU felt justified in exercising violence to gain the power needed to defend them. The suffragettes portrayed themselves as willing victims sacrificed for the collective defense of the women of England. Maxwell Taylor claims that women come to a terrorist strategy usually through political idealism and the desire to force change in the interest of others. Some terrorist acts appear in their extreme form to be a means of avenging the oppressed as well as a means to end their oppression.[12] Frederick Hacker may be close to defining this aspect of union justifications when he says, "Terrorists from below are injustice collectors who use terror from above as their model."[13] In any event, Emmeline Pankhurst used what Paul Ramsey calls the Western "presumption against injustice" to strengthen her case that militant attacks against property were justified defensive actions taken in response to initial violence against the union and against women and children in general.[14]

Therefore, throughout the guerrilla militancy phase, the union exercised this process of "guilt transfer"[15] to make the government culpable for any violence undertaken by union members. Maurice Tugwell claims that guilt transfer works for the terrorist by shifting public focus "away from the embarrassing acts of its originator toward the embarrassing acts of the adversary."[16] Not only terrorists must "redirect attention away from [their] violent act[s] toward the action of others," but also those who wish their violence to be viewed within the outlines of justified warfare.[17] According to Ivie, because just wars must be entered into with reluctance, there exists "a burden on advocates of war to establish the enemy's culpability and [this burden] leads them to engage in what Kenneth Burke has called 'the victimage ritual.' " Reform and revolutionary movements both pose a particular challenge to the hierarchical order occasioning, according to Burke, the guilt that requires redemption. Part of that redemption was purchased through the self-mortification of union members, through their victimage in the cycle of police and crowd violence, prison, hunger strike, and forcible feeding. But as the suffragettes sought a different means to "pay" for the disruption to the hierarchical order other than their own victimage, they naturally placed the guilt outside the movement and sought redemptive payment there. Ivie maintains that "the rhetoric of warfare is a natural extension of this tendency to promote 'social cohesion through victimage.' That is, a people strongly committed to the ideal of peace, but simultaneously faced with the reality of war, must believe that the fault for any such disruption of their ideal lies with others." The Liberal government, with its tendency to make facile pledges, easily broken, and with its intense repression of early and largely symbolic militancy, made a "suitable and plausible scapegoat" for the rhetoric of victimage. This rhetoric "draws upon 'substitution [as] a prime resource of symbol systems' in order to create 'catharsis by scapegoat.' "[18] In the case of the WSPU's justifications, the process of scapegoating served to make the Liberal government ultimately responsible for the "crisis-producing actions" undertaken during the guerrilla militancy phase.

Finally, because of the serious and irrevocable nature of violence (whether conducted as warfare or as terrorism), justification must be sought by proving that the actor lacked other viable choices. Part of the stance of the justified belligerent lies in the proof of his or her own reluctance. Violence must be undertaken only as a last resort and not merely as the most expedient means of accomplishing a goal. The suffragettes used this approach to complete their argument portraying their violence as purely defensive in nature. Because the suffragettes needed to defend themselves and English women and children against unwarranted attack and because an unscrupulous government refused to heed reasonable demands, the suffragettes were, therefore, left with no other viable alternative but the resort to violence. Through these arguments, the suffragettes sought to regain the moral initiative they lost by taking the step into violence.

Just Cause: Self-Defense

In later years, Frederick Pethick-Lawrence claimed that militant methods should "create the greatest difficulties for the Government" and "win the support of the bulk of the population by casting odium on the Government for its repressive counter measures." Constance Rover has pointed to this statement as proof that the suffragettes were playing to win and were determined not to be the nice guys who finish last.[19] Others have identified this method of forcing repressive countermeasures as essentially unfair and as a means for the suffragettes to cause trouble and then play the injured innocent. Pethick-Lawrence was, of course, writing about the movement across its entire existence. As I discussed in the previous chapter, it was certainly the goal of the guerrilla militancy phase to create a crisis, and the union made much of all governmental attempts to suppress its guerrilla militancy through coercive tactics. The way the suffragettes punctuated the sequence of events, guerrilla militancy was an act of self-defense in response to attacks on the union by the government, the press, and the courts.

The union claimed that, long before windows were broken or private property attacked, "the Government had been waging a most cruel warfare upon the Suffragettes."[20] The WSPU pointed out that women initially went to political meetings to ask questions (as men did), but, unlike men, they were brutally manhandled out of the meetings and often arrested for protesting their treatment in an orderly meeting outside.[21] In legal deputations, Christabel Pankhurst claimed, "unarmed women would proceed to the House of Commons. . . . Before they reached their destination they were set upon and driven back by police—mounted and on foot—until it became evident that they would not go away until they had performed their mission."[22] The suffragettes were aware that, as Frederick Pethick-Lawrence claimed, "had a deputation of men, half as influential as this deputation of women, gone to see the Prime Minister on what to them was a vital and important question, that deputation would undoubtedly have been received." At the Conspiracy Trial against the suffragette leaders in 1912, where charges of conspiracy to commit offenses against the law were brought against the union leadership, Pethick-Lawrence could point to a deputation of men from Woolwich who sought an audience with Asquith on a labor question. When told that the prime minister had a dinner engagement, the men made clear their intent to come for an audience anyway. Not only were the men *not* met with police and charged with obstruction, they were met by Mr. Asquith, who made time for their deputation.[23] On the other hand, the deputations by women, their questions at political meetings, and even by-election work by the union were all labeled "raids" and thus brought the same heavy legal penalties as if the women were engaged in violent militancy. Lord Robert Cecil made his opinion known in the House of Commons "that had men in this country been treated as women had been in that matter, there would have been insurrection."[24]

The intense physical violence at police hands encountered by the suffragette deputation on Black Friday in 1910 was a turning point for the union. However, Black Friday was only the worst instance of police and crowd attacks at suffragette demonstrations. Union members were accustomed to mob violence, to the tendency of some elements in Hyde Park to turn into, in suffragette Mary Richardson's words, "ferocious, howling animals" as soon as the union colors were displayed or the words "Votes for Women" uttered. Richardson discussed the men who wore in their lapels locks of hair torn from suffragette scalps, the factory workers who kept suffragette papersellers "in touch with whatever fruits or vegetables were in season," and the respectably dressed men who inevitably sidled up to the papersellers to whisper obscenities in their ears before hurrying away.[25] The union expected more restraint from the English police and was genuinely shocked by the Black Friday treatment of a legal deputation. The Conciliation Committee of Parliament made a careful investigation of Black Friday and concluded:

The clearest proof that the aim of the police . . . included the terrorizing of the women, is supplied by the overwhelming evidence that they resorted to various painful and dangerous methods of torture. The more common devices were to bend the thumb backwards, to twist the arm behind the victim's back, and to pinch the arm continually and with evident deliberation. . . . The intention of terrorizing and intimidating the women was carried by many of the police beyond mere violence. Twenty-nine of these statements complain of more or less aggravated acts of indecency.[26]

The police in this instance violated the "minimal force ethos traditional in the British constabulary," which T. A. Critchley says began with the police "practicing non-violent methods of crowd control against the Reform Bill demonstrators and the Chartists." Critchley speaks of the police utilizing "a controlled application of force, scrupulously careful to offer no provocation" in a situation where "the *bona fides* of protestors are taken for granted."[27] Certainly, the women in the deputations expected this, and they viewed Black Friday and the continuing practice of "buffeting" by police as a sign that any "effective challenge of the political supremacy of the other sex" would bring into play "the physical force measure at the disposal of the State."[28] Members of the WSPU later claimed that their move into violence was a result of their learning the political lessons taught to them by the government. Such researchers into terrorism as Richard Rubenstein have claimed that terrorists choose the modern state as the model for their violence and "derive their exaggerated respect for violent action in large part, from the state itself—the modern, 'progressive' state that emits an endless stream of words while bludgeoning its enemies into submission."[29] In the case of suffragette reformist terrorism, Emmeline Pethick-Lawrence claimed that "the weapon of physical force was thrust upon [the union] by the other side," and suffragettes had no choice but to reply in kind or see their movement crushed.[30]

Historian Ray Strachey claims that the suffragettes "knew well enough that they suffered real violence in return for merely technical offences," but they also knew that the press sheltered the public from this fact.[31] The press had initially conducted a boycott on news about women's suffrage, broken only by mild early militancy creating stories that could not be ignored. But, the women found that breaking press silence did not guarantee fair coverage. The Rev. E. H. Taylor, in a sermon entitled "Christian Atrocities," stated that "all these women have said, all they have done, has been misrepresented and distorted" by the press.[32] The "Suffragette Alphabet" took on press distortions of the actions of suffragettes: "**B** is for Bites that have never been bitten, / Though the journalist finds that they pay when they're written."[33] The union was aware of the effect of bottom-line issues on press coverage, and the Reverend Taylor claimed that "the Press to-day is governed by the political and social world, by the capitalist and financier, and its editors have to do what they are paid to do."[34] Government control over the papers was satirized in a cartoon of December 8, 1911, where personified newspapers labeled "Daily Express," "Manchester Guardian," "Daily News, " and "Globe" are bowing down before a Buddha with Asquith's face.[35] Though the union members claimed awareness of links between government and press, they still experienced frustration that their message did not reach the average person in the street. Although the press directed no actual violence at the suffragettes, members apparently felt that they had to defend themselves from the violence done to the truth. Of course, undertaking violence against property did not cure this problem, and the WSPU still found press coverage contradictory: "There is the old, old conspiracy of depreciation, minimising what has been done, suggesting that it is just a temporary and negligible thing; there is the old, old conspiracy of vindictiveness, exaggerating what has been done, making out that it is so terrible and so intolerable that it must at all costs be stopped. . . . If the destruction of letters is a trivial thing, why this hysterical raving for repression? If it is a powerful thing, why this simulation of contempt?"[36] The union claimed that the government then added injury to insult by intimidating wholesale newsagents, attempting to coerce them into no longer carrying *The Suffragette.* Printers of the union paper were also threatened for printing controversial articles, and at least one issue contained large sections of blackened out articles because the printer feared government prosecution. There were two major raids on the paper in attempts to close it down. These efforts to suppress the free speech of the union were viewed by many as provocation and were considered a part of what Mary Richardson would call, in retrospect, "the stupid treatment meted out to [the suffragettes] that fostered the militancy of their movement."[37]

The union also viewed the courts as a tool used by the Liberal government to crush the suffrage movement, and the judicial mistreatment of suffragettes became a part of their rationale for defensive violence. As described previously, the sentences meted out during the early, nonviolent phase of militancy for "obstruction" (the term used to prosecute such otherwise legal actions as interrupting meetings with questions or taking part in deputations) were really quite extraordinary. When simple stone-throwing to force arrest was undertaken, the sentences continued to escalate. Emmeline Pankhurst received, for example, a two-month prison sentence in the criminal division for breaking one pane of glass worth 2s. 3d.[38] The 1912 Conspiracy Trial was seen by the union, and portrayed by the defense, as a purely political attack against the WSPU's right to exist. Mr. Healy for the defense spoke of each of the sentences—"two months, four months, six months"—meted out for breaking windows and told the jury that "for every pane broken, for every act committed, some woman had lain upon the plank bed, some female had eaten bread and water." If the acts of militancy had already been punished, what was the Conspiracy Trial but an effort at political repression? "I have not the smallest doubt," said Mr. Healy to the jury, "it would be a very convenient thing, if they had the courage to do it, to shut up the whole of His Majesty's Opposition while the present Government is in office . . . as it would be to end women's agitation in the form of the indictment."[39]

If the government was shown as exercising coercion through the judicial system, the policy of forcible feeding was the physically violent manifestation of that coercion. Union speakers often discussed from public platforms their personal experiences with what Emmeline Pankhurst sardonically described as "the tender mercies of a Liberal Government, in its efforts to coerce women and break their spirits."[40] There is a relative consistency in descriptions of forcible feeding, both in contemporary descriptions and in later autobiographies, that leads me to conclude that the speakers were not exaggerating the pain of the procedure. Some of the most graphic descriptions of the process were presented by C. W. Mansell-Moullin, M.D., who was vice president of the Royal College of Surgeons and who had conducted a study of forcible feeding published in *The Lancet* in 1912. He read to his Kingsway Hall audience the statement of one forcibly fed suffragette: "The passage of the tube caused me at first but little inconvenience, but its further passage caused me to retch violently and to choke to such an extent that in my struggle for air I rose to my feet and stood upright, in spite of three or four wardresses holding me down. . . . The passage of the tube caused me excruciating pain. . . . After the operation, two wardresses took me back to my cell. . . . I vomited milk, which eventually became tinged with blood."[41] The forcing of the stiff nozzle of the tube up the prisoner's nose apparently caused much of the pain. Mary Richardson said that "as the nozzle turned at the top of my nose to enter my gullet it seemed as if my left eye was being wrenched out of its socket."[42] Dr. Mansell-Moullin reported to his audience on specific instances of mistreatment during the feeding process. In one case the prisoner told the "operator" of the feeding tube that one side of her nose was blocked and she had never been able to breathe through it. They persisted in "forc[ing] the tube up that side of the prisoner's nose three or four times until the operator was compelled by the blood that poured out to desist." He mentioned another feeding in the Winston Gaol, Birmingham, where the food was driven into the lungs of a suffragette, causing such severe choking that the feeding had to be stopped, and resulting in pleurisy and pneumonia in the prisoner.[43] Annie Kenney testified in one speech that "one woman has never been able to speak on a public platform [since being forcibly fed], because every time she speaks great clots of blood collect in her nose and throat. Another woman had her stomach displaced."[44] It was not so much these extraordinary injuries but the grinding away at the prisoner's health that was the real torture of forcible feeding. Dr. Mansell-Moullin quoted Home Secretary McKenna, who claimed, despite all evidence to contrary, that there was no pain involved in the feeding process: "Time after time has he told the Members of the House that there was no pain or injury, and almost in the same breath—certainly in the same evening—he has told how one of these prisoners has had to be turned out at a moment's notice, carried away in some vehicle or other, and attended by a prison doctor, to save her life. One or other of these statements must be absolutely untrue."[45] McKenna's statements and the apparent insensitivity of the government to the suffering being caused to these women led notables such as George Bernard Shaw to speak out against forcible feeding. Sharing the same platform with Dr. Mansell-Moullin, Shaw challenged Mr. McKenna to prove that "forcible feeding is rather pleasant than not" by allowing himself to be forcibly fed. Shaw sarcastically offered to use McKenna's favorite food and to provide a skilled surgeon to administer the process, pointing out that such niceties were not offered to the suffragettes.[46]

As forcible feeding continued, Asquith was increasingly pictured in union cartoons with one hand around a woman's throat and the other raised in a fist to punch her.[47] The suffragettes viewed this coercion against them as very personal violence, and some expressed doubt about where the government would stop in its measures. In the light of movement history, Emmeline Pankhurst's worry about her personal safety does not seem unreasonable. To an open-air crowd in Chelsea, Pankhurst mentioned the government arrest of a decoy disguised to look like herself:

Men rushed upon a small group of women, and singling out to one of those women whom they imagined to be myself, first struck her violently upon the head, and then threw her upon the ground. This happened at night, and, you know, on a dark night "accidents may happen," and how convenient it would have been, friends, to have got rid of a militant leader by an accidental blow on a dark night! The Government would have expressed great regret, some man would have been dismissed for excess of zeal, and there would have been an end of Mrs. Pankhurst.[48]

Whether the attacks on the WSPU came from the government, the press, the courts, or the prison system, the suffragettes felt that their own guerrilla acts were a means of self-preservation. Union violence was justified, in Emmeline Pankhurst's eyes, as "protest against the infamous coercion of women naturally lawabiding, who have taken to the weapons of rebellion" only reluctantly.[49] Expanding militancy was merely a response, arising out of the need for self-defense in a war declared by others and waged unjustly.

Just Cause: Collective Defense

Union members may have declared their violence a defensive response to the initial coercion of the government, but their primary justification described WSPU violence as a collective defense against the violence done to the women and children of England. According to the union, the franchise was not desirable in and of itself but in "regard to the things we are out for—reforms for women, for old and for young women and for little children, who are dying through the absence from legislation of the effective influence of women."[50] WSPU rhetors formed a sense of identification, in the Burkean sense of the word, with the women of England; that is, they identified themselves with English women in general, "largely through sympathetic attitudes."[51] A sense of identity, according to Hacker, "denotes and connotes that community in whose defense aggression can and must be mobilized when threats arise."[52] Through identification, the WSPU formed a sense of the English woman in the abstract: assaulted by the laws of her country, fearful for her children, yet allowed no hand in improving her own life or the lives of those dependent upon her. The coercion against women brought by the laws of the country formed the central theme for the WSPU and provided the major justification of its "war" as defensive in nature.

Throughout the life of the movement, and not simply following the advent of guerrilla militancy, Emmeline Pankhurst considered England's marriage-age law "a wrong so intolerable, so dreadful, that we feel ourselves justified in using very strong measures indeed in order to get power to alter that law."[53] Pankhurst told an American audience of her trial where a twelve-year-old girl was brought in as witness to an act of suffragette arson: "It was said that it was a terrible thing to bring a little girl of twelve years of age and put her in the witness box in a court of law. I agreed, but I pointed out to the judge and the jury that one of the reasons why women were in revolt was because that little girl, whose head just appeared over the top of the witness box, was considered old enough by the laws of her country to take upon herself the terrible responsibilities of wifehood and motherhood, and women could not get it altered."[54] Under English law, a woman also fared badly during the course of her marriage. A woman was not considered the equal guardian of her child along with her husband and had no legal say over the way her child would be raised. Should she outlive her husband, a woman could find that he had willed all the family money—even money that she helped earn in the family business—to others besides herself and the children. Again, she had no legal recourse.[55] The divorce laws were so one-sided that, as Emmeline Pankhurst told one audience, if a woman found that her husband was "not all she in her love for him thinks him, . . . he may even bring a strange woman into the house, bring his mistress into the house to live with her, and she cannot get legal relief from such a marriage as that."[56] Pankhurst found the law of divorce in England to be, as she told one jury, "the most scandalous in Europe. . . . Talk about revolution and rebellion! Why, I tell you, gentlemen, that that law in itself, once women are convinced that revolution is necessary to alter it, is sufficient justification for any revolution that women may adopt."[57]

Pankhurst and the other union speakers claimed often that theirs was a disinterested battle, because the women of the suffragette ranks were "the women who are held to be fortunate, the women who have no special personal grievance of their own." However, the suffragettes could not ignore, they said, the economic coercion that women felt in English society. Wages were extremely low for women workers, many of whom were the sole support of their children or a sick husband. The sweated homeworker, making three or four shillings for eleven hours of work, was an ill familiar to most of the audiences addressed by the union. Because city rents could not be met with such an income, several families were often forced to crowd in together, increasing the chances of disease.[58] Lloyd George "spoke of 'cottages reeking with tuberculosis,' of 'damp, wretched, dark dismal' abodes; he spoke of 'women condemned to death for the sole crime of sticking to their homes,' and 'little children who have the germs of death sown into their system by abominable housing accommodation.' " Yet, *Votes for Women* maintained in reporting the chancellor of the exchequer's words that, while Lloyd George was aware of the disease, he was blind to the cure and did not mention "the cruelty and crime of depriving women of the vote—that means of protecting themselves and their children."[59] As evidence that the female franchise could truly serve as a means of self-protection for women and children, Frederick Pethick-Lawrence favorably compared the infant-mortality figures in England to those in Australia, where women had the franchise. In 1893, Pethick-Lawrence explained, South Australia had one of the highest infant-mortality rates in the civilized world. The following year, women, having just received the vote, pressed through a considerable amount of legislation, with the result that by 1909 the infant-mortality rate was cut in half.[60] These arguments differed little from those put forward by nonmilitants, and they show that throughout the militant campaign the rationale for the vote itself was not entirely abandoned in favor of the rationale for militancy.

The forms these arguments took were often literary. For example, *Votes for Women* published an excerpt from *The Woman with the Pack*, an execrable little play by Gertrude Vaughan. The opening, in which a group of twentieth-century people are visited by "a mysterious symbolic Woman, carrying a cross, a child, and a lantern," gives some sense of the heavy-handed symbolism. The scene takes place in a room in London where the mother and children (one of whom is blind) are making matchboxes and are beset by a drunken father who delivers such lines as "Damn you and the children! (Hits her with his fist.) Get my supper, I tell you!" The play presents, crammed into one scene, a myriad of very real social problems: sweating, child and wife abuse, intemperance, prostitution, and malnutrition. By the end of the scene, the heroine, Phillippa Tempest, has decided to become a suffragette, and at the close she appears in tableau as Joan of Arc.[61] The printing of this scene in *Votes for Women*, albeit early in the guerrilla militancy phase, is interesting mainly because it is an aberration. Following the move to greater violence, the suffragettes favored the factual example over the fictional compilation when talking about the various kinds of coercion women faced in their daily lives. The examples they gave increasingly developed an angry edge, and they became more willing to speak bluntly about sexual coercion against women.

The argument that women were protected from violence in life simply by virtue of their *being* women particularly galled the union. Christabel Pankhurst called it hypocrisy to say that "the name of woman was a defence against violence. It was to many men an invitation to violence, else why the wife-beating, the assaults upon women and girls. . . . Violence and brutality at women's expense have lurked in corners and in darkness, but . . . the Suffragette has . . . drawn violence and brutality out into the light of day where they can be seen and destroyed."[62] Speaking about sexual violence against women was particularly difficult, for many audiences found the subject inappropriate for discussion and the suffragettes were forced to walk the line between euphemism and bluntness in their descriptions. Union rhetors relied on the factual example, generally being careful to refer only to incidents about which they had personal knowledge. For example, George Lansbury spoke of "one of the most pathetic letters I have ever received in my life." It was from a young girl forced to supplement her income of six shillings per week from a confectionery shop. She was "driven to get the balance made up otherwise," Mr. Lansbury stated, "We all know how."[63] In the speech that inaugurated the guerrilla militancy policy, Emmeline Pankhurst had served for several years as a member of the board responsible for disbursing to the poor money from the Poor Rates (taxes). In the speech that inaugurated the guerrilla militancy policy, Pankhurst gave considerable time to relating incidents she had observed during her years as a Poor Law Guardian:

Never shall I forget seeing a little girl of thirteen lying in bed, playing with a doll, and when I asked what was her illness I was told that she was on the eve of becoming a mother, and she was infected with a loathsome disease, and on the point of bringing, no doubt, a diseased child into the world. . . . I had occasion to visit a Salvation Army hotel in [Leeds] and in the matron's room there was a little child eleven years of age. She didn't look older than eight, and I said: "How was it she was there? Why wasn't she playing with other children?" And they said to me: "We dare not let her play with other children. She has been on the streets for more than a year." These, women in this meeting, are facts. These are not sensational stories taken from books written to attract the attention of those who like to think about matters that we have been accustomed to believe ought not to be spoken about.[64]

Pankhurst used her considerable ethos to verify sexual horror stories while speaking quite convincingly of her distaste at even pondering "the degradation of the helpless little children."[65]

This aspect of the militant suffrage campaign is often portrayed as anti-male, but it should not be overlooked how ardently union rhetors worked to transfer the blame from the average man to the government and the judicial system. Emmeline Pankhurst made, in one address, reference to magistrates convincing young prostitutes to plead guilty so that evidence that might indict the powerful would not be made public. This, Pankhurst maintained, was "the policy of 'hush up,' " and the antisuffragists in the House of Commons were "the men who want things hushed up. And the Government wants things to be hushed up because there are too many tarred with the same brush."[66]

The Defensive Response to a Culpable Opponent / 69

The union compared the sentences given to the suffragettes with those given to men convicted of child molestation to prove that women's and children's lives were held cheaply. Emmeline Pankhurst, at her trial in 1913, compared an earlier sentence she was given of six weeks as an ordinary prisoner for breaking a three-shilling pane of glass with the sentence of "a man in a city I know very well, occupying a high position," who "was sent for six weeks in the First division for having corrupted several little girls." In that same trial, Pankhurst pointed out that, if convicted for an attack on property, she could be given a maximum punishment of fourteen years, but a man morally or physically injuring a little girl could receive a maximum of two years.[67] Annie Kenney rattled off a list of actual "sentences that make women indignant, and which cause them to rebel," among them "three months' hard labour for ruining a child six years old. . . . Then we get a child five and a half years of age; six months' hard labour for carnal knowledge. . . . Another child of five years; carnal knowledge; seven months' hard labour. . . . A child of three; indecent assault; five months' hard labour."[68] In reference to the disparity between sentences protecting property and sentences protecting children, Emmeline Pankhurst claimed that, "If there is in the framing of the laws and the administration of the laws so wide a gulf set between women's feelings and men's feelings on moral matters, that in itself is a justification for what we are doing."[69]

Much has been written about the morality crusade, which was particularly active in the union during 1913 and early 1914.[70] Christabel Pankhurst's book, *The Great Scourge and How to End It,* turned venereal disease from an unfortunate social problem into another instance of physical assault on women as a group. However, venereal disease per se was subsumed often in union rhetoric by the concern over the issue of white slavery. White slavery technically was the procuring (or otherwise "purveying") of young girls into brothels or foreign countries where they would be forced to serve as prostitutes. The extent of the actual problem was far less important than the place it had in the fears of women of the time; white slavery became, for some, a term that encompassed such other sexual issues as economic coercion leading to adult prostitution. The White Slave Traffic Bill, before Parliament since 1909, was pretty well "mutilated" in 1912, providing proof to many that the issue would not be dealt with until women acquired the vote.[71] A *Votes for Women* cartoon with the headline "Set the White Slaves Free!" showed a woman wearing a WSPU sash and standing before a locked jail door labeled "White Slave Problem." Two gaolers (Asquith and Lloyd George) stand before the door. Asquith holds five keys, "Waiting and Seeing," "Indirect Influence," "Man's Protection," "Back Door," and "Chivalry." Lloyd

George holds the key, "Votes for Women," behind his back. The caption read:

Gaoler Asqu.th: "We don't seem to have the right key."
Gaoler Ll..yd G..rge: "I've got another, but don't let's try it."
WSPU (pointing to the key in the hand of Gaoler LL G..rge): "THAT is the only key; will you give it to me?"
Both Gaolers: "The answer is in the negative!"[72]

The issue of white slavery became emblematic to the WSPU women when they were physically attacked during deputations, for they saw themselves suffering to prevent the suffering of other women. One woman assaulted in Wales during a suffrage demonstration described her assault to Emmeline Pankhurst and mentioned that she could not even tell her husband and son the true nature of the assault. Mrs. Pankhurst described to an Albert Hall audience her reaction to the woman: " 'How could you bear it! It seems to me that is the hardest thing of all to bear.' And she said, 'All the time I thought of the women who day by day, and year by year, are suffering through the White Slave Traffic—("Shame!")—and I said to myself, "I will bear this, and even worse than this, to help to win power to put an end to that abominable slavery." ' "[73] Thus, the litany of grievances that English women had against the law and against their treatment by men was accompanied by images of mortification. The suffragettes portrayed themselves as willing victims sacrificed for the collective defense of the women of England.

The strength we accord to the justification of violence in defense of the oppressed is shown by those who wish to denigrate Pankhurst and the union. The primary move made by critics, both at the time of union activity and in later scholarly writing, is to claim that Pankhurst was acting for personal aggrandizement, not in the interests of women and children. However, the suffragettes saw Emmeline Pankhurst and themselves as having "always stood and worked for the bottom dog."[74] This view was reflected in the inscription that suffragette Lady Constance Lytton wrote on the wall of her prison cell: "To defend the oppressed, To fight for the defenceless, Not counting the cost."[75] If we can believe the suffragettes' self-view and public portrayal, then their identification with the oppressed tells us a great deal about their sense of justification. As Hacker says, "Identity legitimizes aggression customarily denied to the individual, thus liberating him from anxiety, inhibition and guilt concerning his formerly restrained or repressed aggressive impulses."[76] Far from feeling guilty over the new violent aggression, Emmeline Pankhurst redefined restraint in the negative: "Those grievances [ones concerning women and children] are so pressing that, so far from it being a duty to be patient and to wait for evolution, in thinking of those grievances the idea of patience is intolerable, and we feel that patience is something akin to crime when our patience involves continued suffering on the part of the oppressed."[77]

Enemy Culpability

By claiming that the WSPU's program of violence was defensive, union members attempted to position themselves as co-victims with other oppressed members of the public. Redefining themselves as victims rather than perpetrators of violence was a vital step if the WSPU hoped to regain the moral ground lost in attacks upon the public. The union held that the "fault" for guerrilla militancy belonged to the government, "which admits the justice of our demands, but refuses to concede them."[78] The basic stance of the suffragettes was that the government, by its trickery and conspiracy against the suffrage movement and by its incitement of the union to greater militancy, became responsible for the union policy of violence against property. This argument of government guilt was often presented in the same terms as God's case against Israel (Hosea 8:7) by using the phrase "Reaping the Whirlwind." Just as Israel had merited punishment in its disobedience to God's will, the Liberal government had "Sown the Wind" by its actions and was now "Reaping the Whirlwind."[79]

The union became particularly irritated by the admonitions of the Bishop of Lincoln, who said of the militants, "Who takes the sword shall perish by the sword." Surely, Christabel Pankhurst said, the bishop "spoke without reflection," for it was the government that had the choice of weapons and which first took up the sword against the women's suffrage movement. If anyone was to perish by the sword, it would be that government.[80] The maintenance of the defensive posture by the union and its characterization of government responsibility could be readily seen in the headlines that accompanied the weekly two-page report of militant damages:

"Reaping the Whirlwind. No Peace for Women Torturers"
"As a Man Sows—So Shall He Reap"
"The Retort Militant. Women Answer the Government"
"Devastating Fires, Grave Responsibility of the Government"
"One Year's Militancy Ends. No Peace for the Wicked"
"Retribution"
"Coercion the Counsel of Fools, and the Spur to Rebellion"[81]

In each instance the "retort militant" was the responsibility of the government for its acts of coercion. A cartoon reprinted from *The*

Woman's Journal out of Boston reflected this same theme. In the cartoon short, fat John Bull is talking to tall, thin Uncle Sam while behind them is the scene of the English police arresting women who have just broken some plateglass windows. The caption reads: "John Bull: 'I call it disgraceful! The women ought to be ashamed of themselves!' Uncle Sam: 'Ya-as. Mebby so. But how about you, John? Who drove 'em to it?' "[82]

Anger over the Manhood Suffrage Bill led to the first attack on private property in the massive window-breaking of November 21, 1911. To union eyes, the Manhood Suffrage Bill was "trickery and chicanery," and the government took it up not in good faith but, as Christabel Pankhurst maintained, even while "preparing for us the slip that lies 'twixt cup and lip."[83] The offer of yet another "sham opportunity of enfranchisement" could, Annie Kenney claimed, "never bamboozle us," since women of the union "always know when to strike a bargain, but we are not going to buy shoddy."[84] This duplicitous nature of the Liberal government was deeply felt by those who had continuously bargained, called truces, and waited in vain for a women's suffrage bill to be passed. Doubtless, the union members felt, as Rubenstein has described other terrorists, "like victims of deception," for they began their movement "so trustingly, believing in their message of hope, their power to deliver it, and the capacity of others to listen and respond."[85] It did not help that the movement was always allowed to reach a peak where success seemed inevitable before the government would yank the political rug from beneath their feet.

This view of a conspiratorial government was the basis of the analogy used by Emmeline Pankhurst in her speech at the May 1912 Conspiracy Trial. She described a case of a young girl tried for infanticide (most likely in this context a euphemism for abortion). The analogy implied that the child was illegitimate and that the girl, abandoned by the child's father, had turned in desperation to "infanticide." The judge in the case refused to try the girl until the "participator of her guilt" was also brought to trial. Drawing the analogy to her own case, Pankhurst claimed, "If we are guilty of this offence, this conspiracy, other people, some of the members of His Majesty's Government, should be in the dock by our side."[86] The analogy is a clever one: the young girl (the WSPU) has been forced to the desperate measure of infanticide (the union's use of violence against property) because she was tricked and abandoned by an unscrupulous man (the government).

The trickery of the Liberal government became the theme for some of the finest editorial cartoons produced by the movement. One cartoon portrayed the tea party scene from *Alice's Adventures in Won-*

THE MANHOOD SUFFRAGE PARTY.

"Have some Votes for Women?" said the Hare.
"I don't see any," said Alice.
"There are none," said the Hatter.

Figure 5. "The Manhood Suffrage Party," *Votes for Women*, January 19, 1912

derland but called it the Manhood Suffrage Party. The WSPU as Alice looks from a paper toward Lloyd George (complete with rabbit ears) as the March Hare and Asquith as the Mad Hatter. The caption reads: " 'Have some Votes for Women?' said the Hare. 'I don't see any,' said Alice. 'There are none,' said the Hatter"[87] (Figure 5). Perhaps the most pointed cartoon showed a lovely Edwardian little girl (wearing a WSPU sash) standing on a street corner in winter. Around the corner are Lloyd George (still with his mustache) and Asquith as two little bully-boys. Asquith holds a large snowball marked "Manhood Suffrage Bill," and Lloyd George holds a tattered doll, "Women's Suffrage Amendment," which is losing its filling through a hole. The caption reads: "Mr. LL..D G..RGE: 'I'll go and give her this and you can throw the snowball at her while she's looking at the doll' "[88] (Figure 6). This cartoon achieves the same kind of diminishment as other cartoons that make the cabinet ministers into children, but in this case there is also a malignant pettiness in the actions of Lloyd George and Asquith, which makes plausible claims that women's suffrage was a personal issue for both men. A cartoon of "The Bravoes of Westminster" shows a young woman turning down the proffered bouquets ("False Promises") of Sir Edward Grey and Lloyd George. The caption

Mr. LL - - D G - - RGE: I'll go and give her this and you can throw the snowball at her while she's looking at the doll.

Figure 6. The Doll and the Snowball, *Votes for Women*, December 22, 1911

informs the reader that "telephone girls are officially warned against accepting drugged bouquets offered them by men—there is no need to warn our readers of a like danger in the political sphere."[89] These scenes played to recognizable types, the little bully and the evil gigolo, and were well calculated to make particular cabinet ministers appear malicious and duplicitous.

The union compared itself favorably to the constitutionalists, who were portrayed as blind to their own deception by the government. Although not directly stated, there appeared to be an underlying contempt for those women who still allowed themselves "to be tricked by the excuses of politicians [and who] have not yet awakened to a realisation of the situation."[90] At the time of the Great Pilgrimage (a massive procession of the nonmilitants to prove public support for women's suffrage), the union put on the front page of *The Suffragette* a wicked little cartoon. The scene depicts the Walrus and the Carpenter from *Through the Looking Glass*, but with the Walrus labeled "Lloyd George" and the Carpenter labeled "Asquith." The little oysters all in a row are labeled "N.U.W.S.S." (National Union of Women's Suffrage Societies). Above the picture it read " 'O Oysters, make a pilgrimage,' The Walrus did beseech. (Advice to the Suffrage deputation at Swindon, on 23rd October, 1913)," and underneath was

"O Oysters, make a pilgrimage,"
The Walrus did beseech.

(Advice to the Suffrage deputation
at Swindon, on 23rd October, 1913.)

(With Apologies to "Alice Through the Looking-Glass.")

THE SAD RESULT.

" It seems a shame," the Walrus said,
" To play them such a trick,
After we've brought them out so far,
And made them trot so quick!"

Figure 7. "The Sad Result," *The Suffragette*, October 31, 1913

the verse "THE SAD RESULT. 'It seems a shame,' the Walrus said,
'To play them such a trick, After we've brought them out so far,
And made them trot so quick!' "[91] (Figure 7). Thus, the union made
known its view that the much-vaunted Great Pilgrimage was simply
another instance of duped women allowing the government to make

them look ridiculous. Fortunately, Christabel Pankhurst offered, "The W.S.P.U., by constant protest, has upheld the honour of women in the face of the Government's insult, intrigue and treachery. But for the attitude of the W.S.P.U., Suffragists would have stood before the public duped and humiliated beings."[92] The government was an enemy lacking honor; the constitutional suffragists were an ally lacking dignity. Union actions were justified by the treachery of the one and were necessitated for the redemption of the other.

Not only did the government members by their treachery merit WSPU violence, they also were responsible for inciting union members to escalate the level of their violence. Early on, the WSPU had focused upon the words of former home secretary and Liberal M.P. Herbert Gladstone when he said that it is "*force majeure* which activates and arms a Government for effective work."[93] But the most direct incitement, and one often pointed to by union members in justification for violence, came from antisuffragist cabinet minister Mr. C. E. H. Hobhouse in a 1912 speech at Bristol, where he said: "In the case of the suffrage demand there has not been the kind of popular sentimental uprising which accounted for Nottingham Castle in 1832 or the Hyde Park railings in 1867. There has not been a great ebullition of popular feeling."[94] Dr. Ethyl Smyth, testifying at the 1912 Conspiracy Trial of the suffragette leaders, claimed that this speech made her change her mind and decide to take part in a massive March 4 window-breaking because she "did not see how any self-respecting woman could stay at home after that."[95] The editorial cartoon of the March 8, 1912, *Votes for Women* showed a shopwalker in front of a shop with broken windows. He is indicating a gentleman standing nearby to an approaching policeman. The caption says: "Shopwalker: 'Please take Mr. Hobhouse in charge; it is he who has incited the women to violence' "[96] (Figure 8). Emmeline Pankhurst characterized other "incitements" as "insults to do more serious things," using as an example the questions posed by the minister of war when he was interrupted by women: "Why do you content yourselves with pin-pricks? Why don't you do something serious?"[97] It was the government's "expressed contempt of militancy in its first mild phase" that Christabel Pankhurst indicated as a factor in the decision to employ greater militancy in order to obtain the desired pressure.[98] An equally direct incitement came from a "professed Suffragist" who claimed, as many did at the time, that "women cannot terrorise—cannot use violence volently [sic] enough."[99]

Showing the government members' lack of scruples was part of a broad vilification that portrayed the government as "a powerful, malignant force" that deserved the violence brought against it. The union followed many of the vilification patterns favored by revolu-

SHOPWALKER: Please take Mr. Hobhouse in charge; it is he who has incited the women to violence.

Figure 8. The Shopwalker and Mr. Hobhouse, *Votes for Women*, March 8, 1912

tionary terrorists who use hyperbole and metaphor in showing their enemy as "conniving, conspiratorial, and pervasive."[100] About the best that could be said for the government members was that they were all talk and precious little action. Theirs were "the fair words that butter no parsnips."[101] A recurrent image equated Asquith with Pharaoh, who could not be appealed to in his moral sense or higher nature (presumably because he had neither). The union claimed, "As easily would the Israelites have softened Pharaoh's heart without the Plagues, as would Suffragists without militancy soften that of Mr. Asquith!"[102]

The WSPU turned to this favorite analogy of the plagues of Egypt to make the point that the attacks on private property were not "new militancy" but only the necessary and predictable evolution of the old: "Ever since militancy began with a question to a Cabinet Minister it has gradually increased in severity just as each of the plagues of Egypt was more severe than the one before it had been."[103] Laurence Housman detailed the analogy of the plagues of Egypt in a way that anyone familiar with the escalation of suffragette militancy could appreciate:

Then, further, it will be remembered that the earlier plagues took rather the form of a nuisance and a discomfort than of actual damage to property. First, the water-supply was interfered with; clean stomachs found it undrinkable,

78 / The Defensive Response to a Culpable Opponent

things would not wash in it, and much dirty linen was in consequence exhibited to the public gaze. This was followed by certain unwelcome intrusions into Kings' chambers of voices that croaked omens; and this, again, by parasitic attentions which produced intense personal irritation. After this came a swarm of flies, which the magicians simply could not stand; and only after this, at long last, came damage and destruction to property.[104]

The unspoken analogy to the early militancy of the WSPU is very clever. The union began by airing the dirty linen of the Liberal government leaders by revealing the duplicitous way they handled suffrage legislation. Soon the union members moved to speaking out at political meetings and making their presence felt through mass demonstrations and other means. All of this effort was of intense irritation to the government, in the same way that Moses and the plagues of God caused irritation to "that Cabinet of Egyptian magicians." But the government was really responsible for the damage to English property, just as the hardness of Pharaoh's heart was responsible for the plagues visited upon the Egyptian people. There was ample opportunity for both to prevent destruction of property, for "the signs of the Heavens are mild in their operation, and judgment does not descend from them without warning."[105]

During the spring of 1913, the government instituted a new policy that verified, in suffragette eyes, their low opinion of the current cabinet ministers. With many of the union members in prison at that time, public discomfort over the government policy of forcible feeding was building. With opposition to forcible feeding on the increase, the authorities needed a tool to prevent the death of the prisoners from starvation without resorting to forcible feeding. In April 1913 there passed into law the Prisoner's Temporary Discharge for Ill-Health Act. This act made it possible to release a prisoner for ill-health—usually due to a hunger strike—then rearrest and send her directly back to prison when her health had recovered sufficiently. Lord Robert Cecil called it the "Cat and Mouse Act," a name that stuck with both the suffrage movement and the press.[106]

This act instituted a system of virtual house arrest. The special police "Cats" would keep watch over a location where a formerly incarcerated "Mouse" was recuperating from her hunger strike. Theoretically, the prisoner was to return voluntarily to prison when her days of temporary release expired. None of them did, of course, nor were many of them recovered in the usual one to two weeks they were granted. The "Cats" would pounce as soon as the suffragette ventured from the house or nursing home in which she was hiding. At least some of the public backing the WSPU lost in its move to guerrilla militancy reappeared as the Cat and Mouse Act was enforced.

The union used the Cat and Mouse Act to prove that its characterization of the government as brutal and repressive was correct. The "murderous policy" of the Cat and Mouse Act was likened, again, to medieval torture, to "the Iron Maiden of the Middle Ages, whose spikes closed slowly upon its victims with terrible pressure until life was crushed out."[107] The best-known poster of the English suffrage movement may have been the one showing a giant cat holding in its fangs the limp, dangling body of a young woman wearing a WSPU sash. The poster read: "The Cat and Mouse Act passed by the Liberal Government—The Liberal Cat, Electors Vote Against Him! Keep the Liberal Out!"[108] (Figure 9). Another cartoon, under the headline "The Quality of Mercy," showed an apparently dying woman on a bed in Holloway. Over her stand two men (one of them Prime Minister Asquith): "The doctor: 'This woman is very weak, but I think at a pinch she could stand another twenty-five minutes.' The Prime Administer: 'Twenty-five minutes! Ah well, never let it be said we do not temper our injustice with mercy, let her out in twenty!' "[109] The Cat and Mouse Act revealed the brute behind the mask of ministerial dignity and restraint. Thus, the Cat and Mouse Act, although instituted after guerrilla militancy began, became part of the proof suffragettes offered that their violence had always been a response to violence directed at the women reformers.

As forcible feeding continued and the Cat and Mouse Act began, the metaphors of vilification mounted. Leaders of the Liberal government were "veritable Turks in their attitude towards women" and "are assailed by a gallant band of women struggling to be free."[110] The government was aided by the police, who were characterized as "Cossacks."[111] The Liberal government was the repeat of a "type" who could be found throughout history, "the counterparts of the men who nailed Christ to the Cross, who sent Joan of Arc to the stake, who killed Marie Spiridonova, who have sent thousands of reformers to living death in Siberia, who in Turkey have massacred men and women of another faith."[112] For such men to criticize women for the use of militancy was absurd; it was "very like beasts of prey reproaching the gentler animals who turn in desperate resistance when at the point of death."[113] Such hyperbole served not only to justify violent actions against a remorseless and predatory enemy but also to make the immediacy of such actions imperative.[114] This vilification strives toward making the "perfect villain," the ideal "political scapegoat" who may be sacrificed in the victimage ritual and thus provide perfect catharsis.[115] If the evil of the enemy provided a measure of justification to external audiences, the internal audience of union members could feel bound closer by hatred, what Eric Hoffer has called "the most accessible and comprehensive of all unifying

Figure 9. "The Cat and Mouse Act," *The Suffragette*, May 22, 1914

agents."[116] In the justification of their "war," the union presented the Liberal government as "the savage" who must be sacrificed so that men and women united for the common good could purify the world of "sins that have caused their fall from the Eden of peace and redeem themselves as defenders of freedom and reason."[117]

Union rhetors thus based their claim that they had just cause for their women's war on two arguments: first, the women's war was fought in defense of the union and women in general against the initial aggression of the government; and second, union violence was the direct result of government coercion, incitement, trickery, and lack of character. By focusing on the blatant coercion the government exercised over the early movement, the apparent duplicity of the legislative process, and the taunting by government members that union violence was negligible, the union was able to give its actions a gloss of relative innocence. As Emmeline Pethick-Lawrence put it: "This great movement is . . . gathering momentum every day like a great flood. Now, when a tide is dammed back it overflows, and inevitable destruction is wrought. But men do not argue with a flood; they do not put the responsibility on the flood; they put the responsibility upon, and they argue with, those who have dammed back the stream and prevented it from flowing in its ordinary channel."[118] The union identified itself as a great natural force involved in a just cause against an unjust enemy. In a blend of the words of Jesus, a folk saying, and the oft-used words from Hosea, the union claimed that women had "asked for bread and been given a stone. The stones have come home to roost, like chickens. The Government had sowed the wind, and now they are reaping the whirlwind."[119]

Last Resort

Thus, union proof that its belligerence was truly reluctant lay in the characterization of suffragette violence as defensive and directed against an unscrupulous enemy. The WSPU also needed to prove that the suffragettes lacked alternatives to violence and that they had fulfilled a "presumption against violence and war," which must be met, according to Ramsey, by proving that the reluctant belligerent has adopted violence only as a "last politically reasonable resort."[120] Despite ready declarations by governments and movements alike that all peaceful methods have been exhausted, "no clear criteria emerge by which one determines when peaceful efforts to the crisis have been pursued sufficiently."[121] The WSPU claimed that its violence

DOUBLE-FACED AGAIN !

Mr. ASQUITH (to Suffragette asking for Votes): "Two Months' Hard Labour !"
Ditto (to Miner threatening with Votes): "One moment, sir, what can I do for you?"

Figure 10. "Double-Faced Again!" *Votes for Women*, March 15, 1912

was undertaken as a last resort—a sole remaining option for the unenfranchised who had exhausted constitutional methods.

A major argument used by the union to prove that it was driven to violence as a last resort was based on the belief that "legislatures have no time to listen to the opinions and the desires of people who have no votes."[122] This view was strongly expressed in an editorial cartoon of March 15, 1912 (Figure 10). Under the headline "DOUBLE-FACED AGAIN!" Asquith is shown with two faces. One face rants at a suffragette holding an empty purse labeled "No Votes." The other face calmly addresses a working-class man holding a bag labeled "1,000,000 votes." The caption reads: "Mr. ASQUITH (to Suffragette asking for Votes): 'Two Months' Hard Labour!' Ditto (to Miner threatening with Votes): 'One moment, sir, what can I do for you?' "[123] The reason put forward by the union for the disparity in treatment between male and female reformers was simply the constituent stature of the latter. All electors shared the power the franchise conveyed and were therefore less justified in using violence to redress their grievances. "The electors do their fighting by marking a cross on a ballot paper," said Christabel Pankhurst, "but for the voteless there is no weapon save that which the Suffragettes are using."[124] Along this

The Defensive Response to a Culpable Opponent / 83

same line, Frederick Pethick-Lawrence provided an excellent analogy at the Conspiracy Trial:

Supposing you had some trouble with a tradesman; supposing your butcher supplies you with some bad meat; supposing some one cheats you in a business transaction; supposing your landlord behaves improperly to you in some way—you don't go and break the windows of the person who has dealt with you improperly; you don't do anything of the kind. . . . If your butcher sends you bad meat, you go to him and say, "I won't have it," and, if he persists in sending you bad meat, you have your remedy, you tell him that in future you will deal elsewhere. Everyone has that power over his tradesman. . . . If people have votes they can turn out the government. If they have not got votes, they are deprived of the ordinary means of redress which one has in ordinary everyday life of bringing pressure to bear upon those against whom they have a grievance. And that is why, as a matter of fact—whether it be right or whether it be wrong—we people are fighting for the franchise and that is why we have adopted methods which under ordinary circumstances would be absolutely unjustifiable.[125]

I have chosen to quote this passage at such length because it provides in one place the gist of the entire argument justifying the union's forcing of a crisis through violence. The agitation for the franchise is portrayed as a unique political situation, for the demand and the tool needed to acquire that demand are one and the same. When other means of obtaining redress are cut off, Emmeline Pankhurst claimed, the reformer must turn as a last resort to "the argument of the broken pane of glass . . . the most valuable argument in modern politics."[126] Union members also considered the choice of guerrilla militant methods to be, not a matter of their own initiative, but a final, desperate response to an untenable situation. Women were not creating anarchy: "Anarchy is there. There is anarchy in a country which professes to be under constitutional and representative government, and denies the benefits of the constitution to more than half its people."[127]

The suffragettes thus developed the argument that the necessity of violence lay in its power as a bargaining chip. The most eloquent rendering of this argument came from Emmeline Pethick-Lawrence, who quoted an 1878 speech of German Chancellor Bismarck in which he declared that "the basis of all political negotiation was the principle *do ut des* (I give that you may give)" (emphasis in original). Pethick-Lawrence pointed to the determination made by Ireland to withhold its political support from the Liberal government in 1910 unless a guarantee for submitting a home-rule bill was made. When the leadership of the Welsh Party no longer held liberalism as their highest political value but insisted that their own concerns be dealt with, then Welsh disestablishment became a viable political issue. In both cases, Pethick-Lawrence claimed, the parties with a grievance said, "We have given, in the belief that you were prepared to give; henceforward we shall withhold if you withhold." The weakness of the women's political position was their lack of anything of political value with which to negotiate on a *do ut des* basis. In Pethick-Lawrence's view, whether the "bargaining medium" was a gift or a weapon did not matter, as long as the women did not "come empty-handed" to the negotiating table. Militancy was the weapon that allowed bargaining on a political basis. While Pethick-Lawrence was willing to admit that it was "a weapon with a double edge, and wounds the hand that uses it," she declared that proof of its value lay in the negotiations it had forced thus far and in the government's desire to force the suffragettes to lay down this weapon. Yet, she claimed, the weapon of militancy remained "stronger and sharper" than ever and would only be surrendered when "we shall be able to conclude an honourable and a lasting peace upon the firm political basis, *do ut des*."[128] In effect, with this argument the suffragettes made militancy an extension of their argument that government rested on the consent of the governed. Until they were given full political rights, militancy would give them the power to withhold their cooperation in exercising their political responsibilities. They would withhold the power of militancy only when the Liberal government proved willing to give them the power of the franchise.

This, then, was the first foundational argument justifying attacks on private property as part of a just cause. Property damage was described as the last effective resort open to the powerless and as a tactic forced upon the union in defense against the attacks of an irresponsible government. The suffragettes were not aggressors but responded as a peaceful nation would to an unwarranted invasion by a foreign power. The personal autonomy of women had been repeatedly violated by the aggression of a more powerful force, and they lived as a country under occupation. Under such conditions, the use of violence was not merely justified but was also the appropriate action dictated by conscience.

4

The Suffragette as Just Warrior

Perhaps the biggest stumbling block for the Women's Social and Political Union in its justification of reformist violence was the public perception that women lack the authority to declare war. According to Robert Ivie, war, in order to be justified, must be "waged under the auspices of legitimate authority."[1] Paul Ramsey speaks of this stipulation as historically meaning that "initiating the use of armed violence in defense of the public good was placed on the topmost legitimate political authority." Over time the right to call for a justifiable revolution extended down to the private citizen acting in a magisterial capacity. That such legitimate authority could conceivably rest in the common person was a Calvinistic byproduct, an extension of the concept of "the priesthood of all believers."[2] The right of men to oppose tyranny by calling for revolt or to oppose an aggressive enemy by declaring war was thoroughly established in Western thought. However, the right of women to do the same was another matter entirely. The problem for the WSPU was summed up by the response of a heckler at an outdoor address by Emmeline Pankhurst at Campden Hill Square. When Pankhurst compared the women's movement to men's earlier franchise campaigns, saying "When your forefathers fought for their liberty they took lives," a voice from the crowd called out, "You are only a woman."[3] Union rhetors faced a double difficulty in justifying their violence, for they lacked the authority for violence, which rested in the state, and they even lacked the authority for justified rebellion, which rested in male citizens. Therefore, the union, needing to manufacture its own authority, faced the rhetorical problem, detailed by Garver, of discovering how "invention can be the source of legitimacy."[4] In this chapter, I examine the attempt by the union to achieve the legitimate authority in public eyes that would justify its use of violence. Primarily, union rhetors reached for this legitimacy by borrowing the ethos of a standard male army conducting warfare, by appealing to their unique character as women, and by calling upon religious justifications for their acts.

The Army of Militant Women

Reformist terrorists face the same problem of legitimacy as revolutionary terrorists, because, as Richard Rubenstein points out, even to call an organization "terrorist" is to judge it as illegitimate. Generally, in Rubenstein's view, the terrorist or reformist terrorist organization is caught between two metaphors that cast its actions in terms of "terrorism-as-crime" or "terrorism-as-warfare." The tendency for those who do not sympathize with a terrorist organization's goals is to view terrorists as "criminals with a political axe to grind." What tends to tip the scale away from a definition of terrorism as warfare is the small number of actual terrorists working for a cause. The terrorists are viewed as "an isolated minority," and their claims to be the vanguard of a mass movement are generally viewed as irrational. If terrorists do not represent the masses, then their acts are individual crimes rather than acts of warfare, because "mass violence may sometimes be justified, individual violence virtually never." This perception of an isolated minority committing crimes rather than warfare is enhanced by the territory in which the terrorist must operate. An organization seeking internal change within its own country must conduct its rebellious acts within a society that is ongoing and apparently peaceful. There is no war zone or clear, contested area of ground where the "war" may be conducted. Therefore, actions that are considered routine and justifiable in war are viewed as crime in the civilian territory where the terrorist must operate: "the capture of prisoners is considered kidnapping," and attacks on enemy holdings are viewed as simple vandalism.[5]

These special rhetorical pressures, faced by the suffragettes because of their choice of a terrorist strategy, led the union to appropriate the image of an army and to place its acts of reformist terrorism under the justifying concept of warfare. If the suffragettes could convince others to see them as they saw themselves, as a "suffrage army in the field," then their attacks on property and the autocracy of their leadership could both be justified.[6] As Emmeline Pankhurst put it,

"Directly you talk of a revolution or a civil war, then you understand the breaking of glass; then you understand every kind of weapon, and the use of every weapon in our warfare."[7] To legitimate the claim of warfare, there needed to be a declaration of war, but one in keeping with the defensive nature of the conflict. At the Albert Hall on November 16, 1911, during the week preceding the first official attacks on private windows, Emmeline Pethick-Lawrence addressed the union as follows:

After a long period of truce with the government, we meet to-night, a united army on the eve of battle; not because we have chosen to fight, not because we desire militancy, but because the Government has broken its terms of peace. The announcement of the intention of the Government to bring a Manhood Suffrage Bill is a declaration of war upon the womanhood of the country. To refuse to take up this challenge would be to turn our back upon public honour and public duty. We are going to put through this fight for women's emancipation, cost what it may.[8]

In the same speech, Pethick-Lawrence described the forcible feeding of the then only nominally militant union as a "new kind of civil war," a war to which the WSPU would now respond in kind.[9]

Early in 1913, Emmeline Pankhurst pointed to men's struggles for freedom "opposed by the forces of organised government" and stated, "Our women have shown as much heroism and resource as any of these men, and our war is of a similar kind. It is guerilla warfare that we declare this afternoon."[10] This declaration introduced the stronger measures of arson and bombing and completed the gradual move into violence against private property, which began in late 1911 with the breaking of shopwindows.

By the time the union actually took the step to guerrilla warfare, union audiences were accustomed to the army and military metaphors that peppered the speeches and writings of suffragette leaders. At times these metaphors were extended and detailed. Emmeline Pankhurst compared her speaking in the Albert Hall to "assisting at a review, and tonight I feel more than ever that we are reviewing our forces. We are considering and measuring our strength, we are seeing where we stand, considering the force of the opposing army, deciding how our campaign is to be pursued." This was the first meeting since the split with the Pethick-Lawrences, and Pankhurst justified the severance in the context of the army metaphor: "One thing is essential to an army, and that thing is made up of a two-fold requirement. In an army you need unity of purpose. In an army you also need unity of policy."[11] Often the military references were brief, alluding to "the brave women . . . ready to come in our next battle," "the impossibility of the Government induc[ing] us to lay down the weapons that we know are of use," or to a specific suffragette as "that great soldier of our army."[12] The superiority of suffragette forces was often claimed, as when Emmeline Pankhurst referred to the opening of Parliament by saying, "The mock battle of Parliament has begun again. The sham armies are in the field. But there is a real army in the field, and that is the women's army. (A Voice: That is the W.S.P.U.) That is the W.S.P.U., my friends. (Applause.)"[13] Military metaphors argued against the idea that the acts themselves were criminal deeds and pressed the point of inevitable victory of a holy army: "They [the suffragettes] have by sheer fighting carried the suffrage flag further and further into the enemy's country, and by sheer fighting in the future they will carry it and plant it triumphant on the citadel itself."[14] Military language lent not only the legitimacy of viewing terrorist acts as acts of war, but also gave the suffragettes a vocabulary of enemies and brave soldiers, traitors and loyal compatriots, small skirmishes and final victories. To an American audience in 1913, Emmeline Pankhurst referred to herself as "a soldier who has temporarily left the field of battle in order to explain—it seems strange it should have to be explained—what civil war is like when civil war is waged by women."[15] The heroic image of the battlefield found its way into union poetry as well as its speeches, editorials, and artwork:

Woman! Arise! And take thy fitting place,
Amid the armies of the human race.
Gird on thy sword of justice and of right,
Nor rest till victory crowns the valiant fight.[16]

In much the same way that the Church militant utilized battlefield images in hymns as an appeal to bravery and self-sacrifice, the suffragettes saw themselves as "buoyant, rejoicing, close-knit in fellowship, this army of the holy."[17]

The suffragette militants liked to point out that "even the least militant of Suffragists find themselves using, almost in spite of themselves, the language of militancy. They speak of being armed with the sword of the spirit and with the sword of the flesh." Of course, they continued dryly, "to use the metaphors of militancy and then to condemn militant action is surely a contradictory thing to do."[18] The WSPU shared with the nonmilitants the tendency to speak of "the sword" more in a figurative than in a literal way. A typical pictorial representation of the sword may be found in a cartoon from The Suffragette in June of 1913. A cloaked, "Dantesque" figure carrying a flame is walking forth from Holloway Prison at night. Shackles are around her ankles, and the chains run the entire way back into the prison. She carries a lowered, flaming sword inscribed "Spirit." The caption reads: "The Sword and the Spirit"[19] (Fig-

THE SWORD AND THE SPIRIT.

Figure 11. "The Sword and The Spirit," *The Suffragette*, June 27, 1913

ure 11). This picture was typical in representing the union vision of
"the glorious, indomitable spirit" of the suffrage prisoners, which
served as their greatest asset in the cause. In the battle with the superior physical resources of the Liberal government, it was the suffragettes' "unbroken spirit which is the weapon by which the Government will be overcome. With this sword of the spirit they cleave
a way along which countless millions shall pass."[20] Of course, the
sword, which had a physical as well as a spiritual manifestation, sym-
bolized all methods—violent or not—"taken for the cutting of bonds
and the overthrowing of tyranny."[21] The sword as the figurative

90 / The Suffragette as Just Warrior

weapon of the suffragettes gave a romantic overtone to actual suffrage violence, which was often messy and unglamorous.

The need to recruit members willing to commit acts of reformist terrorism became increasingly urgent and inspired an array of military metaphors: "We are in the position of recruiting sergeants: we want more soldiers. . . . Swarm into the ranks of the militant army. All come and fight, and who is going to stand against us?"[22] In its recruitment for guerrilla militant action, the union focused upon the special nature of the soldiers who would do the fighting. The WSPU, according to Christabel Pankhurst, gave "the call to battle" that would be answered only by "those who have free souls and the warrior spirit." The need for an answer to the battle call was necessitated by the relatively small number of union women actually taking part in guerrilla militancy. The union was self-contradictory on the issue of numbers. Pankhurst claimed to "have no great reverence for numbers. The big battalions are not always victorious."[23] Yet there was a note of urgency to the recruitment of "guerrillists," as the words to one poem by Charles Kingsley revealed:

> Wisdom, Self-sacrifice, Daring, and Love,
> Haste to the battlefield, stoop from above,
> To the Day of the Lord at hand.[24]

Whatever it lacked in size, the women's army claimed to make up in spirit; Mrs. Drummond claimed that "Mrs. Pankhurst has a far more loyal army than Sir Edward Carson."[25] Because such statements were often accompanied by recruitment exhortations or admonishments by Christabel Pankhurst that "the disgrace is to [those] unready" to participate and the "glory is to those . . . willing to carry on the struggle without them," it appears that the union wished to make the best of an imperfect situation.[26] One effective tactic for the WSPU was to set the active guerrilla militants (the ones who actually placed the bombs or fired the letter boxes) into a special category within the union itself. Their bravery and their participation in the "joy of battle" illumined the entire union, raising all of the union women to a special level in the suffrage battle.[27] On the cover of one issue of *Votes for Women*, above a mounted Joan of Arc figure holding the WSPU shield and carrying a flag marked "Prisoners of War," were the words: "At the Old Bailey, May 22, 1912. The Jury: 'We desire unanimously to express the hope that, taking into consideration the undoubtedly pure motives that underlie the agitation which has led to this trial, you would be pleased to exercise the utmost leniency in dealing with the case.' The Judge: 'Nine months in the Second Division with the costs of the prosecution.' " Beneath the mounted figure was the following saying of Buddha: "We wage war, O disciples; therefore are we called warriors. Wherefore, Lord, do we wage war? For lofty virtue, for high endeavour, for sublime wisdom; Therefore are we called warriors"[28] (Figure 12). In this belief that the militant actions transformed the women who performed them can be seen the important point George Lakey made about the American suffrage movement: "What separated the militants from the women who kept to conventional means of agitation was the continuation of the *freedom motif* to the very mode of action itself. . . . The women found themselves defying both convention and the law. In this defiance, and the consequent hardships, they *enacted* their freedom and experienced the elation which went with it. The goal was experienced in the means, and this identification gave their sacrifice its strangely attractive power."[29] Although Lakey was writing specifically about nonviolent action, the violence against property undertaken by the WSPU even more closely resembled the life of the battlefield and drew its participants together in a secretive and difficult endeavor. More than any other autobiography of the movement, Mary Richardson's *Laugh a Defiance* gives a sense of the gamelike quality of some of the attacks on property. While Richardson was very forthcoming about the physical toll of forcible feeding and the depression that accompanied the physical pain, she wrote a lively account of furtive midnight bombings and strategic public appearances where a suffragette would suddenly rise to address restaurant or theater patrons.[30] One thing clear from her account and underestimated elsewhere is the reliance the union placed on individual initiative. Although new efforts were cleared with headquarters, they were often planned and executed by those in the field.

Christabel Pankhurst claimed publicly that "an army exists by and through its individual soldiers" and alluded to the battlefield speech in *Henry V* when she declared, "the fewer, the greater the honour."[31] Pankhurst referred to this same rallying speech of the king when she claimed that "we few, we happy few, we band of Sisters" would know the joy and accomplishment of battle as men did of old, and that this small army would grow "stronger and better women in the process."[32] This literary reference, familiar to English audiences, lauds the bravery of a small army joined in a sacred cause that ultimately defeats an overwhelming foe. The king, in this speech, also promises a future of pride for those who join the battle and regret for those who do not.

The ability of militant action to perfect the lives of the women who participated in it was joined with the image of the sword in one particular story popular with the union. Emmeline Pethick-Lawrence referred to this tale in a 1912 speech: "The story tells how the transforming Spirit of Illumination has visited the ardent expectant soul, has been made one with it, leaving behind as his gift the transfigur-

"We wage war, O disciples; therefore are we called warriors.
Wherefore, Lord, do we wage war?
For lofty virtue, for high endeavour, for sublime wisdom;
Therefore are we called warriors."

— Sayings of Buddha —

Figure 12. "Prisoners of War," *Votes for Women*, May 24, 1912

ing sword. And the soul awed and exultant sings: 'From now there shall be no fear left for me in this world and thou shalt be victorious in all my strife. Thou hast left death for my companion and I shall crown him with my life. The sword is with me to cut asunder my bonds, and there shall be no fear left for me in the world.' "[33] Militancy became, in Pethick-Lawrence's eyes, "a living and a quickening force" that had the power to transform individual lives even as it transformed society.[34]

The reliance on military imagery also allowed the union to redefine for itself and for the public the time that union members spent in prison. The need to define the movement's violence as acts of war (legitimate) rather than crime (illegitimate) led Emmeline Pankhurst to say to the judge upon her conviction for incitement, "I look upon myself as a prisoner of war."[35] Through this relatively minor image of the suffragette as a prisoner of war, union members sought the legitimacy for their actions that would come, in part, if they were officially recognized as political prisoners. The importance of this argument should not be underestimated. The insistence of the suffragettes that they be placed in the first division of prison—an insistence that sparked the initial hunger strikes—has not been given its due as a vital part of their overall strategy of justification. The women's desire to be considered political prisoners is echoed by revolutionary terrorists today who have made extreme protests to force prison officials to grant them political status. This aspect of the reformist or revolutionary argument is a further effort to define terrorist acts as warfare rather than crime. Emmeline Pankhurst insisted that WSPU acts be viewed as political offenses, as illegalities performed "because the offender is satisfied in her or his own mind that it is necessary to break the law in order to get a political grievance remedied."[36] According to Dr. Louisa Garrett Anderson, intent was the determining factor in dividing criminal from political offenses:

Surely, there can be no doubt in anyone's mind as to which category (common criminals or political offenders) Suffragists belong. A common criminal commits his or her offence for personal motives. He may be wrong in his calculations, just as a reformer may make a mistake in judgment; but he believes that the act which he is committing is going to give him something, to gain him some personal advantage. He hopes to escape punishment, and he does not mind how much the community suffers so long as he gains his own end. The exact reverse is the case when a reformer commits an offence. He puts away all thought of self-interest.[37]

This argument was not created by the suffragettes to avoid punishment for their reformist terrorism, but it was the accepted view formalized into law by the separate divisions of the English prisons. The union pointed to the support of the *Times* for "a broad distinction between the offence of Dr. Jameson [the leader of Jameson's Raid in the Transvaal, which preceded the Boer War by five years] and that of 'the vulgar law-breaker who seeks his own enrichment and the satisfaction of his private vices.' This broad distinction certainly exists as between the offences of vulgar law-breakers on the one hand, and of Suffragettes on the other."[38] The union was also able to quote Prime Minister Asquith himself denouncing the treatment of political agitators as common criminals: "We are assembled to denounce the treatment of political and industrial agitators on the same footing as an ordinary criminal. . . . I would rather find myself face to face with the brutal despotism of Russia than see the present prostitution of Constitutional forms, which at one and the same time is dishonest, ineffectual, and demoralising."[39] The union had little difficulty agreeing with such sentiments but questioned why female agitators were not granted this same governmental support in their status as offenders. "A Patriot" drew a wonderful analogy for *Votes for Women* by picturing a train taking on passengers. The bags of male political offenders (Ginnell, Jameson, Councillor Bradford) are being loaded into a first-class compartment. A guard is holding the door to a second-class compartment open to two women and one man (nicely drawn portraits of Emmeline Pankhurst and the Pethick-Lawrences). Their conversation ran: "PASSENGERS (Leaders of the W.S.P.U.): 'But ours are 1st class tickets! Is not this a 2nd class compartment?' GUARD (Mr. McKenna): 'The answer is in the affirmative. But under the Company's by-law 243a it has been greatly improved, and—' PASSENGERS: 'We don't want an improved 2nd class carriage. We want what is ours by right. We have paid for it—at the risk of our lives.' GUARD (losing his temper): 'It is impossible to enter into the minds of these passengers!' "[40] To gain the legitimacy needed to call for a just war (or a just revolution), the women of the WSPU had to have their actions viewed in the same political frame that men's violent actions were placed. As they would argue in trial after trial, the motives of the WSPU had nothing in common with the criminal and everything in common with the male political offender. Theirs was not a crime of personal gain but a women's war of personal loss for the gain of others. As such, they sought to have their violence viewed as justified acts of war and demanded as their "right" that as "soldiers captured in warfare for the Vote due honour" should be given to them.[41]

The Legitimate Authority of Women

The union could borrow a certain legitimation of violence from societally accepted images of warfare, but it still ran up against the fact that its members were women. The incongruity of women using violent tactics needed to be negotiated by union rhetors. In just-war doctrine, the right to call for a justified revolution against tyranny had evolved into a right possessed by an average citizen to act with magisterial authority—that is, to act in the capacity of a concerned citizen for the common good. Women, as the union often pointed out, were not citizens in the sense of rights, only in the sense of responsibilities. Public perception of women having the "right" to call for revolutionary action would be unlikely when women did not even possess the right to choose constitutionally elected officials. One possible way for the union to circumvent this problem was to present images of the militant women that portrayed them as acting not within their "rights" but within their responsibilities to society.

Yet, the dominant images of activist women were not exactly conducive to a sense of responsibility and reasoned action. Lisa Tickner has written persuasively that "the image of the shrew, and increasingly of that locus of medical and popular attention in the nineteenth century, the hysteric, were there waiting for the militant before she had thrown her first stone."[42] Antisuffragist rhetoric was eager to slip the suffrage militant into pre-existing stereotypes: the masculine or "strong-minded" woman, the frustrated spinster, and the unsexed "shrieking sister."[43] Antisuffragist views of suffrage militants took, on the one hand, an awed view of "screaming viragos" caught up in such "hysterical fanaticism" that Home Secretary McKenna compared "the militants to the natives of the Sudan, fearless of death in the cause of the Mahdi."[44] On the other hand, the militants were portrayed as "bungling incompetents," flailing futilely in a poor imitation of men's superior physical force.[45] Tickner makes the vital point that "the *Times* . . . along with the rest of the press, was talking about 'maenads' and 'hysterical hooliganism' before the first window was broken and five years before the arson campaign of 1913."[46] The images the union had to combat to gain legitimacy were, initially at least, somewhat disconnected from actual militant actions and were applied to any women seeking an active role. To counter the images of hysteria, the WSPU largely used the image of the Militant Woman, an amalgam of the Allegorical Woman (represented by such common figures as Justice or Liberty) and the Historical Militant (generally represented by Boadicea or Joan of Arc).[47] The iconography of the Militant Woman was an attempt to reclaim a higher female image that had been appropriated by men as a symbol for a variety of abstractions. Now this image was to represent real women, although it remained, for the most part, an equally abstract symbol of the Spirit of Womanhood. The image of the Militant Woman covered the untidy acts of actual violence with "the mantle of Boadicea or Joan of

Arc" and replaced the deviant and "hysterical" perpetrator with "the image of an active (and phallic) if unearthly agent of moral, social and political reform."[48] The images of Allegorical Woman were (and still are) familiar in city sculptures and war memorials, and this familiarity lent a ready recognition to the figure of the Militant Woman, whether she appeared in cartoon form or at the head of a parade.[49] There is something clean in the image, as if the Militant Woman retained the marble of statuary in whatever guise she appeared and could impart that purity to the militant women she came to represent.

Joan of Arc stood as the most potent symbol for the WSPU. Timing may have been a factor in her popularity with the militants, for she was beatified on April 16, 1909, when the suffrage movement was in full swing.[50] But this beatification of the historic Joan of Arc was a mere coincidence compared to the value she held as an icon for militant women. Christabel Pankhurst claimed that she left the suffragettes "a great inheritance. She has taught them the loveliness of simplicity, purity, courage, and militancy."[51] In Tickner's view, the true value of Joan of Arc was that "she defied order, division and convention in all the aspects of her marginality and strange, militant sanctity. . . . She was and was not a woman. She transcended the limitations of her sex and yet it was from the position of femininity— however unorthodox—that she posed a challenge to the English and to men."[52] Yet, I believe the most useful aspect of Joan of Arc was that she was real. That is, there was a historic woman who followed heavenly voices in a holy crusade, who challenged her time's view of the proper behavior for women, and who was martyred by forces unable to understand her greatness and the importance of her vision. It is little wonder that Christabel Pankhurst would speak of the Liberal government as "500 years behind the times. Their predecessors burnt Joan of Arc, and they themselves are now persecuting her spiritual descendants."[53] This same point was made by John Masefield, who compared the persecution of the suffragettes to that of Joan of Arc:

I blush for what our grandchildren will say of the men of my generation. Our grandsons and granddaughters will ask: "Were they sane in those days? Were they human beings? Were they not crazy and blinded? What was it in them? They cried out and raged and stormed upon those who burned Joan of Arc. . . . Yet when they had Joan of Arc among them they lacked the living eyes to see her. They thrust her into prison with the rest as an unsexed shrieking sister. . . . And when the martyrs were among them—in the dock, in the gaol-yard, in the gaol hospital, speaking in the parks among horse-play, or selling papers in the streets amid chaff—the men of that generation took no heed."[54]

The fact that Joan of Arc had existed and been rejected by her day provided the suffragettes with their closest link of identification. She offered a vision of what Tickner calls "spiritualised militancy," allowing Christabel Pankhurst to describe the suffragettes as "warrior saints—women of the breed of Joan of Arc!"[55] Joan of Arc was a figure of unquestioned purity, providing an image of "the reforming spirit of Evangelicalism in a newly militant and feminist guise."[56] Yet, unlike the purely allegorical woman (Justice, Liberty, etc.), Joan of Arc had actually lived and fought and, therefore, offered evidence to Christabel Pankhurst that "militancy is not unwomanly," as proved by the many "who reverence the memory of Joan of Arc, and are prepared to applaud the women who fight side by side with their fathers, their brothers, and husbands in every war."[57]

The iconography of Joan of Arc allowed Emmeline Pankhurst to reframe union acts of reformist terrorism as "not the hysterical manifestation" usually portrayed but as "carefully and logically thought out."[58] The carryover from the image of Joan to the actual militant women can be seen in Christabel Pankhurst's assertion that "the militants are not desperate, driven, frantic women. They are soldiers with a soldier's high and gallant heart, with a soldier's joy in battle, with a soldier's cool brain, steady courage, and iron will."[59] The Militant Woman image (and Joan of Arc in particular) gave the suffragettes a model of calm and resolute daring. As Tickner put it, "The Hysterical Woman was a deviant or pathological type, and the Militant Woman its allegorical antidote."[60] Union leaders valued a sense of coolness and calculation; at the Conspiracy Trial, Frederick Pethick-Lawrence pointed to his wife and Emmeline Pankhurst as the embodiments of this attitude: "Now, gentlemen, you have seen the two women who are here in the dock with me. You have been told in your newspapers that the women in this movement are hysterical and excited, and that they do not know what they are doing. You have seen the two women who are here with me, and I think it must have come to you, perhaps as a surprise, the calmness and deliberateness and the self-possession which those two women have shown."[61] The decision to take guerrilla militant action was reached "calmly and thoughtfully and deliberately" and compared well with the "male hysteria" that characterized the government's attempts to stop it.[62] "The hysteria," claimed union member Annie Besant, "is on the bench rather than in the dock, and the loss of self-control is to be seen more in the magistrates than in the prisoners."[63] Not only did "flustered officialdom" compare poorly with the suffragette militants, but militant men in past revolutions were also of a lesser caliber.[64] Annie Kenney stated in one speech, "When men go in for revolution, the first thing they do is to try to take human life. Men are not so calm as women. They don't keep their heads like women."[65] Instead of viewing the prohibition against harming human life as a sign of women's weakness and ineffectiveness, the union presented men's lethal violence as a form of hysteria. Women, on the other hand, "are prompted to rebellion not by mere waves of emotion nor by excitement, but by the steady, unwavering, unchanging and unchangeable command of their soul, and will, and very being."[66] The suffragette, "serene and strong in the knowledge that . . . [her] militant crusade is founded in right and is destined to triumph,"[67] was, in Christabel Pankhurst's characterizations, the antithesis of the desperate hysteric and was instead the spiritual inheritor of the qualities of the "armoured maid."[68]

The union urged women to "cease to regard themselves as victims of circumstance, and as helpless before the whims, prejudices and treacheries of politicians," and encouraged them to "show all the self-reliance, all the resolution, all the courage, all the fighting spirit that used to be, and let us hope still are, the attributes of those of the British race."[69] Christabel Pankhurst exhorted union members, "Who would be free herself must strike the blow," and reminded women inside and outside of the movement that "the conditions of modern life are merciless to the dependent."[70] Asking women to take upon themselves actions that directly challenged the predominant societal view was a hard sell. In an article entitled "Militancy a Virtue," Christabel Pankhurst tried to redefine the traits that were attractive in a woman. She expressed her belief that women, as human beings, need "to possess all human virtues": "It is right for them to be fierce as well as mild, to be strong as well as gentle. . . . The gentleness of a strong man is hailed as lovely, and it is the gentleness of the strong woman that is lovely, too. In fact, the gentleness that cannot in the face of wrong be transformed into aggression is not gentleness at all, but only weakness. It is not right for women, any more than for men, to have characters of tepid milk and water, to be incapable of a divine rage and to be impotent to resist oppression."[71]

One way the union sought to convince women within the movement (or contemplating membership) that violent militancy was justified was to claim that it stirred in men an answering admiration. Though this was not a major part of its rhetoric, the union claimed that "militant methods, the moral and physical daring shown by women in these last six years, have awakened in men impulses of real chivalry, and feelings of human sympathy and respect that were unknown to them before." Taking militant action was also shown as improving the soul of the woman herself, for militant methods "swept away the evils of 'ladyism,' of timid gentility, of early Victorian effeminacy as distinct from womanliness."[72] Union rhetors, it seems, felt compelled to combat any inroads made into the hearts of the union members by antisuffragist stereotypes. Suffrage militants, they assured their members, were more womanly for their use of militancy and, they implied, more attractive to men for their daring. It is interesting to find these occasional appeals to the very human need to respect oneself and to feel respected by the opposite sex. Considering the abuse the militants suffered at the hands of predominantly male crowds, it is not surprising that this type of rhetoric, directed to the internal audience, appeared so rarely during the guerrilla militancy campaign.

Ordained by God

Considering what Tickner calls the "heightened religiose rhetoric"[73] of the suffragette leaders, it would have been surprising had the WSPU *not* claimed that its methods were sanctioned by God. A reform group can do little that is more legitimizing of goal or method than to claim that God sanctions either (or both). Such union supporters as Joseph Clayton claimed that, speaking generally, "religion over and over again has sanctioned rebellion."[74] Specifically, Christabel Pankhurst spoke of the movement as not merely approved by God but ordained by Him, for "revolutions are the divinely appointed punishment of unjust rulers."[75] The suffragettes were answering "the Divine call . . . to yield [their] li[ves] and [their] service in the deliverance and redemption and uplifting of the human race."[76]

The biblical aspect of reform violence was presented by the Rev. E. H. Taylor in a sermon preached at Norfolk. Taylor was speaking to the faithful, giving his imprimatur particularly for those who might be uncomfortable with the personal use of violence. His contention was that "every great reform that has ever come into the world has come by the power of the sword, corruption has been driven from the kingdom by the violent who have taken it by force." Thus the Reverend Taylor could support suffragette methods "because the entrance of any great reforms necessitates a condition of warfare, it raises a standard which divides those who fight under it from those who fight against it."[77] This division between the reformers and those opposed to reform was, in this view, predicted by Christ: "Think not that I am come to bring peace on earth. I came not to bring peace but a sword. Suppose ye that I come to give peace on earth? I tell you nay, but rather division."[78] In using these words of Christ, the union compared His "purely spiritual warfare" to the need of the suffragettes for "militancy on the material plane." The suffragettes, "who are seeking to win political liberty, which is a kingdom of this world, must use the weapons of this world."[79] The union therefore declared its surprise at the constitutional suffragists, who could speak of a spiritual warfare and a spiritual army but insisted that there be no physical expression by this army. The same was said, claimed the union, to Joan of Arc by the church, which maintained that God had "no need of soldiers to deliver France." The suffragettes joined in Joan of Arc's answer: "The soldiers will do the fighting. God will give the victory."[80]

This image of the humble tool of the divine will was captured in a poem entitled "The Reformer," published in *Votes for Women:*

I am a tool in mighty hands;
    Though of myself no strength have I,
Yet, if He strike with me, the lands
    Shall reel and the great mountains cry.

And if He use me as His torch,
    My heat shall drink the eternal waves,
And the hot tongue of flame shall scorch
    The hidden depths of ocean caves.

If as a lamp He make me shine,
    My glow shall pale each fire afar,
Irradiate with light divine,
    The space beyond the utmost star.

And if, when He His power has shown,
    He lay me by, as is most meet,
I take the place that is my own
    Amongst the dust beneath His feet.[81]

What was true of the generic reformer was more especially true of the militant, leading Emmeline Pethick-Lawrence to claim that "we individually and collectively have been caught in the meshes of a Will that we may be used in the accomplishment of its purpose. By the decree of this Will, the time has come for a new birth of humanity, the hour has struck for the redemption of Woman." The militants, in effect, portrayed themselves as conduits of the divine will for humanity: "To play the game, while conscious that the game is being played through us!"[82] As such, their suffrage goals were approved by the divine will, and George Lansbury believed their acts of reformist violence were part of a justified war, "a holy war," declared by the ultimate legitimate authority.[83] The suffragettes' appeal to religion was a further justification of the individual militant. As Perelman points out, "God is the incarnation of supreme justice, and the just man is the one who obeys God."[84] In preaching their "new gospel," their "new good tidings," the suffragettes claimed to share "the spirit that prompted the early Christians to do what they believed right" and to possess "the faith that will remove mountains."[85]

One religious image that proved popular with the militants was that of David and Goliath. In fact, the inaugural issue of *The Suffragette* used as the first political cartoon the image of a small, feminine David wearing a WSPU sash, standing on the rock of "Militancy," and holding a slingshot at the ready. Toward David, through the water of "Broken Pledges," strides a three-headed giant of the Coalition government, wearing the sword of "Forcible Feeding" and swinging the mace of "Coercion."[86] Another pictorial representation of David and Goliath appeared after the late-night raid and destruction of orchids at Kew Garden. A small figure of a woman is shown breaking windows in the "Westminster Hot (Air) House" while a shocked Lloyd George (in gardening attire) looks on. The caption read: "THE GARDENING GOLIATH (as the Suffragette David breaks another pane in his hothouse): 'This is terrible! terrible! If she lets any more of the cold air of day into those Party System orchids they'll never survive it!' "[87] David, in particular, appears in various places in union rhetoric, as in this description of the November 21 demonstration: "Another rush, and far away you see a small green, round cap between two black Goliaths. A little David arrested—a proud and happy little David, no doubt."[88] Obviously, the link between David and stone-throwing was a primary reason for the initial use of the image, but the David/Goliath reference did more than place one union protest tactic in a familiarizing context. Identification with David, of course, put the union on the side of God and left the government to the ranks of the Philistines. It gave a sense of nobility (rather than comedy or contempt) to the smaller ranks of the suffragettes and made the point that "ever since David there have been times when the weak have been made strong to conquer."[89]

There were dire warnings for those who did not hear or heed the divine will. One headline on the weekly account of reformist terrorism in *The Suffragette* borrowed once again from Christ's admonitions to the lawyers and Pharisees: "The Government Answered, 'Woe Unto You, Ye Hypocrites!' "[90] Most of these warnings used biblical allusions and appeared written on walls or left on notes at the scenes of suffragette violence against property. During the aftermath of the destruction of a Somerset mansion, several postcards were found with such sayings from Psalms written on them as "Oh, come hither and behold the works of the Lord, and what destruction He hath brought upon the earth"; "Upon the ungodly the Lord shall rain snares—fire and brimstone, storm and tempest. This shall be their portion to drink" (Psalm 11:6); and "He maketh His angels spirits, and His ministers a flaming fire."[91] In these biblical references, the suffragettes take on a prophetic voice and foretell the heavenly vengeance awaiting those who would delay justice.

Following a suffragette raid at Town Hall at Newcastle-on-Tyne, the biblical expression "Mene, Mene, Tekel, Upharsin" ("God hath numbered thy kingdom and finished it. Thou art weighed in the balance and found wanting") was found written on the walls.[92] In this reference to the Book of Daniel, the government is equated with the doomed King Belshazzar, who watches a heavenly hand write the same words on the wall of his banquet hall. In this allusion, the suffragettes take on the role of Daniel, called to prophesy the future to a king who would not humble his heart and is, therefore, destroyed.

Poetry presented in the union paper reflected, if not this apocalyptic vision of what awaited those closed to the spirit of reform, then at least a sense of God's contempt for those slow of heart and mind. The final verse of the suffragette poem "Out of the House of Bondage" read:

> Sentence: "A month in second-class division
> For breaking plate-glass windows in the Strand"!
> Hear ye no laughter of the Lord's derision?
> O fools, and slow of heart to understand![93]

One rather infamous little piece of verse, by James Barr, was directed at Home Secretary McKenna:

> St. Peter spoke: "The gate's ajar,
> Enter McKenna!" "No," groaned he
> "So many souls I racked are there
> Heaven would indeed be hell to me."[94]

Considering the overall amount of union rhetoric, there was surprisingly little of this type of Judgment Day hyperbole, and it is important not to overemphasize the few examples that exist. However, they do help to establish that union members felt their movement to be sanctioned by God and that they saw themselves as cooperators with the divine will. God both legitimized militant actions and would wreak His vengeance on those who hampered His work.

It is natural to ask whether the apparent "millennial zeal of the WSPU," as Tickner puts it, was a genuine expression of religious feeling or a more cynical appeal to societal norms. It is true that "the 'language and style of religiosity' surrounded the altruism of . . . the late Victorian and Edwardian period."[95] David Mitchell was apparently correct in observing:

The identification of the Hosts of Light with one's own side has always been a human failing, and in Edwardian England was by no means confined to the WSPU. Lloyd George, a great oratorical bible-puncher, claimed that the Insurance Act was "doing the work of the Man of Nazareth." James Larkin referred to his "divine mission" and spoke of employers "crucifying Christ" (the workers) in Dublin. Religious overtones were traditional in the women's movement, from Mary Wollstonecraft to Josephine Butler, Annie Besant, and Florence Nightingale, who had written of the need for a "female Christ."[96]

Evidence indicates, however, that strong religious feelings existed within individual members of the union. Christabel Pankhurst spent her life following World War I as an Adventist evangelist (although this fact tells us little of her religious beliefs during the time of the suffrage campaign). It is perhaps telling that, when one suffragette playfully made up a creed—"I believe in Emmeline Pankhurst—founder of the Women's Social and Political Union. And in Christabel Pankhurst, her eldest daughter, our Lady, . . . She descended into prison; the seventh day she returned again to the world. She was entertained to breakfast, and sat on the right hand of her mother . . . , etc."—Emmeline Pankhurst was reportedly not amused. Though not all the suffragettes were "strict church-goers," Antonia Raeburn tells us, the majority "had a religious faith, and many had become interested in Theosophy."[97] Mary Richardson reported the consternation of the Anglican suffragettes imprisoned at Eastertime when the Anglican chaplain refused to allow them to take Holy Communion (a condition soon lifted by the Bishop of London).[98] Some of the religious tone of movement rhetoric surely came from the Pethick-Lawrences, who were so comfortable with Christian allusions that Frederick could whisper to his wife, as they were arrested for conspiracy, "This is their hour and the power of darkness!"[99] Emmeline Pethick-Lawrence, when criticized for the Sunday demonstration in Hyde Park, replied, "Ours is a moral and spiritual movement based on fundamentally religious conceptions."[100] More important, such union members as Mary Richardson clearly considered their movement rhetoric "a gospel" and felt that they were serving divine ends (whatever their individual conceptions may have been of the divine).[101] Although, as Paul Ramsey has pointed out, "a just cause need not be holy (indeed should not be deemed holy)," the need of the suffragettes to legitimize their authority as agents of justified revolution led to a self-sanctification of their acts.[102] By making themselves an extension of divine authority, whose right to call for war was unquestioned, the union attempted to justify to external audiences even violent actions taken in their holy crusade.[103]

Images of martyrdom, of the spilling of innocent blood, appeared early in the movement and lent a sense of inevitability to the union's emphasis on self-sacrifice. For example, the designs by Sylvia Pankhurst for the 1909 exhibition in the Prince's Skating Rink included images of the sacrifice that yields great abundance. Images of a female sower were accompanied by the text from Psalms: "They that sow in tears shall reap in joy. He that goeth forth and weepeth, bearing precious seed, shall doubtless come again with rejoicing, bringing his sheaves with him." Even more illustrative of physical sacrifice for others was the image at the same exhibition of a pelican piercing her breast in order to feed her young.[104] The self-mortification of the hunger strikes and forcible feeding were, perhaps, an inevitable repayment for the challenge to societal order by a group lacking the resources to force victimage upon the enemy. Union members saw their physical sacrifice as a weapon in the struggle for political equality. In this view, the suffragettes are united with later terrorists who have adopted the hunger strike in prison. Terrorist Gudrun Ensslin described hunger strikers as using their bodies as "our ultimate weapon."[105] But if, as Tickner believes, "militancy and martyrdom went hand in hand" and physical self-sacrifice was, in union eyes, a viable weapon of the powerless, the hunger strikes were viewed more equivocally by others. Many viewed the hunger strikers as bringing their suffering on themselves and believed "that the militants had so far degraded themselves that they could scarcely claim to be victims innocent of any part in the circumstances in which they found themselves."[106] The WSPU was well aware of this viewpoint and sought to regain the moral high ground by portraying the suffragettes as "tortured, martyred, for their political faith" and by presenting Emmeline Pankhurst, in particular, as "giving her life for the womanhood of the nation."[107] Christabel Pankhurst directly answered Home Secretary McKenna's charge that "these women . . . are determined to make martyrs of themselves in order that their cause may receive a further stimulus from their heroic example." "Yes," replied Pankhurst in an editorial, "all martyrs are self-made, for no one need be a martyr who will recant, who will submit, who will break the law of God in order to keep on the right side of the law of man." Pankhurst turned the accusation back upon the government, claiming that "forcible feeding is torture, and the Government themselves admit that those who suffer it are martyrs. From this it follows that the Government who inflict this agony are torturers."[108] If the suffragette martyrs were self-made, the union argued, the Liberal government had a hand in their creation.

It was one thing to implicate the government and quite another to make the public care about the fate of the suffragette martyrs. One means used by the union to inspire interest and sympathy in the public consisted of verbal and visual portrayals of the act of forcible feeding. Such a direct approach had, as Tickner has perceptively pointed out, the downside of possibly appealing to a sadomasochistic element who enjoyed the spectacle of women's suffering.[109] The suffragettes needed to prove that they were not masochists seeking self-aggrandizement, were not "fanatics smarting under personal injuries, but heroic figures fighting to redress the wrongs of others and defying the Government and death."[110] To remove the sense that the suffragettes were acting on personal grievances, Emmeline Pankhurst expressed her belief that the "people who are crushed by personal wrong are not the right people to fight for reforms. The people who can fight best are the people who have happy lives themselves, the fortunate ones." In a move that also countered the image of suffragettes as soured spinsters, Pankhurst continued by describing the suffragettes as "the happy women, the fortunate women, the women who have drawn prizes in the lucky bag of life, in the shape of good fathers, good husbands and good brothers," and who fought the suffrage battle "for the sake of others more helpless than themselves."[111] The suffragettes were not suicidal fanatics, and Pankhurst claimed that union members shared a common love of life with the general public: "Life is sweet to all of us. Every human being loves life and loves to enjoy the good things and the happiness that life gives."[112] What explained the suffragette's willingness to martyr herself for others was her identification with women who were *not* lucky and who had children for whom life was *not* sweet. In this view, the suffragettes' was truly innocent blood, for they risked sacrificing their otherwise happy lives in the effort to save the lives of others.

Predictably, this emphasis on sacrifice for others led to identification of the suffragettes with Christ. The union was relatively restrained on this point and tended to make the comparison indirectly. In the 1912 Christmas edition of *The Suffragette*, Christabel Pankhurst made reference to the celebration of "the birth of One who set the example of individual action and individual sacrifice" for the militants.[113] The suffragettes, too, wrote Emmeline Pethick-Lawrence, "have tasted, each in our own measure and degree, the bitter cup, and have found it sweet."[114] Primarily, the comparison to Christ was made by likening the rejection and persecution of the suffragettes to the rejection and persecution of Christ in His day. Annie Kenney was particularly forthcoming in this comparison during one speech: "Yes, you people, do you know that if Christ were on earth to-day and putting His principles into practice, the people who are hooting us would hoot Him! What did they do to Christ when He was on earth? They did the same thing that you are doing to us. They spat on Him, they abused Him, they ridiculed Him, they imprisoned Him, and they crucified Him. This is the crucifixion that you are making the women undergo at the present time."[115] In the arguments of Kenney, Naylor, and others, the audience is asked to make a series of identifications: Christ is identified with the oppressed, the suffragettes are identified with Christ, and the audience member is asked to identify with the suffragettes. By refusing to identify with the suffragettes, the audience member rejects not merely the suffragettes but the Christ within them who gives them the impetus to suffer for others. The modeling of proper identification came from an unusual source, to say the very least. George Bernard Shaw delivered a speech at Kingsway Hall on March 18, 1913, protesting the forcible feeding of the suffragettes. At the close of his speech, while he admitted to being "not altogether what is called an orthodox man," he remembered an "old sentence which runs, 'Inasmuch as ye have done it unto the least of My brethren, ye have done it unto Me.' " Claiming that " 'brethren' includes sisters as well," Shaw continued:

We are all of us very fond of talking about what people call altruism, and about our duty to others. I have always understood that altruism is the final identification of the least of these with me. If you take a woman and torture her, you torture me. If you take Mrs. Pankhurst's daughter and torture her, you are torturing my daughter. If you take Miss Pankhurst's mother and torture her, you will be torturing my mother. I go further than that. If you torture my mother, you are torturing me. These denials of fundamental rights are really a violation of the soul. . . . I say that the denial of these fundamental rights to ourselves in the persons of women is practically a denial of the life everlasting.[116]

Shaw did not miss the most important identification sought by the suffragettes. If the public could identify with union suffering, could see it somehow as a violation of natural human rights, then the humanity of women (with all its attendant political ramifications) became a concept no longer requiring debate.

Union members claimed as their inspiration "One who, for the sake of mankind, was numbered among the transgressors and met a criminal's death."[117] Emmeline Pethick-Lawrence spoke at the London Palladium of taking a crucifix with her to a demonstration, which reminded her of the movement's "fight for the deliverance of humanity—crucified humanity." According to Pethick-Lawrence, women shared with Christ in His suffering, for they were "doubly

"Her children shall rise up and call her blessed."

Figure 13. "Votes for Working Women," *The Suffragette*, January 17, 1913

crucified—crucified on the cross of humanity and crucified also on the cross of motherhood."[118] It was a common idea that mothers were Christlike. In a time of high maternal mortality and inefficient pain control, a mother suffered the "little death" of childbirth in order to bring new life to another. The political cartoon on the front of the January 17, 1913, issue of *The Suffragette* showed a working woman with her arms extended in the cruciform position. Across her shoulders and haloing her head are the words "VOTES FOR WORKING WOMEN." Under her sheltering arms her healthy, happy children sit on the ground, picking flowers and making daisy chains[119] (Figure 13). Again, this was woman as a Christus figure, but revered for the sacrifices of daily life not death.

As can be seen from this amalgam of Christian imagery, the linking of the suffragettes with Christ was extremely fluid, depending on the point the rhetor hoped to make. Christus imagery was used to describe the suffering of women (the object for reform), the sacrifices of the suffragettes (the agents of reform), and the need to bring not peace but a sword (the method of reform).[120] This latter reference was to Christ's warning that He would bring division on earth and that His followers would share in His own rejection. The mobs that attacked the suffragettes were often equated with the mobs "that yelled: 'Crucify Him! Crucify Him!' "[121] When doing so was convenient to the rhetor's point, the suffragettes were transformed in religious imagery into the "prophets and wise men" whom Christ foretold would be killed and persecuted.[122] This image had the advantage of linking the sense that the suffragettes were the advance guard of change to the notion that they represented traditional (and eternal) values.

The ultimate martyr for the suffrage cause was Emily Wilding Davison, whose fatal act of protest on June 4, 1913, "secured for the WSPU its unlooked-for martyr saint."[123] During the derby at Epsom Downs, Davison ran onto the track as the horses rounded Tattenham Corner and grabbed the bridle of the king's horse. Her skull was fractured, and she died on June 8 without regaining consciousness. Whether suicide was her goal is uncertain, but reports indicated that the purple, white, and green of the WSPU were sewn inside her coat. Other reports said that she was wrapped in a WSPU flag underneath her coat and that she initially planned only to wave the colors at the horses and thus disrupt the race.[124] She was always a step ahead in her militancy. She was the first to firebomb a letter box and was the reputed bomber of Lloyd George's country house. She had stated at an earlier time that only one great tragedy, one great sacrifice, would end "the intolerable torture of women." Her funeral was the last grand procession of the suffragettes through the streets of London. Spectators deeply lined the streets to watch women dressed in white, black, or purple—carrying laurel wreaths, purple irises, or crimson peonies, respectively—as they marched with the funeral cortege.[125]

Despite the uncertainty that exists to this day regarding whether or not her death was accidental, Davison was clearly involved in a suffrage protest when she brought down the king's horse. Her death served to galvanize the movement members and even "caught the public imagination," in Laurence Housman's estimation at the time.[126] There seems to be good evidence that such was the case, for despite large public crowds lining the path of her funeral procession, there were surprisingly few (and then only minor) disruptions. Although Davison's death may not have won many long-term converts, it gave temporary pause to many in the public, if only because it proved the serious intent of the union members. Her death provided a point of legitimation for the authority of women to act in the interests of the oppressed, or, as one minister put it, "A woman has laid down her life for her friends . . . has done so of her own free will, has done so in the midst of overwhelming difficulties, in order to remind her country with the whole power of her being of the injustice, the cruelty, the wrongs, the sufferings of women."[127] Christabel Pankhurst noted the "superhuman generosity and courage [of one] who can die for those unseen, unheard, unknown. . . . It was a tremendous imaginative and spiritual achievement! A wonderful act of faith!" Davison became a Christus figure for the movement, equated by Christabel Pankhurst with Christ in her concern for the oppressed and in the offering of "her life as their ransom."[128] The Rev. Gertrude Von Petzold claimed that, like Christ, "Emily Wilding Davison also died for sinners," for those who opposed women's suffrage, who remained uninformed and indifferent, or who did too little in its behalf: "It is for these—all these—that Emily Wilding Davison laid down her life. It is to these that her mangled body has made its piteous appeal; it is for the redemption of these that she surrendered her beautiful, glorious life."[129] Although the union attributed other suffragette deaths (such as those of Mary Clarke and Cecilia Wolseley Haig) to serious injuries received during demonstrations, these deaths occurred some time after the initial injuries and a causal relationship could never be proven. In Emily Wilding Davison the movement had an undeniable incident of self-sacrifice for the suffrage cause. As such, Davison became the embodiment of "innocent blood" who united the religious image of Christ in His crucifixion with the allegorical image of Joan of Arc in her immolation and linked them to the currently negotiable image of the militant suffragette.

Thus, the WSPU presented women in a new guise as the Just Warrior. In this view, the militants were not criminals whose violence is independent and selfish but soldiers whose acts of war are collective and altruistic. Theirs was the sacrifice of innocent blood; theirs was the guardianship of the race; and theirs was the satisfaction of knowing that they led the way to freedom for future generations of women. As agents of the divine will—as the warriors of God in the holy cause—success could not elude them in the final accounting. Through these personal images the union sought legitimation in the public mind as competent to initiate and conduct a justifiable revolution. The true dispute of the suffrage issue had always been over the nature of women and the rights appropriate to them in society. With the Just Warrior image, the union made the final move from request to demand and placed the burden of proof on those who would deny the right of self-determination to women.

5

The Value of Violence

In some quarters the suffragettes' equation of their movement with a just war was rejected out of hand on the basis of the choice of targets for suffragette violence. The problem of noncombatant immunity poses a particular problem for both reformist and revolutionary terrorists. Terrorism by its very nature takes place not on a distinct battlefield with clearly differentiated combatants and noncombatants but in the midst of an ongoing society that is often unaware of the terrorist's issues. Because of its third-party nature, terrorism relies for its expressive impact upon the innocence of its victims. However, the selection of a neutral target in itself violates an important tenet of the just war, the principle of discrimination, or what Paul Ramsey defines as "the moral immunity of non-combatants from direct attack."[1] The reason that war (or participation in violent conflict) is justified—the need to protect the innocent from unjust assault—is the very reason that war must be limited in such a way as to avoid harm to the innocent. Interestingly, in just-war reasoning, the protected population (the noncombatants) are considered innocent and deserving of special consideration not because they have a natural right as human beings to protection for life and property but because they have a *non-relation, or remote relation, to the conduct of war.*[2]

Some scholars have attempted to assess what Ramsey calls the "morality of means" of individual terrorist actions by the degree of societal responsibility (or decision-making power) of the victims.[3] Martha Crenshaw, for example, looks at the selectivity used in the choice of victims. Crenshaw differentiates between those victims who "are decision-makers or uniformed agents who are responsible for the state of injustice the terrorists combat" and those "harmless" citizens who lack a public role or exercise "negligible influence over the policies of the offending state."[4] The Women's Social and Political Union ran straight into this problem of discrimination at the moment when its target moved from official government property (or that symbolically connected with the government) to private property. Thus, the union was caught in the dilemma facing many terrorists who claim to hold the moral high ground yet use as their victims those who are apparently innocent. Like most terrorists, the union needed to justify supporting the innocent victims of societal injustice through acts which themselves victimized the innocent. Terrorists have a tendency to solve this paradox through the same means used by other protestors. According to Maxwell Taylor, justification is achieved "either by reinterpreting the qualities of the victim, making him or her conform to the overriding world view, or by denial of responsibility because of some other agency's inaction."[5] The WSPU used both of these tactics, placing a primary emphasis on redefining the public less as an innocent victim and more as a collaborator in government injustices. Assigning guilt to the general public removed the innocent victim from suffragette attacks. Thus, a measure of illegitimacy was extracted from the violent acts themselves. Union rhetors combined this tactic with the argument that violence was necessary in order to combat greater evils. And, finally, they claimed that the violence of the militant women compared favorably with that violence deemed acceptable when exercised by men. With these arguments, the WSPU hoped to remove the onus from the acts of violence themselves and to redefine violence as a valuable tool when used in a just cause.

Public Guilt

An act of violence becomes far less heinous in the public mind when the targets deserve such treatment. The interesting difficulty faced by the suffragettes in justifying their acts against public property was the need to convince the British public of its own guilt. Extension of guilt to the public was a tactical move of hardheaded practicality. Before the public would act to pressure the government to yield to union demands, the public needed to be convinced of its own power and the responsibility attendant on that power. In making this argument of public guilt, the union appeared to desire a mass mea culpa that would stimulate public action on the suffragettes' reform agenda. Although it may at first appear to be so, the union's extension of guilt to the general public was not nearly so sweeping as the extension of guilt in wartime sometimes made to civilian populations. A good example of the common view of civilian guilt is provided by Lawrence L. McReavy, who claimed that "the vast majority of the enemy's noncombatant subjects is cooperating in aggression." Viewing only infants as wholly innocent of providing support to the country's fighting forces, McReavy used the civilians' cooperation as providing justification for attacks upon their property (although not support of their "direct slaughter").[6] The WSPU assigned a certain amount of guilt to the general public for their acquiescence in the treatment of the suffragette prisoners. As Emmeline Pankhurst told an audience at the London Pavilion, "When people say, 'Why do you touch the property of people not responsible?' we reply, They are responsible. They are all responsible unless they put a stop to the way in which women are being treated."[7] It particularly rankled the union that the destruction of letters by the suffragettes was considered more heinous by the public than the physical destruction of the suffragette prisoners. In *The Suffragette*, the WSPU remonstrated the public: "Those who clamour in private or public about the 'cowardice' of destroying letters had perhaps better consider how little protest they made about the cowardice of torturing women in prison!"[8] One of the ongoing analogies used by the union concerning the destruction of private property was with the plagues brought by God against the Egyptian people to force the release of the Israelites from bondage. Laurence Housman detailed the culpability of the Egyptian people:

If this lesson be a moral one, its moral lies in the assertion that the whole community stands responsible for the injustice of its accepted rulers, and that those who maintain injustice in high places must not expect their indifference to the establishment of justice to be without cost to themselves. Had the Egyptians taken any trouble in the matter, had they appealed to Pharaoh for the release of the Israelites from bondage, he would not so long have hardened his heart; the pressure of public opinion would have been too great for him to withstand.[9]

This rhetorical tactic of blaming the *entire* public was—and had to be—a minor one, for it was a primary argument of the union that women, in their voteless condition, were powerless to affect public policy.

Guilt for collusion with the government fell, therefore, upon the male elector. Although claiming that in every war, the general public had to suffer, Christabel Pankhurst continued, "The electors, at any rate, have brought it all upon themselves by putting and keeping in office a Government guilty of resisting the enfranchisement of women."[10] It was really the enfranchised male whom the union referenced when it claimed, "If the public doesn't like militancy—and who does?—it can stop it. It can give the vote."[11] Considering the power attached to the ballot in a democracy, Christabel Pankhurst called it an "amazing statement" when the *Daily News* claimed that the shopkeepers whose windows were broken were "private citizens, totally unconcerned with this or any other political question." Pankhurst begged to differ, stating that these shopkeepers were "citizens, and, as such, the masters and employers of Cabinet Ministers. They have allowed their servants to deal in disgraceful fashion with the question of women's enfranchisement. Are they not, therefore, to be held responsible? We think they are."[12] One of the fascinating aspects of union rhetoric on this point was its bluntness in blaming the victim to his face. In the WSPU leaflet "Window Breaking: To One Who Has Suffered," the "victim" was clearly apprised of his guilt:

"Well," you may say, "I sympathise with the women, but what have I got to do with it? Why should my windows be broken because Cabinet Ministers are a pack of rogues and tricksters?"

My dear Sir, you have got everything to do with it. You are a voter, and, therefore, the Members of the Government are your servants, and if they do wrong, you are really responsible for it. That is why your windows have been broken—to make you realise your responsibility in the matter.

Let me remind you again that women are your best supporters. You can get on very well without Mr. Asquith and Mr. Lloyd George, but you can't get on without the women who are your good friends in business. Surely one good turn deserves another! The women have been having a very hard time in this Votes for Women fight. **What have you done, what are you doing, and what are you going to do to help them?**[13]

When speaking in Hartford, Connecticut, Emmeline Pankhurst gave a rather pointed assessment of the innocence of some of the victims of property damage. She explained to her American audience that one instance of window-breaking involved shopkeepers' windows and the windows of many of "the smart clubs in Piccadilly," including the Guard Club. As Pankhurst explained, "The ordinary army man is not much in politics, but he very often, because of his aristocratic and social connections, has considerable influence if he would use it." It was a young actress who had broken the windows of the Guard Club, and she stood quietly until the porter seized her. During the wait for the police to come and arrest the woman, several guards came out to see who it was who had broken the club windows. Indignant, these army men said, "Why did you break our windows? We have done nothing." The young actress replied, "It is because you have done nothing I have broken your windows."[14]

In the preceding arguments, union rhetors put their slant upon a major issue still troublesome in modern protests, both violent and nonviolent. Limitations upon protest tactics are often defended on the basis of the "innocent bystander" theory. According to Franklyn Haiman, in this view "protest is permissible only so long as it is confined so as to affect the legitimate targets of the protest but not to inconvenience others." Presumably, the WSPU would have agreed with Haiman that "there is no such thing as an innocent bystander. Every citizen who supports the status quo, either actively or by passive acquiescence, is a legitimate target for the communications of the dissenter."[15] The WSPU believed that the male citizen was responsible for public concerns through his possession of the franchise, although "the average voter wants to be allowed to go on with his business. He does not put himself very much out of the way about any grievances except the grievances that come right home to himself."[16] The only way to make the elector aware of his responsibility in public matters and to bestir him out of his "distinguished ossification" was to bring the battle home to his own doorstep.[17] Again, the suffragettes' tactic was to make their grievances both "present" and salient to the male elector. It was a consistent union belief that the "innocent bystander" was *not* innocent and could no longer be permitted to remain a bystander.

The move to guerrilla militancy was accompanied by a considerable change of tone in union descriptions of the British public. In the earlier phase of militancy, the public (more accurately, the male enfranchised public) was given the benefit of the doubt as to their open minds and chivalrous intentions toward women. Sandra Holton has pointed out the appeal to male chivalry in union rhetoric and the emphasis placed on "the blackguardly character of the Liberal government" that had failed to respond appropriately to this appeal. Emmeline Pankhurst was one who maintained a rhetoric of chivalry in various forms throughout the movement, for "though Mrs. Pankhurst spoke often of the wrongs of women and children at the hands of men, she also continued to rely on men's capacity to rise above their lower natures when confronted with the 'sorrowful wrath' of women."[18] Yet as the movement ground on and the public remained insufficiently moved by the plight of the suffragette prisoners, union rhetoric increasingly reflected a loss of patience with "John Bull." Emmeline Pankhurst described as "literally true" an old proverb: "You cannot rouse the Britisher unless you touch his pocket."[19] It became the WSPU view that "a public opinion not susceptible through its conscience must be approached through its pocket; if it cannot understand why women suffer, it must in common fairness be given a chance of understanding why they act!"[20]

To the British public and the Liberal government, the revolt of women seemed a distant concept, certainly not of the same probability or serious nature as the revolt of the Orangemen in Ulster or the workers on the London docks. In its early days, the WSPU had apparently come to the same conclusion as Chaim Perelman, that "the prime concern of publicity and propaganda is to draw the attention of an indifferent public, this being the indispensable condition for carrying on any sort of argumentation."[21] Lisa Tickner states, "The Pankhursts were indifferent to public opinion," and cites in support the union statement, "If the general public were pleased with what we are doing, that would be a proof that our warfare is ineffective. We don't intend that you should be pleased."[22] This statement should not be taken as an indication that the union was indifferent to or did not understand public opinion. Rather, the union strategy of violence was intensely reliant upon public opinion, but not in the conventional manner, which equates success with *favorable* public opinion. Flora Drummond bluntly told one audience: "We do not want you to like militancy. We want you to hate it, to loathe it, and practically rise and put a stop to it by getting votes for women. We are not an entertaining society; but we are a society to make things intolerable, so that the average man and woman in the street will say, 'For Heaven's sake give the women what they want, and let's have peace.' "[23] This strategy set on its ear any notion that a movement seeks popularity and performs deeds with which the public agrees and is then rewarded by compliance with any reasonable demands. Instead of approbation on the part of the general public, the union wanted anger. The anger elicited by attacks on letter boxes or golf greens was preferable to the electors' "former state of blank indifference."[24] Emmeline Pankhurst spoke of lifelong supporters of female suffrage who came to her and said, " 'You are completely alienating my sympathy.' I reply to them: 'What did your sympathy do for us, my good friend, when we had it? . . . It is better to have you angry than to have you pleased, because sooner or later you will come to the conclusion that this intolerable nuisance must be put an end to.' "[25] The WSPU is often portrayed as either unaware of the hostility raised by its actions or unaware that it was the object of this hostility. Yet, the triggering of public anger was part of a set purpose that the movement knew to be a gamble. As Emmeline Pankhurst put it, "We had enough of sympathy for fifty years; it never brought us anything." She expressed her preference for the angry elector who, when all else failed, would demand that the government give women the vote rather than see his business interrupted. Pankhurst claimed that the union did not care if the vote came "out of sympathy or . . . out of fear, or . . . because you want to be comfortable again," just as long as it came.[26]

This bluntness and contentiousness, unexpected in women reformers, was matched by their refusal to apologize for the stance they felt compelled to take. When speaking in America, Emmeline Pankhurst said, after expressing her thanks to the audience for their attention, "I want to say that I am not here to apologize. I do not care very much even whether you really understand."[27] Approval was not openly sought by the movement, and the union claimed that "militant Suffragists themselves are under no obligation to give justification of [their] action."[28] Of course, the refusal to seek approval or provide justification was itself a part of the WSPU's justification. The union took the stance of the already-justified by refusing to pander to public opinion.

When the cynicism directed toward the male elector was combined with the negative view of public morality seen in the purity campaign (again, primarily directed at men due to the sexual double standard), the union rhetoric of violent militancy took on what many have described as an "anti-male" flavor. Although there appear to be more negative comments directed specifically at men during the guerrilla militancy phase, what I see as predominant is a darkening of the union's attitude toward the British public as a whole. With the years of frustrated effort and the sometimes tenuous help of supporters, the enmity of opponents and difficulty of success became predominant for some union members until, as Mary Richardson later described it, "the movement seemed to be all 'night.' All darkness. A hopeless groping through the fogs of human hatred."[29] With this change of attitude, reflected in a more negative rhetoric, came the ability to justify attacks on private property.

A Necessary Evil

As action itself was hallowed as godly, the focus shifted from the "evil done" by violent militancy to the promise that "good may come" from the suffragette acts. The WSPU claimed that the "evil" of violent militancy was diminished by the greater evil against which the union was fighting. In one editorial, Christabel Pankhurst presented the following metaphor: " 'Cruelty flung broadcast over the community' is a recent description of Suffragist militancy. If that militancy is cruel, it is with the cruelty of the surgeon's knife. It is a stern remedy for a mortal disease."[30] In a later editorial she claimed that, as women learned more about "woman slavery" and about "the Social Evil" which was its "chief fruit," their view of militancy would change: "As their knowledge grows they will look upon militancy as a surgical operation—a violence fraught with mercy and healing."[31] Ideally, Pankhurst maintained, "we may wish that fighting were not needed, and that those who bar the way to the kingdom would offer no resistance to our entering in; but the principle of evil exists as well as the principle of good, and it has to be fought and conquered."[32] In her speech in Hartford, Emmeline Pankhurst portrayed the suffragettes as caught in a dilemma that forced them to make "a choice of two evils; they would either have to submit indefinitely to an unjust state of affairs or they would have to rise up and adopt some of the antiquated means by which men in the past got their grievances remedied."[33] What the WSPU found, according to Christabel Pankhurst, was that "the morally blind and the dead of soul who condemn militancy" did so on the basis of "the well-worn spiritual fallacy of ranking sins of omission higher than virtues of commission." Men who "shudder at the thought of a letter lost and a house burnt" should "make haste to redeem your own sex," for not to do so was to choose, by omission, the greater evil of social wrongs over the lesser evil of militancy.[34]

"Militancy," in Christabel Pankhurst's view, was "a law of life. Without militancy there is no life. Life is a battlefield. Who will deny all that?"[35] Such statements make the suffragettes sound like "realists," the term commonly used to denote those who have a pessimistic view of human nature and who believe that war and violence are regrettable but necessary parts of human life.[36] Yet, the union members' support for militancy and their belief that life is a battlefield were based solely on the concept of war fought for the oppressed. Because the battle for the *right* was a natural part of life and the suffragettes were struggling over vital issues, neutrality was impossible. Christabel Pankhurst maintained that not to be with the union in the fight was to be in league with the evil against which the union fought: "Non-militancy is tolerance of evil. To tolerate evil is to strengthen and to encourage it. Militancy, therefore, is the highest virtue."[37] The decision to support the militancy of the suffragettes became, for the individual, part of a conversion experience with all of its attendant religious and moral implications.

In attempting to prove that violence was not necessarily forbidden to the just, the WSPU turned once again to biblical proofs as a key form of justification. The union used the example of Christ overturning the money changers' tables to show that Christianity did not forbid the effective use of militancy against property for a higher cause, even when that property was in private hands.[38] Along the same biblical lines, one of the strongest supports for the use of militancy against private property was the one provided by Laurence Housman. Housman, while not a member of the all-female union, provided highly literate arguments in *Votes for Women*. In one article he enlarged upon his analogy between the suffragettes and the Israelites in their attempt to seek freedom from bondage. In the case of the plagues of Egypt, the "hand of the Lord" was upon the property not only of Pharaoh but also of the Egyptian people. The story of Moses and the plagues of Egypt was "a statement of the militant action taken by Heaven against an unjust government which continues to hold a people in bondage; and the blow falls . . . not upon the head of the government itself, but upon the property of the whole community. In each case after due warning, law abiding people are made to suffer for the action, or rather the inaction, of a government."[39]

Opponents of the suffragettes liked to point to the hypothetical charwoman who would be greatly injured if a gift of money or her day's wages were destroyed in the burning of a letter box by the union. At times Emmeline Pankhurst took an apparently cavalier attitude to such difficulties by saying, "You cannot make omelettes without breaking eggs; you cannot have civil war without damage to something."[40] Generally, however, the suffragettes took one of two approaches to answering the question of the impact of a violent act itself. First, reform was shown by Christabel Pankhurst as inherently costly no matter who was conducting the agitation: "Poor working women have before now known what it is to suffer loss in political and industrial struggles in which they were not directly concerned—for example, in the coal strike and in the railway strike, which brought starvation, and at least temporary ruin, to vast numbers of such women." Pankhurst compared the destruction of letters, which could prevent news of illness reaching a family member, with a strike by the railway, which could prevent attendance by a family member at the patient's bedside. Commercial and personal business of many kinds was impeded by the destruction of letters, but this inconvenience was surpassed by the disruption caused by the industrial strikes. Second, the women who suffered were "suffering in their own interests" for a change. Although women had shown themselves as willing in the past to "pay the price" of liberty, this was a rare instance where they would share in the benefits of that liberty. At least the hypothetical charwoman could comfort herself that the loss of her equally hypothetical money order led her a little closer to sharing in the power of the vote.[41]

The immediate reaction of local citizens to news that their railway station had been bombed would be outraged insistence that the malefactors be arrested. The union hoped to insert between the violent deed and the public response to the deed a mediating interpretation of the militant act. Slowly, therefore, the "evil" of violent militancy was recast as a good in itself. I agree with Sandra Holton that in this belief it is possible to see the influence of Carlyle on Emmeline Pankhurst and, through her, the rest of the WSPU. Holton points out that Pankhurst designated (along with Stowe's *Uncle Tom's Cabin*) Carlyle's *The French Revolution* as her most influential childhood reading. Holton provides a nice summary of Carlyle that makes clear his influence on the suffragette view of violent militancy as a positive force:

History was . . . a sequence of disruptive actions creating new worlds. Carlyle likened society to the phoenix, continually dying and being reborn in its own ashes, and he defended the "torching of rotten structures" as a precondition for the building of new foundations. He was the first apologist among historians for the Terror, arguing it to have been at the heart of the French Revolution, and to have borne the hopes of future ages. Carlyle insisted on the beauty of chaos and conflagration, the importance of the irrational and instinctual in creative human action.[42]

Holton sees the influence of Carlyle appearing in Pankhurst as a romantic worldview that greatly valued the individual with all of his or her instincts and courage. Violent militancy was also valued as "the fire of a great struggle" that could hone those individual qualities into a worthy weapon for reform. By passing through the fires of militant action, the individual would develop the personal traits needed to "change the world, and changing the world was the highest calling to which an individual might aspire."[43] According to Christabel Pankhurst, the policy of militancy "purifies and strengthens. A Suffragist who becomes militant passes through cleansing fire. She wins a new freedom and strength of spirit. When the Vote comes, it will set a seal upon a liberty already hers."[44] Union member Edith Zangwill extended the metaphor of cleansing fire and its effect upon the soul of the militant woman:

For the flame of the revolution is burning up all the petty and ignoble things, all the little weaknesses, and deceits and vanities that may have crept into the sheltered woman's soul. You know how, by burning rubbish, it may be turned into clean, new electric power that can be used in the service of mankind. That is what this fire of rebellion seems to me to be doing for womanhood. It is purifying and ennobling our sex. It is tempering it for its work in the world. It is the pillar of flame in the dark night that is leading us into the Promised Land. It is the gleam of hope and of light in all this miserable turmoil and disturbance.[45]

Here we can see a revolutionary worldview domesticated to serve a reformer's needs. The fire happens primarily within the individual as the essential element of reform, and outward acts of arson are merely a secondary manifestation. In this view, the destruction of the old order is not necessary, for the empowerment of the individual and the redemption of society could come through particular reforms. Therefore, in suffragette rhetoric, acts of violent militancy became less an evil, albeit a necessary one, and more an integral part of the good to be wrought in a reformed society.

Just as suffragette arson had been shown by Christabel Pankhurst as promoting "strength and purification" in the individual, it was also portrayed as a "purifying fire" that would cleanse all of society.[46] Hannah Arendt, in her work *On Violence*, ascribes such beliefs to "the infusion of biologism into political discourse." According to Elshtain, this view claims that "destruction is a law of nature and violence a 'life promoting force' through which men purge the old and rotten."[47] Thus, violence was justified to the internal audience of suffrage militants through reference to "the fire and spirit of revolt."[48] The image of fire reflected (and rationalized) the widespread use of arson of empty buildings, "firing" of letter boxes, and explosions from homemade bombs that became primary tactics of the suffragette's reformist terrorism. Accounts of weekly damage were often announced with headlines such as "Militancy—A Spreading Fire" and statements to the effect that "the flame of militancy has blazed forth again, and with more vigour than ever before."[49] The flames of militancy that were to cleanse the world of the stain and disease of immorality were intended to prepare the world for the new relationship between men and women that would rise from the ashes.

The metaphor of fire, as part of the internal talk of union members, formed a ready repository for puns. The humor within the movement has largely been underestimated in favor of a more grim-jawed view of the suffragette. The image of fire was treated humorously by Edith Zangwill in a speech entitled "The Burning Question," where she described militancy as "the burning question of the day." "I think," Zangwill continued, "the coercive measures of the Government are adding fuel to the flame. Instead of pouring oil on the troubled waters, the authorities are pouring it on the fires of rebellion. The Government has met a match."[50] Fire became emblematic of the ardent and consuming nature of the movement and of its special spirit, which had "lit an answering flame in the hearts of other women."[51] It served as proof to the internal audience of union members that their movement was truly the advance guard of the future and, as such, was inextinguishable. As suffragette Hope Jones declared before receiving a six-month prison term for breaking windows during a demonstration, "The light is still burning, and will never be put out by the hand of man."[52]

In the suffragettes' eyes, violence was not always evil, and David

Mitchell reports that the union pointed to "Nature herself, the Arch-Militant" as proof of that fact.[53] Violence, as Christabel Pankhurst described it, was part of the natural order and therefore had an element of the holy in it: "Violence has a place in the scheme of things. The Creator has not disdained to use it. Great storms break and leave a fresh and shining world behind them. Great wars and rebellions have in the past cleansed human society and cut out cancerous wrongs. The militancy of women is doing a work of purification . . . a great blasting away of ugly things—that is militancy."[54] The WSPU reminded women of the words of Emerson: "Nature has made up her mind that what cannot defend itself shall not be defended."[55]

The single act of violence that was the hardest to justify, and which called down the wrath even of supporters, was the attack on artwork. Wyndham Lewis's *Blast* of June 20, 1914, included the following combination of patronizing warning and sympathy: "In destruction as in other things stick to what you understand. . . . We make you a present of our votes. Only leave works of art alone. You might some day destroy a good picture by accident. . . . You and artists are the only things (you don't mind being called things?) left in England with a little life in them. If you destroy a great work of art you are destroying a greater soul than if you annihilated a whole district of London. Leave Art alone, brave comrades!"[56] Despite the insulting assumption that all the women of the movement were ignorant about art, this editorial apparently sympathized to an extent with methods of destruction but drew the line when damage occurred to property that was particularly valued. It is painful even today to read about the attacks upon artwork, for we consider political agitation as time-bound and art as timeless. The political issue may resolve itself, but the damage to the work of art is permanent, and we consider artwork to be unique and irreplaceable. But, of course, this was the point that the suffragettes hoped to make. The destruction of artwork was conducted in protest of the permanent destruction of individual women, who were also unique and irreplaceable. Mary Richardson said that her attack upon the *Rokeby Venus* was made to protest (and hopefully prevent) the "destruction" of Emmeline Pankhurst through further imprisonment under the Cat and Mouse Act.[57] Christabel Pankhurst drew and broadened the same analogy between destruction of art and destruction of women when she wrote in praise of Richardson's act: "Humbug and hypocrisy it is indeed to whine at an attack upon the picture of a beautiful woman, while beautiful womanhood is being defaced and defiled by the economic horrors of sweating and by that other horror of prostitution."[58]

As a final support to the argument that militancy—even reformist terrorism—was not illegitimate in and of itself, the union pointed to the nearly universal tendency by all groups to use militancy when redressing a grievance. Marie Naylor, in a speech at Steinway Hall, used a comical example to prove this point: "You know in Edinburgh after our smashing of windows two ladies drove up to the W.S.P.U. shop, and they tried to break the windows with their umbrellas, because they were so dead against the breaking of windows; it was such a dreadful thing. Well, they did not succeed in doing it, and so they went off and got hammers, and then got in a motor-car and escaped. That is how they showed what a wicked thing it was to break windows. We all believe in militancy directly we have got a grievance of our own."[59] Even those most critical of attacks on private property resorted to the same acts in support of their own beliefs. This shared use of the same methods meant that a blanket condemnation of the acts in and of themselves was impossible.

Women's Comparative Restraint

The WSPU used arguments of reciprocity to provide a major support for the value of violent acts. Arguments of reciprocity attempt to show that "two situations . . . are counterparts of each other."[60] The union particularly wanted to make the argument that its violence was equivalent to that used by men and should be judged in the same manner. In fact, union rhetors repeatedly claimed that WSPU violence was superior in its very nature to male violence and that the union's concern for noncombatants was greater than that found in the wars or political movements conducted by men. Rejection of this claim was fairly widespread. When Christabel Pankhurst "compared letter-burning and other forms of militancy to the Balkan War, and . . . claimed that such militancy has the same complete justification as has that war," she met loud protests from those who viewed war as conducted under terms more chivalrous than the union agitation.[61]

Other suffragists rejected the war analogy also, and *Votes for Women* quoted these words from a follower of constitutionalist Millicent Fawcett: "The late outrages differ profoundly from honourable civil war. War can only be honourably conducted where there is a clear distinction between combatants and non-combatants, and where neither side inflicts injuries which it is not prepared to receive without a murmur in its turn. The present militant tactics ignore all fair rules of war. To burn a man's house over his head as he slept was considered a 'nithing's deed' even in the fierce Icelandic days."[62] The union accused the holders of such views of suffering from incredible naiveté and "arrant sentimentality" in their understanding of war. Not only was war more violent than the actions of the suffragettes, but also, in war, "the distinctions drawn between combatants and non-combatants are imaginary rather than real." The union cited T. E. Holland's *The Laws and Usages of War on Land* to prove that, in the interests of "military necessity," war permitted an army to clear entire areas of countryside, destroy all dwellings, and confiscate all supplies. Any "defended" town was considered fair game for bombardment, and there was no requirement that the civilian population be allowed to escape.[63] The WSPU compared the results of such a bombardment to one of their attacks upon property: "What does a bombardment mean! It means houses in flames. It means that women and children—all innocent—are killed. Babies may be shot to pieces in their cradles! And then men talk of orchids! While members of their own sex are, in the name of freedom, starving and slaughtering children, men talk of golf greens and of letters! To honest, manly men we say: Leave such hypocrisy to the politicians!"[64] Direct attack on noncombatants was one aspect of the wars of men, but equally damaging were the famine and disease brought by war. Christabel Pankhurst reported the rumor that cholera was rampant in the Turkish army in the Balkans, and only time would tell if this disease (which certainly did not differentiate between combatants and noncombatants) would spread to all of Europe.[65] The union claimed that "only a woman who belongs to a nation which has not for generations seen warfare within its own shores" would be unaware of the outrages perpetrated upon the women of a country during the time of war.[66] Comparison "between militancy in Britain and militancy in the Balkans" revealed simply that the militancy of the suffragettes in their search for freedom was more restrained and less violent than that undertaken to gain Balkan freedom.[67]

The Boer War, according to Pankhurst, developed "for the sake of votes for men who would not wait five years for them."[68] Acceptance of this premise made the underlying issue of both the men's and women's war the same and left only methods of violence as a point of comparison. Women, by this reckoning, were a model of restraint. They burned letters and empty buildings in their war for the franchise, while "two hundred and fifty million pounds and at least thirty thousand lives [were] spent to get Votes for Men!"[69] It was the worst form of hypocrisy, in Christabel Pankhurst's eyes, for the *Daily Telegraph* to pay homage to the Boer women in South Africa and not to the militant suffragettes. The South Africa war presented the British generals with the "cruel necessity of burning the scattered farms of the burghers. We saw from this that burning houses was, in men's eyes, quite justified in the cause of votes for men in South Africa, the issue out of which the Boer War had developed, and that militancy on the part of women was admired by men, provided that women were militant for a cause directly affecting men and not in a cause directly affecting women only."[70] Objection to suffragette reformist terrorism was another instance of the double standard, for "when men are militant for the sake of their personal or national freedom, nobody says that they are selfish; nobody says that they are cruel."[71] The veil of concern over the morality of suffragette means was thus ripped away: it was not the methods of the suffragettes to which men objected but the goal of freedom for women.

Throughout the agitation, the union had shown how men in the past had turned to violence as a last resort. Now the union compared its guerrilla militancy with the *level* of violence used by men in their warfare. "It is plain," stated Christabel Pankhurst in an editorial entitled "History Repeating Itself," "that the sole difference between men's militancy for the vote and women's militancy for the vote is one of degree, and of degree only."[72] The WSPU published pictures of Nottingham Castle in flames during the Franchise Agitation of 1831 with the caption, "What Men Did to Get the Vote." The union reminded readers that, in Bristol alone, men seeking the franchise had "burnt the Mansion House, the Custom House, the Bishop's Palace, the Excise Office, three prisons, and much private property." Considering that the franchise goal of the WSPU was the same as the goal of men in the past, the union expressed its belief that "the Government may indeed be thankful for the moderation shown by women."[73]

The adoption of a strategy of violence against property alone was undertaken, not out of weakness as some implied, but out of a moral strength that limited the extent of violence that women were willing to undertake. The leaders of the union, Annie Kenney claimed, "realised that we should have to use men's methods, only we said, 'We won't go as far as men go,' because you know the men in revolutions have always killed people. We don't like the idea of killing people, so we thought we would stop at that."[74] Union rhetoric extolled this restraint by women as a proof of natural superiority. Women were careful to choose nonlethal strategies, Emmeline Pankhurst stated, "because women care more about human life than men, and I think that is quite natural that we should, for we know what life costs. We risk our lives when men are born." Pankhurst presented the restraint of women as difficult at times to achieve but as a point of pride: "Now, I want to say this deliberately as a leader of this movement. We have tried to hold it back, we have tried to keep it from going beyond bounds, and I have never felt a prouder woman than I did one night when a police constable said to me, after one of these demonstrations, 'Had this been a man's demonstration, there would have been bloodshed long ago.' "[75] In just-war tradition there is an analysis of the "morality of means," which Thomas Murray has called "the rule of minimal means." According to Murray, if war must be fought, "we should make every effort to wage it according to the rule of minimal means, instead of operating from the very first hour according to the dialectic of wild excess. We should attempt to hold the use of force down to the minimum necessary for accomplishing the multiple ideas inherent in the moral idea of war."[76] The suffragettes had only gradually escalated into violent activity, and even then they restricted themselves to property damage. Men could not make the same claims, and Christabel Pankhurst mused: "Strange, indeed, does it seem to single out the Suffragettes for condemnation. Their violence is comparatively mild, and they respect human life, but the policy of male warmakers is first and foremost to *destroy* human life. Moreover, their aims are not always so pure as those of the Suffragettes, and they have been known to wage war for sheer envy and greed."[77]

The amazing flexibility of the rules of the game when applied to men and women was particularly galling for the suffragettes when they compared their movement not to war or to men's movements in the past but to another current movement. Ulster violence—and the perceived governmental hypocrisy of differing policies toward militant men and militant women—was a particular sore point with the union. Union speakers long complained—and with just cause—that Sir Edward Carson and the Ulster rebels could make speeches that even advocated the spilling of blood if need be and yet not be arrested for incitement as the suffragettes were.[78] Where suffragette free-speech rights were impinged by a ban on their speaking in Hyde Park, no such ban was imposed upon the Ulsterites. The union argued that even the Phoenix Park murders, although widely condemned, did no irreparable harm to the Irish cause.[79] The WSPU portrayed Asquith as afraid to act punitively toward Ulster because "the insurrectionists" had votes (as did their male friends and relations), and any violence could prove "politically dangerous to Mr. Asquith."[80] Sir Edward Carson was considered by Emmeline Pankhurst as a fellow rebel, but he was portrayed as less justified in his rebellion because he had a constitutional avenue open to him through his franchise.[81] This point was used to great effect by union rhetors, for they could also show that the Ulster rebels were treated with respect rather than coercion because they had the political protection of the franchise.

When it came to Ulster, the participants in the uprising themselves had a blind spot concerning the use of militancy, as Flora Drummond comically related to one audience: "It just reminds me of my experience in Derry. A man there came back to the organiser with the ticket for the meeting, and he said, 'I am sorry I cannot come to your meeting to-night because I am drilling, and I have made up my mind I cannot support your organisation because I do not believe in militancy.' . . . He believes in militancy by men for the benefit of men, and by women for the benefit of men; but when it is militancy by women for women it is a differnt [sic] matter."[82] Union cartoons reveled in the inconsistency between government treatment of militant women and the militant men of Ulster. In a cartoon entitled "The Liberals' Idea of Justice," Asquith is shown personally force-feeding a suffragette. In the panel below, he is bowing and holding out an olive branch to an Ulsterman in battle gear. The caption described the scenario as "Coercion for Militant Women. Surrender to Militant Men"[83] (Figure 14). The union thus pointed to a double standard of general morals (equivalent to the double standard of sexual morals) where, Emmeline Pankhurst said, "men's blood-shedding militancy is applauded and women's symbolic militancy punished."[84]

Christabel Pankhurst evinced particular anger at a comparison made by Lord Hugh Cecil to defend the obvious variance in legal treatment between the women agitators and the Ulstermen. Lord Cecil said:

The members of the Women's Social and Political Union are fond of comparing themselves to rebels. But they forget that rebellion and terrorism are entirely distinct.

When the Ulstermen, for instance, threaten that they will resist Home Rule by force, they do not mean that they will resort to a campaign of crime and outrage on their Roman Catholic fellow-citizens. They mean to set up some form of government in North-East Ireland independent of the Home Rule Government, and certainly not less careful to maintain law and order.

It is no part of their plan to destroy Home Rule by inflicting injuries on private individuals.[85]

Christabel Pankhurst responded by saying, "A course of 'reasoning' more extraordinary we never read. Rebellion and terrorism entirely distinct! What, pray, is the object of a rebel if not to terrorise a tyrant! What indeed is the object of an army if not to terrorise the enemy!" Lord Cecil's opinion was the crux of the difficulty the suffragettes had in legitimizing their methods in terms of a just war. Warfare according to his view (one commonly held) was conducted between established governments over established and defendable territories using the standard methods. Or, as Christabel Pankhurst put it, to find legitimacy in this view the suffragettes would have to establish a rival government, "pounce upon . . . [a] definite bit of territory" to defend, and become "armed and drilled" in the manner of a standing army.[86] Acceptance of these criteria would make illegitimate all revolutionary violence (and/or terrorism), for, although the revolutionary

The Liberals' Idea of Justice.

Coercion for Militant Women.
Surrender to Militant Men.

Figure 14. "The Liberals' Idea of Justice," *The Suffragette*, May 8, 1914

seeks a new government, he or she does not have a separate territory to defend but is fighting from inside the territory controlled by the existing government. Reformist violence would be placed even farther beyond the acceptable, for the reformer has neither separate territory to defend nor a desire to set up a new government.

The government claimed that Ulster was a different case from the suffragettes, and, as Christabel Pankhurst said, some government members tried to show "that the Ulster rebellion will be milk-and-water and gentleness itself compared to the militancy of the Suffragettes."[87] Annie Kenney used the words of the judge in a suffragette case to throw doubt upon the common argument that Ulster was "all talk" and the suffragettes were only punished because actual acts of militancy followed their incitement: "What did Judge Phillimore say to us? He told us when we were in the dock that it was not the mere making of militant speeches that counted; it was because militancy followed these militant speeches. What about Sir Edward Carson? He made a militant speech the other day, and what happened yesterday? People were shot; riots were numerous in Belfast."[88] Although it seems clear today that there was a double standard for militant men and militant women, this was an issue against which the union constantly shadowboxed. However common it was in a volatile reform period for male syndicalist strikers and Ulster radicals to use violence, the notion of women as perpetrators (rather than victims) of violence was jarringly new and thus loomed large in the public perception.

This was a point of prime contention for the suffragettes, for they needed to show that they were not a "case apart" but a part of the ongoing "great tradition" of a people seeking liberty through every means available.[89] Emmeline Pankhurst expressed her frustration on this point to an American audience: "If I were a man and I said to you: 'I come from a country which professes to have representative institutions and yet denies me, a taxpayer, an inhabitant of the country, representative rights,' you would at once understand that that human being, being a man, was justified in the adoption of revolutionary methods to get representative institutions. But since I am a woman it is necessary in the twentieth century to explain why women have adopted revolutionary methods in order to win the rights of citizenship."[90] The union clearly had trouble influencing audience perception so that the suffragettes were included in the same category as male revolutionaries. They also had difficulty finding inclusion in the public mind with the great revolutions in the past. Christabel Pankhurst suggested that the average person carefully consider "the applause given to those bye-gone revolutions that have been crowned by worldly success."[91] The Rev. Edwin Mould requested that the public "apply the same standards and values to the living present as you apply to the dead past."[92] The WSPU considered itself to be using means that were more restrained and in better proportion to the ends it hoped to attain than had the much-vaunted male revolutionaries of the past. Christabel Pankhurst argued that the suffragettes' status as "just revolutionaries" should not be lessened either by their gender or by the closeness of their fight to home: "If revolution is right for men, it is right for women. If revolution is right in China, it is right in Great Britain."[93] And if revolution, even accompanied by lethal violence, was justified in the past, then reform, with its controlled violence against property, was justified in the present.

6

Evil That Good May Come

The WSPU asked the public, in judging union militancy, to look behind the act of violence to the motives that inspired the act. It is in this type of justification that intention weighs in and, according to Paul Ramsey, it becomes important that "the evil, secondary effect [the act of violence] . . . not be out of proportion to the good effect one intends to obtain."[1] This idea of "proportionality," described by Robert Ivie as the intention "to achieve a good that is in proportion to the evils of the act of war itself," makes accountants of those involved in waging war, forcing them to "count the cost" of each act of violence.[2] Ernest Ruede called it "the proper work of calculation, comparing effects, weighing their gravity, estimating the sufficiency of the reasons for them, and balancing greater against lesser goods or lesser evils."[3] It is a "test of expediency" that compares the good that an act of violence may accomplish with the unavoidable evil inherent in the act.[4] Ramsey makes clear that counting the costs of an act of war involves more than a "body count" or assessment of property damage; it also weighs in the balance the effect upon the soul of the community, the impact upon the "values and heritage" of a people.[5]

This question of motive constituted the union's final major defense of guerrilla militancy as proportionate with the good that was intended. Justifying violence based on consideration of the *motives* behind the use of armed force grew, according to Ramsey, from "the interior of the ethics of Christian love." By this phrase, Ramsey means that, historically, Christians had to come to grips with the notion that they would be forced to choose "between the perpetrator of injustice and the many victims of it." *Not* to act when injustice is perpetrated is to choose the former, because, as Ramsey put it, "While Jesus taught that a disciple in his own case should turn the other cheek, he did not enjoin that his disciple should lift up the face of another oppressed man for *him* to be struck again on *his* other cheek. It is no part of the work of charity to allow this to continue to happen" (emphasis in original). The use of motive to justify acts of armed resistance came in this view from an expansion of the story of the Good Samaritan. Clearly, a sense of social charity led the Good Samaritan to help the man found beaten by the side of the road. However, it might also be an act of social charity to "serve in a police patrol on the Jericho road to prevent such things from happening." And once that concept is accepted, the notion of what actions are legitimate in resisting injustice broadens. As Ramsey puts the intriguing question, "What do you think Jesus would have made the Samaritan do if he had come upon the scene while the robbers were still at their fell work?"[6] Such speculations provide room for reformist groups to situate and justify their acts of violence on behalf of the oppressed.

During a speech at Steinway Hall, Marie Naylor provided the best summary of the suffragettes' general view of proportion and of the relativity of good and evil. She indicated to her audience that the question of whether one should do evil that good may come was complicated by the fact "that even evil is a matter which cannot be settled absolutely." To show that evil varied according to the viewpoint of the observer, Naylor used the example of the spy during time of war. To the camp that sent him, the spy is a hero; to the camp being spied upon, he is the epitome of evil, "only fit to be shot or to be hanged." Life would be simplified, Naylor continued in her argument, if our choices were "between absolute good and absolute evil." Instead, the reality was that people end up choosing between evils, only hoping to choose the lesser of the two. Naylor used as her example the choice made by Japan to go to war with Russia to protect its "national existence." Knowing that the choice would result in the death of thousands, Japan considered its potential loss of sovereignty as the greater evil and chose warfare over submission. Building dreadnoughts and keeping an army (issues of great importance during an era worried over a possible invasion) were shown by Naylor as the logical precautions taken in the belief that occasionally a nation must choose the evil of warfare over the greater evil of surrender to an unjust aggressor.[7]

The union viewed the need for violence to bring about peace as a paradox of biblical proportions: "The new idea, beautiful as it is, cannot be born into the world without suffering and pain and conflict. Because we love happiness, we have learnt that we must not shrink from suffering; because we love peace, we have learnt that we must not shrink from conflict. Those who would preach a new gospel know always that they come not to bring peace on earth but a sword."[8] This image of suffering leading to new birth is a common mothering image that was repeated in the poetry the union chose to quote:

> The night is darkest before the morn;
> When the pain is sorest the child is born,
> And the Day of the Lord at hand.[9]

The union did not deny the pain of its methods but argued that the good that would result was proportionately greater: "The violence done by Suffragists is directed against property, and surely Liberals care little for property when weighed in the balance against freedom."[10]

The suffragettes developed three primary arguments that their strategy of forcing the crisis met the criterion of proportion. First, the union argued that its motives were pure and, through a series of clever analogies, presented the case that violence was necessitated by the desire to end current evils. Second, union rhetors used an argument of reciprocity (comparing suffragette violence with that used by the government and church) to show that WSPU violence was actually in better proportion to the importance of their goal than was the violence of men. Only the hypocrisy of government and church prevented their acknowledging that union attacks were of the same means/end ratio as that of men in equivalent situations. And, finally, the union turned to an appeal to the future, arguing that, although the current age could not appreciate the good to be attained through the necessary evil of strategic violence, future generations who would reap those benefits would laud the union's tactical choices.

Purity of Motive

The Women's Social and Political Union argued that its acts of violence against property were undertaken solely in an effort to gain the franchise power necessary to improve the nation. The motives of the suffragettes were pure, Christabel Pankhurst claimed, and free of self-interest: "What is the object of the letter-burners? It is to abolish White Slavery. It is to put an end to hideous assaults on little girls. It is to stop the sweating of working women."[11] The motives of the union purified illegal acts and brought them within the realm of jus-

THE END JUSTIFIES THE MEANS.

Figure 15. "The Outlaw," *The Suffragette*, December 20, 1912

tice. This notion was illustrated in a political cartoon published in *The Suffragette*. Over the words "The Outlaw," a woman in robes carrying the banner "Votes for Women" stands beside a fire call box, apparently having placed a false alarm. She stands with her hands raised under her chin in a prayerful attitude as she watches a fire engine race past her into the night. She is wearing the headband, "Justice." The caption to this cartoon read, "The End Justifies the Means"[12] (Figure 15).

Through a series of analogies, some of them quite complex, the union insisted that its violence was undertaken with pure motives. One of the simpler analogical arguments compared the crime of the reformer with that of the criminal. The motive behind the violent acts moved union attacks against private property out of the arena of crime and into the realm of political action: "Both reformers and criminals are alike in that they break the established law of the land. They differ only in their motive. The criminal breaks the law to the injury of the State and for his own profit; the reformer breaks the law to his own injury, but for the salvation of the State."[13] The union used as an example of political offense the Swiss who shot a member of the Swiss government and was given asylum in England because his act occurred during a political uprising. Had the man, the union explained, "murdered his employer in order to rob the till he would have been an ordinary criminal, and would have been extradited."[14] Such an example allowed the WSPU to make the point that an act (even killing) could not be judged apart from the motives that actuated it.

Because, as Christabel Pankhurst maintained, the prevention of injustice was "our great end, shall we shrink from the means because those means are hard and bring pain and perhaps death to those who use them?"[15] This equation of a difficult means to a greater end led, perhaps inevitably, to an evoking of the image of Christ, as in this exchange between Emmeline Pankhurst and a heckler: "I challenge those who denounce our violence, and I say to them that if our violence is wrong then the violence of Christ was wrong, for did He not turn the money-changers out of the Temple; did He not drive the Swine into the sea? (A Voice: He did not break windows.) We break windows, my friend, to get the power to save broken lives."[16] To keep this important justification for violent militancy before the public, the union used many rhetorical images, all clustered around the notion of breaking windows: "This breach of faith [by the government] could only be responded to by another breach of faith, which took the form of the breaking of glass"; "Better broken windows than broken promises"; "I want you to see behind those broken windows what the women saw who broke them. I mean, I want you to see the broken human lives"; "I tell you the holes in those windows were mouths, calling the attention of the public to the fact that 100,000 little children's lives are destroyed every year."[17] These images linked the broken promises of the government, the broken windows of the suffragette demonstrations, and the broken lives the female franchise would redeem. To see or hear of one would call to mind the other two and provide the motive needed for the justification of violent militancy.

One highly developed metaphor recurred in union rhetoric to justify violence, window-breaking in particular. This image relied for its effectiveness on a preliminary notion that England was a nation that was "asleep" to the oppression of women and children and the desperate need for female enfranchisement. Headlines in *The Suffragette* used biblical allusion to describe deputations to the bishops of Islington and Stepney: "Awake, Thou That Sleepest."[18] This concept was repeated constantly in the movement and set the stage for the notion that some act was required to rouse the sleeper. One WSPU writer claimed that "thinking of Suffragette stone-throwing always brings to the mind these lines:—'Awake! for morning in the bowl of night / Has flung the stone that puts the stars to flight.' The stone has in very truth put to flight the dark hours of women's subjection. It gives the signal to women of awakening and emancipation. It lets in the free air of hope and liberty."[19] When describing in one speech the "blowing up" of Lloyd George's summer home, Emmeline Pankhurst was interrupted by an audience member who asked, "Why did you blow him up?" To this question, Pankhurst replied, "To wake him up, my friend. We have tried blowing him up to awaken his conscience."[20]

A more complex analogical argument was developed and used by union rhetors based on this same idea of the need to awaken the nation. In this analogy, a helpless victim (of the type that female enfranchisement was supposed to help) is in need of immediate assistance, and the only way to provide aid is to break a window. While there are numerous examples of this image, the finest was the one provided by Frederick Pethick-Lawrence at the Conspiracy Trial. I will quote it in its entirety:

> Supposing you are passing a house in which is a little child. Through the windows you hear its piteous cries. You know it is seriously ill, and you know that if you can only get at it you can save its life. You knock at the door. It is opened by some contented and portly old gentleman. He says, "What do you want? What are you knocking for? You can't get in here." You say, "There is a little child inside whose life is in danger, and I want to save it." He says, "Go away; I am too busy; you can't come in here." You say, "I must get in, it is imperative that I should get in." He won't let you in; he stands in the way. You argue with him for forty minutes, and you think you have argued long enough. The wail of the child is in your ears. You call on the neighbours to help you, and you force your way in. Suppose the neighbours are all asleep— do you think you would be doing anything very terrible if you broke one or two of their windows to waken them up? Don't you think you would be doing something quite justifiable?[21]

This analogy was directed to a jury charged with determining whether suffrage leaders had conspired to commit acts of violence. Because the jury was unlikely to sympathize with the violent acts themselves (or even the goal of the female franchise in most cases), the story explained in homey terms the feelings that animated the suffrage militants. This compelling little melodrama features a portly (i.e., well-fed and upper-class) villain, a helpless child, and the listener cast in the role of the frustrated rescuer. The forty minutes the hero spends arguing with the villain is a translation of the forty years the suffragists of various stripes had spent arguing with the government. In this story, the "victims" of window-breaking are willing allies of the hero if only they are awakened to his purpose. Any irritation or anger they may feel at the damage to their property is presumably swept away as they help him to force open the door (of legislation) and save the child. In other variations of this story, a woman sees "a young girl in the clutches of a White Slave Trader, or a sweated worker dying of starvation, or a baby being murdered" and is prevented from helping by a bolted window. The logical thing for her to do is to break the window, even if it means going against her natural "law-abiding instincts."[22] This version of the analogy is not as strong a defense for reformist terrorism, for it does not account for the necessity of damage to the property of a third person.

A visual variation on the basic rescue story was presented in the political cartoon of the April 5, 1912, *Votes for Women*. In this version, there are two firefighters (in vaguely female form) wearing sashes identifying them as the WSPU. One firefighter is on a ladder breaking a window; the other is putting out the fire with a hose that sprays "Votes for Women." The fire and smoke coming from the window is labeled "Sweated Workers," "White Slaves," and "Child Victims." This cartoon was placed over words of George Bernard Shaw to the effect that, while breaking the windows of a stranger without permission was a crime, the fire brigade did it all the time. Were a firefighter to be brought up on charges for this "crime," Shaw maintained, the jury would "find him 'not guilty,' with, probably, a rider expressing high commendation. If they did anything else, they would be sent to a lunatic asylum." In this variation of the analogy, the ills of white slavery et al. are a conflagration that threatens to destroy (as the headline reads) "The Englishwoman's Home."[23] Once again, this story justifies an apparently illegitimate act by virtue of the motives behind the action.

One final variation of the rescue story is worth noting, more out of historical interest than out of the quality of the argument. During the Conspiracy Trial defense, Frederick Pethick-Lawrence presented the example of the *Titanic*'s sinking, which was then under investigation. He expressed the wish that "people could have been wakened up to the seriousness of the need for precautions beforehand" and bemoaned the fact that so many people died for lack of adequate lifeboats. Warming to his analogy, Pethick-Lawrence pondered:

But supposing that some public-spirited people had said: "We are very much concerned about these regulations. If they are not attended to there will some day be a terrible accident." Supposing they went to the Board of Trade and broke a few windows to rouse the officials to the urgency of the matter. Don't you think that would have been better than doing nothing and allowing these 1,500 people to lose their lives on the *Titanic*? Let me put it another way. There was another ship close by. She had a wireless installation, but the operator was asleep. If she had received a message the lives of the people on the *Titanic* would have been saved. Supposing someone had wakened up that operator and that in doing so it had been necessary to break a few windows, don't you think it would have been worth while? I think you would.[24]

While this analogy lacked the clear justification of breaking a third party's window that Pethick-Lawrence's earlier story provided, it used current fears to minimize the importance of property (those "few windows") when great numbers of people were in danger. As Christabel Pankhurst said later to minimize the crime of letter-burning, "Which are the more precious—letters or lives? When the *Titanic* went down, huge mail bags stuffed with letters were lost. But who cared about those letters when they thought of the men and women who were drowned?"[25]

The WSPU's violence against property was the peripheral damage to be expected in a rescue mission to save vast numbers of oppressed women and children. Guerrilla militancy was planned in secrecy and carried out with suddenness; its very form spoke of the seriousness of its mission and captured the public's attention. In her memoirs, Emmeline Pethick-Lawrence described the sound of breaking plate-glass windows as "a sound as of fate knocking at the door and coming in without waiting for an answer!"[26] In seeking to cast its violence against property as a legitimate act of war, the union wished to draw the public attention past the sound of breaking glass to a focus on the just intentions behind the destruction.

The Lesser of Two Evils

Christabel Pankhurst dealt with the issue of proportion in a surprisingly direct manner, asking, "Is militancy morally right? That is the important question for women who, more than men, dislike doing evil that good may come. Yes, militancy is morally right and a thousand times morally right!"[27] The charge that the suffragettes were "doing evil that good may come" was directed at the union from two primary sources: from fellow suffragists who supported the union's cause but decried its militant methods, and from the church, specifically from the bishops of the Church of England. The union responded to the latter in no uncertain terms through Marie Naylor's reply to the bishops: "You, too, oh bishops! have done evil that good might come." Naylor pointed to the rushing of the Cat and Mouse Act through the House of Lords by the bishops as an evil done to promote what the bishops perceived as a "good" (the ending of militancy). Naylor suggested to the bishops that, if they considered suppression of militancy as God's act, then "they had better do this

God's act in God's own way. What is the way to put down militancy? Let them do it in God's own way by doing justice."[28] Emmeline Pankhurst reminded one audience that the Bishop of London refused to tender the same advice about not doing evil that good may come to Sir Edward Carson, and asked rhetorically, "How is it that he reserves his advice for women?" In the same speech, Pankhurst answered the bishop's charge that the suffragettes did evil in the pursuit of good: "I want to say to the Bishop of London, and to all those who talk as he does, that we do no evil. He says that to do violence is evil, and yet he supports the State where we maintain armies to kill human beings; he blesses warlike banners; he prays in cathedrals for the success of our armies. How, then, can he condemn women who are fighting for that which is most sacred—for human liberty? Our armies fight for possessions and property; women are fighting for human rights."[29] It was a fine example of hypocrisy for the bishops to support men's armies—which were superior only in the amount of violence they were willing to inflict upon others—and to deny that support to women.

Over the issue of the amount (and nature) of "evil" that could be done in support of the good, the suffragettes levied charges of hypocrisy in multiple directions. Some hypocrisy over militant methods was evinced by former supporters who declared themselves unable to accept the new policy of reform terrorism of the suffragettes. These erstwhile friends of the union were given a place in the "Suffragette Alphabet": "**O** for the Others who were always in favour / Till they witnessed our rude and impatient behaviour."[30] Such fair-weather support was not missed, the union claimed, and the movement was actually healthier for the removal of tenuous sympathizers. A cartoon that appeared on the cover of *Votes for Women* pictured a woman wearing a country bonnet and a WSPU sash. She has a firm grip on a limb of an apple tree and is giving it a healthy shake. Falling apples are labeled "Disgusted Liberal," "Chivalrous Supporter," "Mr. Sydney Buxton, M.P.," "Sir W. Byles, M.P.," and "Former Sympathiser." The caption read, "The Suffrage Tree has had a good shake at the hands of the militants, and the rotten fruit has fallen off"[31] (Figure 16). It was undeniable that a certain number of supporters were upset over the turn to violent militancy and withdrew their support from the union (if not from the suffrage cause as a whole). For some former supporters, a certain amount of their hostility was mitigated by the continued accounts of forcible feeding and the institution of the Cat and Mouse Act. George Bernard Shaw made an intriguing argument in a 1913 Kingsway Hall speech when he claimed that the suffragettes, whether openly supported by the majority of the public or not, had touched the collective conscience even of their enemies:

THE SUFFRAGE TREE.

The Suffrage Tree has had a good shake at the hands of the militants, and the rotten fruit has fallen off.
(Suggested by a speech made at the London Opera House last Friday.)

Figure 16. "The Suffrage Tree," *Votes for Women*, March 22, 1912

What the women have also proved is that the conscience of the community is on their side. What they have proved is . . . that the conscience of the very men who are doing this is on their side. See the continual suppression that is going on; see the uneasiness, and the shame. See the miserable excuses that are made about this matter—excuses that would not impose upon an intelligent frog. . . . If you take, for instance, the case of Dr. Crippen. Supposing Dr. Crippen had been sentenced to penal servitude for life, and if he had refused his food, do you suppose that anybody in the community would not have said, "Very well; let him starve."[32]

Shaw had earlier challenged the government leaders, if they were sure they were in the right in the matter, to let the suffragette prisoners hunger strike until they starved to death. The fact that the government refused to do so was an admission, in the eyes of Shaw and others, that the government could anticipate the hue and cry certain to be raised over the death of a suffrage prisoner. There was a hesitancy and discomfort in punishing the suffragettes that was not present in dealing with criminal women in general. The government and the public, suffrage supporters and opponents alike, thus tacitly acknowledged that the suffragettes were not in the same category as other criminals and that their violence was undertaken in order to achieve a greater good.

The Judgment of Posterity

To persuade its members to engage in violent acts, the union portrayed its terrorist tactics as guaranteed to succeed. Yet as time passed, the goal seemed to some to be further from hand, while the furor over the new methods seemed to grow. This obvious lack of progress—highlighted by the lack of a third Conciliation Bill or any other viable alternative legislation—needed to be negotiated with union members if their violent efforts were not to flag. When beset from all sides, it is comforting to project a hypothetical audience that will agree with your actions. In justifying the proportionality of its reformist terrorism to its goals for a better society, the union turned to the common device of an appeal to the future. Christabel Pankhurst put forth the following prediction, one particularly intriguing for current readers: "Lapse of time dignifies and magnifies events; or perhaps more truly, it shows them in their due proportions, and just as in these days, eighty years afterwards, the militancy of men is deemed epoch-making, so in the year 1990, when the Votes for Women battle is long since fought and won, the Women's militancy of 1913 will be recognised as the wonderful revolution that it is."[33]

As the physical difficulties of forcible feeding and the Cat and Mouse Act mounted and as the union's militancy was questioned on many sides, the suffragettes' rhetoric increasingly turned to assurances that vindication of their goals (and particularly their methods) would come through posterity. If the current generation could not see that the good to be obtained proportionately outweighed any evil wrought by militancy, then later generations would grant the suffragettes justification in retrospect. Shortly after the death of Emily Wilding Davison, the Rev. E. H. Taylor gave words of comfort to the besieged suffragettes: "Next, never forget what the verdict of posterity will be on all this. You are passing through great and wonderful times, and your names will live on the page of history as the violent who took the kingdom by force, as the drivers-out of its corruption, and as those who, at so infinite and great a cost to themselves brought the new regenerating power into the world of social and political life. The world does not know yet, but it will then, and then your names will be on the lips of its children's children through all the ages."[34] In 1913 and 1914, a stronger note of fatalism in the present day, but accompanied by an optimism for the future, entered suffragette rhetoric. A little more than a month before the death of Emily Davison, Christabel Pankhurst declared in an editorial, "Human life is in danger, but the cause of Votes for Women is not in danger. A Militant woman may be killed, but her cause will live and triumph."[35] A poem by James Lowell, reprinted in *The Suffragette*, described the reaction of the future to the martyrdom of the present:

> For Humanity sweeps onward; where to-day the martyr stands,
> On the morrow crouches Judas with the silver in his hands;
> Far in front the cross stands ready and the crackling faggots burn,
> While the hooting mob of yesterday in silent awe return,
> To glean up the scattered ashes into History's golden urn.[36]

The union pointed to history's revised view of everything from Cromwell's army to the Dorchester laborers (who were transported for starting a "Friendly Society of Agricultural Labourers") as examples of time's tendency to make heroes of the "criminals" of yesterday.[37] In this view of the justification of posterity, the WSPU's rhetoric of reformist terrorism closely resembled modern revolutionary terrorist rhetoric. Both address the issue, discussed by Richard Rubenstein, of "violent vanguardism," with each type of terrorist claiming that "the minority that now organizes violence against the state will become the majority. I speak and act in the name of this future majority." It is difficult during an actual crisis of violent reform or revolution to know which "isolated extremist may become tomorrow's legitimate leader." Therefore, all terrorists claim "that they are the statesmen and women of the future" and that the label of "terrorist" is little more than a word used by the winners in a revolution to delegitimize the losers. It is the old claim put forward (and challenged) endlessly in the terrorist literature, that "One man's terrorist is another man's freedom fighter."[38]

It is little wonder that Emmeline Pankhurst made the claim that history may well rewrite the view of women's militancy. In the foreword to her autobiography, published soon after the start of World War I and the suffragette truce with the government but before the WSPU entered into the women's war-work drive with the government, Pankhurst speculated upon this point: "The militancy of men, through all the centuries, has drenched the world with blood, and for these deeds of horror and destruction men have been rewarded with monuments, with great songs and epics. The militancy of women has harmed no human life save the lives of those who fought the battle of righteousness. Time alone will reveal what reward will be allotted to the women."[39] If the suffragettes would undergo revision in the eyes of future generations, then it followed that the verdict upon the government (and its actions) would also change. George Lansbury, M.P., was one who strongly believed that the future would be kinder to the suffragettes than it would be to Asquith and his government. On the memorable day when the policy of forcible feeding was debated in the House of Commons, Lansbury walked up the floor of the House to say to Asquith's face, "You will go down to history as the man who tortured innocent women!"[40] One writer for *The Suffragette* confidently declared that history would be less than kind to other members of the government besides the prime minister: "Mr. Lloyd George, that self-styled champion of the people, who has to go about England guarded like the Czar of Russia . . . even before those hard and greedy eyes of his must occasionally rise a vision of history as it will be written by posterity—a vision of himself, stripped of his pretensions as a liberator, revealed as a tyrant trying to maintain his power by trickery, a bully refusing liberty to the people of England."[41] This form of vilification, which presumed that a wiser future would see the justice of the suffragette side, was highly useful in bolstering the internal audience against the press of current opinion. In the strategy of forcing a crisis, a part of the vision of success became the belief that even the victims of violent militancy would one day thank those who destroyed their property in a higher cause. The pamphlet "Window Breaking: To One Who Has Suffered" concluded: "The day will come when you will be as proud as can be of your broken windows, and of the orders you delivered to the Government to give women the vote. I am, Sir, Yours faithfully, A SYMPATHISER."[42] In the rhetoric of reform, as in the rhetoric of revolution, part of the rhetorical battlefield consists of a projection of the future where a hypothetical victory can be declared and allies can be gathered from the ranks of the not-yet-born.

The view of Mr. Healy that "the criminals of one day are the Cabinet Ministers of the next" and the belief that posterity would kindly judge even the violent efforts of the suffragettes were part of a larger utopian vision of the future.[43] That in the future, the union would be justified, the government would be vilified, and a new world would be wrung from the old by means of the female franchise were all articles of faith in the WSPU. Annie Besant best summarized and drew together these expectations in a 1912 speech at the Royal Albert Hall:

And when history in the future judges the struggle of the present; when women all the world over walk hand in hand with men in equal liberty, in mutual respect, in loving co-partnership, then posterity, looking back on the shameful story of to-day, will crown with shame those who have used strength against the women who are doing hard labour now. And this country—in this country where the Cross, the sign once of ignominy, is now regarded with adoration—the martyrs of this cause will also be crowned with honour, because they realise that to suffer means in the long run to succeed, and to be able to face pain ensures the triumph of the cause for which the martyr is in pain.[44]

To those of us who live in the actual (and decidedly non-utopian) present, the hope and expectation of the Edwardian suffragettes appear as pure romanticism. Yet, in a practical sense, reform must be led by a vision of a better future in order to be effective. More important, in terms of the just-war criterion of proportionality, a utopian projection of future gains is necessary to offset acts of violence. Even a man who would not receive a direct gain for the sacrifice of his mail could have "the knowledge that his letter has been burnt on the altar of freedom."[45] Such a cost/reward ratio was a difficult aspect of the union argument, for any quid pro quo was merely speculative. The WSPU had to summon up by force of its rhetoric an image of a better world that would be brought into being through acts of political violence. According to William O'Brien, revolutionaries tend to "have as their end referent an open-ended utopia," which gives them such leeway in the methods they advocate. When a utopia can be presented as a viable end, that alone serves as "the justification for means that would be very hard to define and limit."[46] As Robert Ivie has pointed out, war or the use of violence in a reform or revolutionary cause "is considered an essentially negative agency that assumes positive characteristics only in the presence of severely threatened ideals; it is portrayed as but a step toward more permanent resolutions such as 'a concert of free peoples' or 'a world where all are fed and charged with hope.' Belligerency, then, is the unpleasant means to a more permanent peace which will insure the security of those principles."[47] Some of the descriptions of the brighter world to come, which the union used to lend proportion to its acts of violence, were painted with the same broad brush as the examples given above. George Lansbury, in a speech at the Albert Hall, spoke of the desire for "men and women to join hand in hand and destroy the hard economic conditions, the harsh political conditions, and bring about that kind of comradeship between men and women which will help us, as Blake said, 'To build Jerusalem, In England's green and pleasant land.' "[48] Much of the general utopian projection of the future dealt with relations between the sexes. The suffragettes felt that reason, rather than force, would form the basis of the new relationship between men and women. The disappearance of the once-common practice of dueling to settle issues was cited as an example of the rise of reason over force in human affairs. In the future, once men and women were given an equality of position "the very memory of domination based on force and resistance to that domination made by force will quickly fade away."[49]

The utopian nature of these arguments is one aspect that the reformist WSPU shared with more revolutionary movements. Yet, the vision of the future presented by union rhetors was primarily a realization of traditional values and was pinpointed toward the outcome of a single reform. In a speech in 1914, while she was under considerable physical strain from repeated hunger strikes, Emmeline Pankhurst emphasized that "out of our struggle, even by the laying down of our lives, will come a time so wonderful for humanity that we can only dimly see that beautiful future."[50] Although apparently broad, Pankhurst's emphasis was upon a specific change in the relationship between the sexes, which would usher in a golden age of respect and trust:

We are fighting for a time when every little girl born into the world will have an equal chance with her brothers, when we shall put an end to foul outrages upon our sex, when our streets shall be safe for the girlhood of our race, when every man shall look upon every other woman as his own sisters, when love shall be lifted to be the noblest thing in life. When we have done that, we can rest upon our laurels, assured that we have passed on to future generations an inheritance worthy of the great human race of which we are humble members.[51]

Because of the nature of the reform sought by the union, its vision of the future was a liberal-feminist utopia, where women were both empowered and cherished. The suffragettes extended their vision of a new relationship between the sexes to a new relationship between the classes in England. Concerning this issue, which was not directly tied to the reform they sought, the union remained vague and romantic. In a poem by Lucius Grant entitled "Springtime," which appeared before the split in the suffrage forces, Mrs. Pankhurst (in prison) sends an imaginary message to Mrs. Pethick-Lawrence. The final verse of the poem dealt with their common future vision for the oppressed:

The day in which work is a joy, my friend,
    And everyone has a full share
Of the gifts God strews with a lavish hand,
    In his boundless pity and care;
When the high shall raise up the low, my friend,
    And the strong by the weak shall stand,
So that this fair England, at last, my friend,
    Shall be *truly* a Christian Land![52]

The union was not alone in its hope for a better future, for many writers on the Edwardian period have noted "expectancy" to be a primary trait of the period.[53] In their vision of a postreform paradise, the suffragettes varied from the other reformers of the Edwardian period only in their belief that the female franchise would be the primary engine that drove the reform.

The WSPU did not restrict itself to using general visions of a post-vote utopia to justify present-day violence but made continuous reference to correcting specific societal ills. According to Annie Kenney, the government was so adamant in its opposition to the suffragettes *"because they are afraid of the effect that the W.S.P.U. will have on private life and public life after the Vote is won"* (emphasis in original).[54] Flora Drummond asked, "Women concerned with the temperance question, how are you getting on until you get votes?" and pointed out that, in the postsuffrage future, candidates for office would have to cater to social reform issues as "bait" to catch the women's vote.[55] Even more important to the union, largely due to the emphasis of the purity campaign, was the effect the women's vote would have upon the incidence of venereal disease. Christabel Pankhurst cited the opinion of one doctor that the elimination of such diseases would lead to a new world as far as medicine was concerned. "A new world!" Pankhurst continued, "That is what women want. By Militancy they are preparing for it! With the vote they will build it. Pessimists may tell us that a world-old shame can never be uprooted. Our answer is that women have never been allowed to try. That we should fly was once declared impossible!"[56] Universal Good would come by means of the vote; the vote would come by means of violent militancy. The union felt confident that, whatever the judgment of the present time, the suffragettes would be justified in the restrained "Evil" of their reformist terrorism once posterity weighed in the balance the proportionate good that had been obtained.

Conclusion

> The truth is that violence and warfare assume a moral complexion
> in accordance with their circumstances and their cause. An unjust
> and oppressive war is the blackest of all crimes. But there are wars
> of liberation, holy wars. Of such is the women's war now afoot in
> Great Britain.
>
> Christabel Pankhurst, 1913[1]

Clearly, the suffragettes felt that, if their "women's war" was judged
by the same criteria generally used to judge the revolutions and wars
of men, they would be considered justified in their use of violent militancy. During the time of their reformist terrorism, the suffragettes
were unable to break through public condemnation of their attacks
on private property and achieve their goal of suffrage. The union saw
1914 as a time of heightened activity and potential progress. Others
saw it as a period of stalemate and believed the militant policy had
been taken as far as it could go without bloodshed. Knowing whether
the union plan of forcing a crisis would have achieved the desired goal
of franchise reform had World War I not intervened is impossible. In
any event, World War I transformed the suffrage movement as far as
the union was concerned. After war was declared on August 4, 1914,
the WSPU called an immediate truce on militant action and temporarily suspended publication of *The Suffragette.* The government
soon granted an unconditional release to all suffrage prisoners.[2]

Suffrage workers differed as much in their response to the war as
they did in determining suffrage strategy. The WSPU leadership—
Emmeline and Christabel Pankhurst, Flora Drummond, Annie Kenney, and Grace Roe—became strong supporters of the government
they had previously opposed. Christabel Pankhurst, who returned in
triumph from Paris in September, and Emmeline Pankhurst threw
themselves into political war work, leading a campaign to encour-

age women to work in munitions factories and essential services. The WSPU became what some called "war extremists," traveling throughout England speaking for universal obligatory service and pressuring men to enlist. Followers of Emmeline and Christabel Pankhurst were among the women who would walk up to a man of fighting age at a restaurant or on a public street and, if he was not in uniform, hand him a white feather as an accusation of cowardice.[3]

When *The Suffragette* reappeared in the spring of 1915, it reflected the new pro-government stance of the WSPU. On October 15, 1915, the paper was even renamed *Britannia* and given the new dedication under its masthead, "For King, for Country, for Freedom."[4] Not all the original militant suffragettes shared this positive view of the war. Emmeline Pethick-Lawrence spoke in Europe and America for peace and was a prime mover in the Women's Peace Conference in The Hague in April 1915. Emmeline Pankhurst, on the other hand, clearly stated her strong opposition to the peace conference in a speech delivered in Liverpool that same April. In fact, the Pethick-Lawrences and the Pankhursts were polar opposites in their response to the war. Emmeline and Christabel Pankhurst made a long series of speeches on war issues during the next four years. Christabel, in particular, spoke weekly at the Aeolian Hall during the summer and fall of 1917. One speech by Emmeline Pankhurst, given at London Polytechnic on June 24, 1915, was reported in the *Times*. Largely on the strength of this speech, Lloyd George, then at the Ministry of Munitions, gave the WSPU a £2,000 grant to stage a Right to Serve parade for women. On July 17, 1915, a highly successful parade of thirty thousand women took place, echoing some of the grand processions of the suffrage movement. Sponsoring this parade was one way for the government to pressure the trade unions to accept lower-paid women workers. The trade unions were opposed to the low wages of women, not out of a sense of equality but because the women's presence could undermine the wages and working conditions of men.[5]

Several years into the war, the opportunity to seriously raise the franchise issue emerged only because of Liberal and Unionist demands to guarantee a vote to every soldier at the front. As things stood, men had to be householders and had to occupy "a dwelling for at least one year prior to the fifteenth day of the July preceding an election." It is not hard to see how both the soldier overseas and the war worker who had moved to areas where he was needed had lost their vote. The Conference on Electoral Reform set up by the Asquith government recommended a variety of franchise reforms, including votes for women. The conference recommended, too, that an age restriction of either thirty or thirty-five be imposed on women to prevent a female majority.[6]

On March 28, 1917, Asquith finally declared himself a convert to women's suffrage under the new Electoral Reform Bill. This support would have been more dramatic had Lloyd George not replaced Asquith as prime minister in December 1916. On May 15, 1917, the bill was introduced in the House of Commons, and the debate on women's suffrage took place on June 19. The bill passed the committee by a vote of 385 to 55.[7]

With only the House of Lords needing to vote on the Electoral Reform Bill, it seemed likely that women would soon be enfranchised. The WSPU leaders formed The Women's Party. Their feeling was that the men's parties had all made mistakes, they had not supported women in the past, and they were now trying to "herd" future women voters into their ranks. The Women's Party platform began with the war, favoring war till victory and harsh peace terms that would deplete German resources and presumably make another war impossible. The platform was very specific in the war measures it supported, from food rationing and communal kitchens to better coordination of the Allied forces. The Women's Party also supported special women's issues, such as equal pay for equal work, equal marriage laws, equal employment opportunity, and a raising of the "age of consent" for girls.[8] The Women's Clause passed the House of Lords on January 8 by a vote of 134 to 71, and the Electoral Reform Bill received the royal assent on February 6, 1918.[9] And so, fifty years after John Stuart Mill introduced a women's suffrage bill to Parliament, women over thirty quietly obtained the vote.

Clearly, the suffragettes made a rapid and successful transition from reformist agitators to mainstream supporters of government policy. In my view, the just-war arguments of the suffragettes presented during the course of their agitation served as a uniquely effective means of rehabilitation for the WSPU during the early years of World War I. This same group of women who spent two and a half years perpetrating secret acts of arson and bombing made the successful return to a conventional support of the same government that they previously attacked. Rather than being met with ridicule and rejection by the government, the WSPU quickly took a major public role in support of the government's conduct of the war. The difficulty facing the suffragettes in achieving rehabilitation following the close of their agitation should not be underestimated. Reform movements may turn to violence in order to find novel ways to communicate their message. Yet, as Schmid and de Graaf write, "when violence is used to communicate, the means often deflect attention from the ends so that the message often does not get through. People then see in terrorism only the violence and no longer the communication. Very few groups have therefore managed to transform themselves from disruptive news-makers into habitual news-makers who are no longer primarily dependent on violence."[10] The WSPU achieved this transformation in the period immediately following the beginning of World War I. However, I believe that the union's rehabilitation was largely accomplished not in the period following the August 4, 1914, declaration of war but during the very time when it was violently attacking the government. As far as tactics are concerned, the story of the union is that of a reform group that "crossed the Rubicon" into violence, apparently burning its bridges behind it, yet managed simultaneously to construct a new rhetorical bridge for its later return to respectability.

With the advent of World War I, the just-war arguments in favor of suffrage militancy blended seamlessly into arguments justifying Great Britain's participation in the war and helped to position the union as an important advocate of British war policy. As Lisa Tickner remarked, "Militant rhetoric and the image of the just crusade remained, but their object shifted, and the Pankhursts remade their allegiances in the face of a new 'Great Scourge': that of German hostility."[11] Although they have not explored the just-war basis of the similarity, several scholars have remarked in passing on the unusual "fit" between the militant images of the WSPU and the new militant images of the "Great War." Joseph Clayton, in his study on English socialism, pointed to WSPU rhetoric as easing the transition into war: "The violence and sabotage of the WSPU were *ad hoc* to get a bill passed for the enfranchisement of women; not revolutionary in themselves, the disorders of the WSPU encouraged the feeling that violence directed to a good end was not to be condemned, and accustomed many minds to the idea of war, and fostered an admiration for the sacrifices that war required."[12] Although many suffragists considered the Pankhursts' support for the war as a betrayal of women's higher nature and desire for peace, a general sense emerged that at least the militant union was being consistent in its belief that violence was sometimes justified in a good cause. Esme Wingfield-Stratford has wryly noted, "As Nietzsche might have put it, the Pankhurst gospel was hardly so much that a good cause sanctified militancy, as that a good militancy sanctified the cause."[13] The nonmilitant suffragists who now supported the war were unable to claim such consistency, for they appeared to justify militancy—but only for the benefit of men.[14]

The irony of the suffragettes' serving as spokeswomen for the government was not lost on Emmeline Pankhurst. In a military recruitment speech made in November 1914 in the Plymouth Guildhall, Pankhurst noted, "Life is a queer topsy-turvy thing, isn't it? Here you have a convict, whose license has expired, and not amnestified, actually asking people to enlist and fight for the country!"[15] Roberta Carson claims that in their war speeches, the Pankhursts continued to present the suffrage argument, but "they restyled it as they might have last season's gown; the look was new, yet the fabric was the same."[16] Certainly the early war speeches contained references to the suffrage fight, and speakers often compared the struggle of Belgium to that of the suffrage workers. But my sense is that it was not a matter of using the war argument to support suffrage but a use of suffrage references to better support the war. The Pankhursts wished to bring the union membership along with them in the new war campaign, and they referred to the suffrage struggle largely to show that, despite their gender, they knew what physical war was all about. In referring to their own physical combat for the vote, the Pankhursts and other union speakers reached for the legitimate authority needed to speak about combat and war. As the recruitment campaign progressed, references to the suffrage campaign quickly dwindled and vanished from union speeches and articles. It is intriguing to see how often, in the early recruitment campaign, the Pankhursts themselves were heckled by audience members (and one woman in particular) who interrupted their speeches with calls of "Votes for Women!"

The Pankhursts' war rhetoric repeated the view of violence (and suffering) as ennobling that was so familiar to union audiences during the suffrage movement. The just war for women had become the just war for the nation, and many of the images from the former (Joan of Arc, Britannia, etc.) would find new life as justifying images for the latter. I strongly believe that the suffragettes owed much of their rapid rehabilitation with the general public to the "fit" between the just-war rhetoric of internal reform and the just-war rhetoric of international conflict. Obviously, this successful transition could not have been planned in advance. It is hard to know how well just-war rhetoric would have served the suffragettes had they achieved the vote and then attempted their rehabilitation into a peacetime society.

Rereading Suffragette Violence

It is only fitting at the close of this study to see how an understanding of the suffragettes' just-war rationale helps us answer those perennial questions raised about suffragette violence in the introduction. First, how could a movement whose object was reform justify, to itself and others, the adoption of essentially revolutionary methods? Reformist and revolutionary terrorists share a belief that conventional methods (and even unconventional methods of militant protest) are played out. It was a feeling of impotence that led the union to appropriate revolutionary methods, if not the revolutionary agenda. This study has shown that when reduced to its essentials, reformist terrorism shares with revolutionary terrorism the need to bring presence to its cause in the mind of the public. Violence applies pressure to the public, who will then, in theory at least, pressure the government to grant the terrorist demands and restore peace. The use of violence, however, brings philosophical pressures to the reformist movement far greater than those experienced by revolutionaries. The basic contention of this study is that the philosophical incompatibility between reformist ends and violent means must be rhetorically negotiated by a movement.

This brings us to the second question generally raised about the suffragettes: How could intelligent women from the social class and historical period of the suffragettes support the use of violence, however worthy the cause? This examination of the WSPU has argued that framing their violence as a just war was incredibly liberating for union members. In her use of just-war doctrine, Pankhurst sought legitimacy for her new vision of politics by, in Eugene Garver's words, "taking over the territory traditionally occupied by the old." It is important, however, to differentiate what union rhetors needed to accomplish from the direct and unaltered imitation of the past utilized by those whose personal authority is unquestioned. In Garver's eyes, "a simpleminded sort of imitation—an unreflective connection between past successes, universal values, and future acts—would be disastrous" for one who still needed to achieve authority in public eyes. Pankhurst and the other suffragette rhetors needed to rely on "a rhetorical method in which invention is the leading office" in order "to manufacture relations between past action, general value, and future action."[17] By interweaving their own images and arguments with the traditional issues surrounding the just war, the suffragettes found the one socially approved justification for violence that allowed them to be simultaneously radical and conventional. The violence that separated the suffragettes from society became the very point of commonality they shared with that society when it was arrayed in the trappings of the just war.

First, because a just war is of necessity defensive, union members were freed from the guilt of instigating violence and could cloak their understandable frustration and aggression in a purely defensive guise. The need to protect both themselves and the women and children of England allowed actions that union members would normally view as unacceptable. It was the role of nurturer, the feminine philosophy of care for others, that was the impetus for violent action. Second, the persona of the Just Warrior transformed the self-image of union members. Army imagery gave the individual and surreptitious acts of suffragette violence both dignity and structure. As soldiers, the suffragettes saw themselves as set apart, possessing a special, indomitable spirit. The WSPU members softened their military self-view with images of martyrdom and motherhood. These images spoke to the public of the traditional feminine role of loving self-sacrifice that the militant women brought to their struggle. The militant was the prototype of the new woman, and she claimed for herself the legitimate authority to wage war in a just cause. Third, the WSPU argued that violence was necessitated by a heedless public, guilty of condoning the greater evils in society. Violence was portrayed as a purifying tool of the just and one utilized by men in both the past and the present. References to the just wars of men clarified for the women who remained as violent militants the historic significance of their cause. They could see clearly that their grievances were every bit as great as many of the grievances that had prompted men to use violence in the past. In their refusal to use *lethal* violence, the suffragettes reclaimed women's traditional assertions of moral superiority even in the conduct of war. The expediency argument of women's higher moral nature, long used to support female suffrage, was thus recast through the just war to support the means used to acquire the vote. Finally, the just-war rationale allowed the suffragettes to shelter their violence behind the purity of their motives. The need for men occasionally to do evil in support of good was widely accepted. By borrowing the just-war rationale from men, the union highlighted the hypocrisy of those who claimed that the suffragettes had gone too far in their pursuit of justice. The answer to the question of how these Edwardian middle- to upper-class women could support violence for a worthy cause now becomes relatively simple. They had, along with most of their culture, always supported violence for a "good cause." Only now, they applied the same criteria to the women's cause that they always had accepted for the concerns of men.

One conclusion I draw from this analysis of WSPU rhetoric is that reformers using violence need not abandon their moral stance. The genius of appropriating just-war rhetoric for reformist violence was that it allowed a spinning out of a fantasy of heroes, of a gallant band fighting against the odds. It challenged the imagination of the public to extend to women a romantic vision usually reserved for men and to accept the new expectations inherent in that vision. What first appeared to be random acts of senseless violence became, when viewed through the transformative frame of the just war, strategic acts of war undertaken with deliberation by the suffragette army. Violence apparently aimed at the innocent was transformed into defensive acts to protect the powerless and undertaken against an unscrupulous and powerful foe. Even more dramatic was the rehabilitation of the public view of the suffragette. An image of desperate and hysterical women (presumably driven insane by their personal and social failings) became the Just Warrior—strong, determined, and virtuous. Acts of arson, bombing, and window-smashing became the purifying fire of the battlefield, a "holocaust" cleansing the world of pernicious evil. The streets of London, the public byways of a society ostensibly at peace, could now be seen to be a battlefield where a covert war against women and children had raged for years, unchecked. Finally, the apparent desire of the suffragettes to force society to yield to extremist demands was transformed into a holy cause, grounded in a desire to inaugurate a just and lasting peace between men and women.

As can be seen in this comparison, the transformation of public perception sought through the use of just-war rhetoric lent a gloss of moral superiority to the use of violence. In this way, the WSPU solved the dilemma of the philosophical incompatibility of reformist goals and violent revolutionary methods for those who remained as soldiers in the union army. For external audiences, too, the specialized ethics of war became the common ground where the system co-existed with those who would alter that system. Too often, the suffragettes' use of military metaphors, their vilification of the government, and their violent attacks on property have been referenced as proof that union members were hysterical and out of control. However, WSPU rhetors put forward a consistent rationale for their plan to force a governmental crisis that would provide the necessary pressure for reform. Their argument that suffragette actions comprised a just war was at least compelling enough to force their opponents and the press to directly refute the case the union made. The Just Warrior was a comfortable, albeit unexpected, persona for a women's movement to adopt, for it clothed violence in virtue and belligerence in self-sacrifice. Finally, by replacing the image of "crime," the competing metaphor for terrorist violence, with that of "warfare," just-war rhetoric allowed closure to the struggle for the vote. A war generally comes to a definitive end as terms of peace are sought between the two sides, and it is this same rapprochement with the larger society that must be achieved by a reform movement following the conclusion of its agitation.

At this point, another question naturally arises from a contemplation of the WSPU's just-war rationale: How effective was just-war rhetoric in mediating between movement violence and public displeasure? During the time of the suffrage agitation, the union's justificatory rhetoric may have been effective in some quarters. There has long existed an image of the WSPU moving deeper into violence and cutting itself off completely from friend and foe alike. Although it is true that the guerrilla militancy tactics caused severe splits in the suffrage ranks and that the daily operations of the union became more suited to clandestine operations, it is not necessarily true that the union lost all its public support. Support actually increased by certain parties (notably George Bernard Shaw and certain members of the clergy) as controversy grew over suffragette actions and the counteractions of the government. The union kept careful financial records and could, in its last annual report, of February 28, 1914, point to a year's income of £36,896. This figure was independent of local fund-raising and amounted to an £8,000 increase over the previous fiscal year.[18] Even if one chooses to discount as suspect the financial report of the union, there exists other evidence that the suffragettes were able to maintain support. During the debate in Parliament over acceptable methods of punishment for the suffragettes, the idea of deporting them was dropped because the suffragettes' "rich supporters" would simply send their yachts and bring them home.[19]

It is difficult to obtain an objective view of suffragette popularity apart from the claims of the government and the press that the union was friendless and apart from the union's view that its support in the public was increasing. One place to look for objective clues as to suffragette support may be found in the advertising in the union paper. Even a brief glance at *The Suffragette* shows that advertisers believed that many of their upper-class clientele continued to read the union paper and patronize shops advertised in its pages. The number of ads in the paper fluctuated primarily based upon the usual changes in seasonal advertising rather than upon the actions of the militants. For example, in the July 3, 1914, issue, during the summer sale season, *The Suffragette* was filled with ads from major stores such as Swan & Edgar, William Owen, Selfridges, Pontings, Peter Robinson, and Waring & Gillow's. Ads also touted Gibb's Cold Cream Soap, Jaeger Wool Coats, and Welford's Dairies. Certain ads could be counted upon for almost every issue throughout the militant campaign, selling Mapleton's Nut Foods, the fare of the Thistle tearoom (or Ye Olde Oake Tea House), W. Clarke & Sons coal, and wigs and hair dyes by Maison Robert of Regent Street.[20] Advertisers are naturally sensitive to controversy and tend toward the conservative in ad placement. To continue to place ads during the times of greatest militant attacks reflected advertiser beliefs that *The Suffragette* had a continuing loyal (and wealthy) readership. But even if we grant the union's justificatory rhetoric as successful in some quarters, it clearly did not yield the suffragettes universal (or even majority) acceptance during the time of the agitation.

Studies of the WSPU are drawn repeatedly to the issue of effect and question whether suffragette reformist terrorism "overstepped the line" and hurt the very cause it purported to help. Constance Rover clearly states the dilemma shared by reformist groups: "To use insufficient pressure is ineffective, but to attack too fiercely arouses antagonism which may both delay the attainment of the objective and make eventual acceptance of the group with the community as a whole difficult." Rover, thus, believes that "suffragette violence after 1912 fell between two stools, being inadequate to coerce the government but sufficiently destructive to antagonize public opinion."[21] This view of suffragette reformist terrorism appears to be shared by the majority of researchers of the WSPU. Brian Harrison devotes many pages in attempting to prove that militancy was not only ineffective in gaining the desired reform but also deleterious to the movement as a whole. He expresses the belief that the "tactical violence" of the suffragettes was very different from the "mass violence" necessary to achieve success.[22] Tickner joins in the opinion that "the difficulty for the suffragettes was not that they were violent, but that they were not violent enough." She further expresses the opinion that violent militancy could work only if the government could be seriously threatened and that "women were never in a position to ensure that it was."[23] Such views of the ineffectiveness of militancy are balanced by the autobiographies of suffragettes who claim in a variety of ways that fear of renewed union militancy was a prime impetus to the government inclusion of women in the "Sailors' and Soldiers' Enfranchisement Bill."[24] In this view, as Annie Kenney put it, the constructive building of the structure of the women's movement was completed early in the movement, but "the tower was built by the extreme Militants" and the complete structure was necessary to the final success.[25]

Although the critics may be correct that selective violence is not as effective as mass violence in accomplishing a reform goal, I would argue that mass violence was never an option for the WSPU. Even if the union had converted the majority of the population to favor suffrage, half of that population would be unable (by law) to bring their desires directly to legal realization. Many in that same half of the population would be unable (by social custom) even to make those desires publicly known. Certainly the average Edwardian woman, even if desirous of the vote, would not join in mass violence to get it. The experience of the suffragettes in seeking reform for the powerless (and disenfranchised) challenges the easy assumption that reformers must convert the public and that reform will be achieved through that conversion. Terrorism (selective and covert violence) attempts to make up for a lack of numbers available to take part in violent action for reform. Reformist terrorism may not be designed just to foist a minority view upon an unwilling public but may be used to circumvent the obstacle of a powerful and stubborn minority. To say this is not to give a tacit approval for the use of violence but to acknowledge that terrorism will probably always remain a strategic choice open to reformers as well as revolutionaries. Taking the step to violence may not be an uncontrollable escalation for a reform group but a decision made "in cold blood."[26]

Reformist versus Revolutionary Rhetoric

Reformist terrorism needs to be separated from its more dramatic revolutionary cousin and examined as a separate entity in terms of its discursive and extradiscursive rhetoric. This examination of union rhetoric suggests not only that reformist terrorists can use rhetoric successfully to defend their moral position, but also that expectations of a return to respectability at some later date have an impact on the form of that rhetoric. The suffragettes envisioned not only their eventual success but also their readmittance with honors into mainstream political society. During the height of the attacks on property, the suffragettes published an open letter assuring the British public that "the Suffragettes are your friends, and will be your allies and comrades in the days when women have the Vote and can help to govern the country better. We have been very patient with you hitherto. Even now we feel no bitterness. When all is over we will give you a free pardon for your neglect of our interests and liberties. But there can be no peace without honour—no end to fighting till the Vote is won."[27] The WSPU subscribed to the basic value system of British government but "dispute[d] the distribution of benefits or power within that value system."[28] That is, the union sought to extend power to women and benefits of the British system to the oppressed. By accomplishing this redistribution of power and benefits, the union believed any disagreements it had with the predominant value system (such as the double standard of sexual morality) would be resolved. The union declared at the time of the agitation that, once the vote was won and the good the vote would bring was accomplished, "how gladly will these women become peaceful and law-abiding citizens. The joy of having the Vote will be almost equalled by the joy of no longer having to fight for it. How gladly will these women beat their swords into ploughshares, and their spears into pruning-hooks."[29] Reintegration into mainstream society was made difficult by the militants' use of reformist terrorism. It was the violence of their extradiscursive rhetoric combined with the desire to blend back into the larger society that necessitated an ameliorating discursive rhetoric to justify and excuse their actions.

In terms of extradiscursive rhetoric, the need to reassimilate into the society also serves as a restraint on the extent of physical violence that reformists may successfully employ. I believe that the WSPU refrained from attacks on human life out of moral commitment, but even from simply a strategic standpoint, lethal violence is an inappropriate means for reformist ends. Rover has spoken of the view of moderate African Americans that the civil rights struggle was "a family quarrel" that would be resolved by their further integration into American society. The attainment of reformist goals and the subsequent reintegration of the reformers into the political mainstream results in a "situation [in which] the definition of the limit to which agitation can usefully be pressed is a delicate manner."[30] The point that needs to be made here is that reformist terrorists in their extradiscursive rhetoric (their acts of violence against property) face the unavoidable balancing of sufficient violence for effect against sufficient restraint for postreform assimilation. There is no formulaic resolution to this problem. One of the most thoughtful contemplations of the use of violent methods comes from Rover. She cites the tendency of governments to "say they will not give way to force" but juxtaposes these claims to the common "pattern of nationalist leaders being imprisoned, subsequently to be released, negotiated with, and to become honoured leaders." Combined with the inability of "those outside the constitution" always to find a "legal means of protest," these instances of success guarantee that reformers will continue to join revolutionaries in viewing violence, and even terrorism, as viable *and justifiable* strategies.[31]

If the need for later assimilation spells the difference between the extradiscursive rhetoric of the reformer and that of the revolutionary, it also serves to differentiate the discursive rhetoric used by both. In many ways the rhetoric of the reformist terrorist has a great deal in common with that of the revolutionary terrorist. In the discursive rhetoric of the revolutionary terrorist there is a heavy emphasis upon "bipolar" justification. According to Richard Leeman, the revolutionary terrorist justifies the use of violence "by constructing a bipolar world which cleanly divides good from evil. Terrorism is legitimate because it 'responds' to an evil, illegitimate enemy." Like the rhetoric of reformist violence, revolutionary terrorism vilifies its opponents (often through metaphoric and hyperbolic language) and points to the need to end oppression as the primary justification for violent action. Revolutionary terrorists share with reformist terrorists an emphasis upon "action" as a God term and a tendency to view those who choose not to join them in violent action as tacitly supporting the oppressor. For the revolutionary terrorist, the emphasis upon bipolar justification and action finds its expression by "exhorting blows against the system."[32] Exhortation, described by Edwin Black as the "stirring of an audience's emotions [as] a primary persuasive force," is common to both reformist and revolutionary rhetoric.[33] However, for the revolutionary terrorist, exhortation for the oppressed to strike violently against the oppressive system becomes a primary element in a meager discursive rhetoric.

The WSPU did utilize exhortation in its speeches and editorials. Often such exhortation formed a conclusion to the speeches and articles that preceded a particular deputation or procession. A typical example of union exhortation could be found in an editorial by Emmeline Pethick-Lawrence:

Women! You whose eyes are opened . . . what are you going to do? Are you going to respond to the call of your colleagues who have suffered imprisonment again and again for the Cause which is yours as much as it is theirs? Or are you going to leave that little band of heroes to the hazards of the conflict? Are you going to let the issues of this great struggle for *your* liberty and *your* honour rest upon *their* courage and *their* sacrifice? . . . Mrs. Pankhurst will place herself at the head of a great demonstration of protest. . . . Let the Union as one woman rise and go with her. Let hesitations, scruples and fears be finally cast aside. Be ready![34]

In speeches such exhortation could be particularly effective. Emmeline Pankhurst's speech at the Albert Hall, which ushered in the policy of guerrilla militancy, roused the faithful to greater action:

You, women in this meeting, will you help us to do it? ("Yes!") Well, then, if you will, put aside all craven fear. Go and buy your hammer; be militant. Be militant in your own way. Those of you who can express your militancy by going to the House of Commons and refusing to leave without satisfaction, as we did in the early days—do so. . . . Those of you who can break windows (great applause)—those of you who can still further attack the sacred idol of property so as to make the Government realise that property is as greatly endangered by women as it was by the Chartists of old days—do so.[35]

Although such exhortation provided a pleasing crescendo in occasional speeches and editorials, it was a very minor aspect of the suffragette rhetoric. On the other hand, Leeman points out, revolutionary terrorists "ground their discourse in the negative emotions of frustration, anger, and hatred of the system," and what brief discursive rhetoric they make available in their communiqués is often primarily given over to exhortation.[36]

Awareness that they will later need to work with the very people they now attack also may have a structuring effect upon reformers' rhetoric. If the revolutionary terrorist uses a rhetorical meat-ax to divide the good guys from the bad, the reformist terrorist wields a scalpel. This difference in discursive subtlety can be seen by comparing the revolutionary's broad-brush attacks upon the "system"[37] to the very specific charges the suffragettes leveled against the Liberal government, the cabinet ministers, or individual politicians such as Asquith and Lloyd George. The entire just-war argument is one of subtlety and nuance and unlikely to be utilized by revolutionary terrorists, who seek a more gut-level justification. Whether or not revolutionary terrorists actually use (or have used) just-war doctrine as a basis for their justifications is an intriguing question that invites further study. My best guess would be that, if just-war doctrine is used in their discursive rhetoric, it would primarily be geared toward the recruiting of fellow revolutionaries. Because revolutionaries plan to overthrow the system completely, they would be unlikely to seek converts within the power structure of that system. Although it is certainly a possibility, I see little sign in revolutionary terrorist rhetoric of a desire to present an in-depth explanation to other countries defending the right to violently attack the system. As mentioned previously, during the actual time of the agitation, the terrorist's criminal status prevents access to media needed to disseminate a detailed rationale for violent action. The need to convince other countries of the terrorist's right to revolution comes after the takeover of the system has been achieved. It would be a valuable study to examine the aftermath of a successful revolutionary action and see to what extent just-war doctrine is referenced as a justification after the fact. When erstwhile revolutionaries teach the history of the revolution to their children in formal educational settings, how do they justify the use of violence to achieve change? To what extent do stories of former oppression grant the revolutionary "just cause," and how do former terrorists defend their acts in terms of proportion and discrimination?

The primary implication of this study has less to do with the specifics of suffragette rhetoric than it does with the recurrent rhetorical need to employ a conservative rhetoric in support of a radical cause. Strategic violence, the rhetoric of the deed, has the power to reformulate a movement's sense of community, to the point where violence actually creates community. The surreptitious planning, the personal danger, and the self-justification necessitated by violent action form a point of commonality reflected in the internal talk among members. However, the very rhetoric that draws a movement together also isolates that movement from the larger community. For the general public, revolutionary change may not be comprehensible if it is promoted by equally revolutionary rhetoric. The WSPU could be considered doubly revolutionary, for it supported the radical goal (in many people's estimation) of female suffrage with radical action. The innovative use of tradition by the union served to fulfill Garver's requirement for an inventional rhetoric that "mak[es] the new politics seem to inhabit the same world as the old."[38] An understanding of the WSPU's just-war rationale provides further proof that the union's voice was conservative even in the justification of radical deeds.

Whether the rhetoric of the just war is a commonality among reform groups or a peculiarity of the Women's Social and Political Union remains to be seen. In their campaign of violence, the suffragettes took upon themselves the mantle of the Just Warrior and later extended it to cover every woman working in a British munitions factory. By incorporating this self-view into their rhetoric, union members who made the step into violent action were able to resolve for themselves the conflict between moral transcendence and political immanence. They were able to answer in some measure the recurrent question facing reformist movements: How can we maintain our moral stance yet do what necessity dictates for success?

In the same way, the rhetoric of the Women's Social and Political Union took centuries-old justifications for war and extended them to reformist terrorism. The union said of its movement, "It may not be war, but it is certainly magnificent." Through its rhetoric of the just war, the WSPU argued wholeheartedly that "the common principle which underlies both war and a revolt such as that of the militants is the use of violence to subserve a cause deemed right."[39] The WSPU's innovation was not so much the use of tactical violence itself but the adoption of a rhetorical stance *toward* violence that quite literally made a virtue out of necessity. Suffragette rhetors systematically took the most conventional justification that Western tradition provides for the use of violence and adapted it to meet their unique circumstances as women utilizing violence for political reform.

Notes

Introduction

1. Midge Mackenzie, *Shoulder to Shoulder* (New York: Knopf, 1975), 221.
2. Ibid., 219–33.
3. Antonia Raeburn, *The Suffragette View* (New York: St. Martin's Press, 1976), 57.
4. Maxwell Taylor, *The Terrorist* (London: Brassey's Defence Publishers, 1988), 58.
5. Lewis A. Coser, *The Functions of Social Conflict* (Glencoe, Ill.: Free Press, 1956), 134.
6. Richard Vatz, "The Myth of the Rhetorical Situation," *Philosophy and Rhetoric* 6 (Summer 1973): 157.
7. Alex P. Schmid and Janny de Graaf, *Violence as Communication: Insurgent Terrorism and the Western News Media* (London: Sage, 1982), 217.
8. Paul Wilkinson, *Terrorism and the Liberal State* (New York: Wiley, 1977), 31.
9. Schmid and de Graaf, *Violence as Communication*, 15, 54.
10. Richard W. Leeman, *The Rhetoric of Terrorism and Counterterrorism* (Westport, Conn.: Greenwood Press, 1991), 13, 46.
11. Schmid and de Graaf, *Violence as Communication*, 176.
12. Richard E. Rubenstein, *Alchemists of Revolution: Terrorism in the Modern World* (New York: Basic Books, 1987), xvii.
13. Harry A. Bailey, "Confrontations as an Extension of Communication," in *Dissent: Symbolic Behavior and Rhetorical Strategies*, ed. Haig A. Bosmajian (Westport, Conn.: Greenwood Press, 1972), 182.
14. Taylor, *The Terrorist*, 130.

15. Robin Morgan, *The Demon Lover: On the Sexuality of Terrorism* (New York: Norton, 1989), 33, 24, 27.

16. Frederick Hacker, *Crusaders, Criminals, and Crazies: Terror and Terrorism in Our Time* (New York: Norton, 1976), 36.

17. Morgan, *The Demon Lover*, 170.

18. Granted, some researchers do not think of "terrorism" as a proper term for reform movement actions. Some researchers would avoid the terrorist designation for any political group that did not take (or threaten to take) human lives. It is this belief that led Andrew Rosen to specifically exclude union members as terrorists: "The inconvenience created [by the arson campaign] was not insufferable, in part because the scope of the campaign was limited. It was not really a campaign of terror, in that the Union took care not to burn down buildings with people or animals inside" (*Rise Up, Women! The Militant Campaign of the Women's Social and Political Union, 1903–1914* [London: Routledge & Kegan Paul, 1974], 222–23). Other researchers, such as Richard W. Leeman, make passing comments that serve to include the WSPU within the terrorist ranks. When discussing the emphasis placed on action by terrorists, Leeman chooses to quote a WSPU leader: " 'Beware of emotion that finds no vent in action,' writes Mrs. Pethwick-Lawrence [*sic*], 'translate every emotion, every feeling into deed, and act' " (*The Rhetoric of Terrorism and Counterterrorism* [Westport, Conn.: Greenwood Press, 1991], 56). In an unpublished dissertation about the WSPU, Roberta Kay Carson also explicitly acknowledges that the WSPU moved not simply into greater militancy in their guerrilla phase but into terrorism. In both her title and her text she speaks of "the transition from teacups to terror," and she mentions the promise made by Christabel in 1912: "We will terrorize the lot of you" ("From Teacups to Terror: The Rhetorical Strategies of the Women's Social and Political Union, 1903–1914" [Ph.D. diss., University of Iowa, 1975], 49).

19. Chalmers Johnson, "Perspectives on Terrorism," in *The Terrorism Reader*, ed. Walter Laqueur (Philadelphia: Temple University Press, 1978), 269.

20. Lisa Tickner, *The Spectacle of Women: Imagery of the Suffrage Campaign, 1907–14* (Chicago: University of Chicago Press, 1988), 135.

21. Robin P. J. M. Gerrits, "Terrorists' Perspectives: Memoirs," in *Terrorism and the Media*, ed. David L. Paletz and Alex P. Schmid (Newbury Park, Calif.: Sage, 1992), 29.

22. Schmid and de Graaf, *Violence as Communication*, 15, 14.

23. Morgan, *The Demon Lover*, 238.

24. George Dangerfield, *The Strange Death of Liberal England* (New York: Capricorn Books, 1961), 158.

25. Antonia Raeburn, *The Militant Suffragettes* (London: Joseph, 1933), 189–91, 200.

26. Martha Vicinus, ed., *A Widening Sphere: Changing Roles of Victorian Women* (Bloomington: Indiana University Press, 1977), x.

27. Kathy Ferguson, *The Feminist Case against Bureaucracy* (Philadelphia: Temple University Press, 1984), 158.

28. For a discussion of feminine style, see Karlyn Kohrs Campbell, *Man*

Cannot Speak for Her, 2 vols. (New York: Praeger Press, 1989); and Karlyn Kohrs Campbell, "The Rhetoric of Women's Liberation: An Oxymoron," *Quarterly Journal of Speech* 59 (February 1973): 74–86.

29. Raeburn, *Militant Suffragettes*, 160.

30. Herbert W. Simons, "Requirements, Problems, and Strategies: A Theory of Persuasion for Social Movements," *Quarterly Journal of Speech* 56 (February 1970): 4, 5.

31. James R. Andrew, "The Passionate Negation: The Chartist Movement in Rhetorical Perspective," *Quarterly Journal of Speech* 59 (April 1973): 202.

32. Jerome H. Skolnick, "The Politics of Protest," in *Dissent: Symbolic Behavior and Rhetorical Strategies*, ed. Haig A. Bosmajian (Westport, Conn.: Greenwood Press, 1972), 157, 168.

33. Eugene Garver, *Machiavelli and the History of Prudence* (Madison: University of Wisconsin Press, 1987), 30, 28.

34. John Angus Campbell, "Scientific Revolution and the Grammar of Culture: The Case of Darwin's Origin," *Quarterly Journal of Speech* 72 (November 1986): 351, 359.

35. Cheryl R. Jorgensen-Earp, "The Lady, the Whore, and the Spinster: The Rhetorical Use of Victorian Images of Women," *Western Journal of Speech Communication* 54 (Winter 1990): 82–98.

36. I am grateful to John Campbell for numerous ideas along this line, which he shared in private conversation.

37. Taylor, *The Terrorist*, 62.

38. Paul Ramsey, *War and the Christian Conscience: How Shall Modern War Be Conducted Justly?* (Durham, N.C.: Duke University Press, 1961), 15.

39. James Turner Johnson, *Ideology, Reason, and the Limitation of War: Religious and Secular Concepts, 1200–1740* (Princeton, N.J.: Princeton University Press, 1975), 75.

40. Ibid., 150, 53–64.

41. Ibid., 254.

42. Robert Ivie provides an excellent summary of the modern just-war doctrine as it appears in the writings of Paul Ramsey. The doctrine specifies four primary requirements for a just war: (1) "that a war be a defensive response to avenge injuries"; (2) "that it be waged under the auspices of legitimate authority"; (3) "that it be conducted discriminately"; and (4) "that it be intended to achieve a good that is in proportion to the evils of the act of war itself" (Robert L. Ivie, "Images of Savagery in American Justifications for War," *Communication Monographs* 47 [November 1980]: 283). These four doctrines may be divided, with the first two (just cause and legitimate authority) forming the criteria for the *jus ad bellum* and the latter pair (discrimination and proportion) composing the criteria for the *jus in bello*. Of course, Ramsey is not the only researcher to discuss just-war doctrine, and other theorists provide other lists of just-war criteria. For example, the United Methodist Bishops' Pastoral Letter "In Defense of Creation" included such criteria as last resort, probability of success, and comparative justice in addition to the four criteria identified by Ramsey (Paul Ramsey, *Speak Up for Just War or Pacifism: A Critique of the United Methodist Bishops' Pastoral Letter "In Defense of Creation"* [University Park: Pennsylvania State Uni-

versity Press, 1988], 89). Richard B. Miller produces a list of criteria: just cause, competent authority, right intention, last resort, relative justice, proportionality, reasonable hope for success, discrimination, and proportionality. Miller categorizes the first seven criteria as determinants of the *jus ad bellum* and the final two criteria as relevant to the *jus in bello* (*Interpretations of Conflict: Ethics, Pacifism, and the Just-War Tradition* [Chicago: University of Chicago Press, 1990], 13–14). Grady Scott Davis provides a briefer list of seven criteria, with proper authority, just cause, just intent, last resort, and reasonable hope of success as elements of the *jus ad bellum* and discrimination and proportion as elements of the *jus in bello* (*Warcraft and the Fragility of Virtue: An Essay in Aristotelian Ethics* [Moscow: University of Idaho Press, 1992], 53–54). In examining these and other criteria lists for just war doctrine, I have concluded that Ivie's list (derived from Ramsey) includes the four primary criteria common to most theorists.

43. Jean Bethke Elshtain, "Refections on War and Political Discourse: Realism, Just War, and Feminism in the Nuclear Age," in *Just War Theory*, ed. Jean Bethke Elshtain (New York: New York University Press, 1992), 266.

44. Of course, the WSPU is not the only terrorist group that has utilized discursive rhetoric to justify its terrorist acts. In recent explorations of the rhetoric of revolutionary terrorism, certain patterns of justification have been identified that account for the need for lethal violence: "(i) any means are justified to realise an allegedly transcendental end (in Weber's terms, 'value-rational' grounds); (ii) closely linked . . . is the claim that extreme violence is an intrinsically beneficial, regenerative, cathartic and ennobling deed regardless of other consequences; (iii) terrorism can be shown to have 'worked in the past, and is held to be either the 'sole remaining' or 'best available' method of achieving success (in Weber's terms 'instrumental-rational' grounds); (iv) the morality of the just vengeance or 'an eye for an eye and a tooth for a tooth'; and (v) the theory of the lesser evil: greater evils will befall us or our nation if we do not adopt terror against our enemies" (Wilkinson, *Terrorism and the Liberal State*, 53). These same arguments appear in somewhat altered form in the rhetoric used by the WSPU to justify its nonlethal violence against property. Although each of these arguments appears in union rhetoric, Emmeline Pankhurst and her followers more closely followed a pattern of argument based on the premise that the militant suffrage cause was a just war.

Chapter 1. A Rhetorical Path to Terrorism

1. Quoted in Susan Kingsley Kent, *Sex and Suffrage in Britain, 1860–1914* (Princeton, N.J.: Princeton University Press, 1987), 203.

2. Samuel Hynes, *The Edwardian Turn of Mind* (Princeton, N.J.: Princeton University Press, 1968), 201, 203, 208, 211.

3. George Dangerfield, *The Strange Death of Liberal England* (New York: Capricorn Books, 1961), 149.

4. Andrew Rosen, *Rise Up, Women! The Militant Campaign of the*

Women's Social and Political Union, 1903–1914 (London: Routledge & Kegan Paul, 1974), 82, 200.

5. Duncan Crow, *The Edwardian Woman* (London: George Allen & Unwin, 1978), 80, 85, 86.

6. J. B. Priestley, *The Edwardians* (New York: Harper & Row, 1970), 42–43, 41, 42.

7. Midge Mackenzie, *Shoulder to Shoulder* (New York: Knopf, 1975), 17.

8. Emmeline Pankhurst, *My Own Story* (New York: Hearst's International Library, 1914), 38.

9. Sandra Stanley Holton, "In Sorrowful Wrath: Suffrage Militancy and the Romantic Feminism of Emmeline Pankhurst," in *British Feminism in the Twentieth Century*, ed. Harold L. Smith (Amherst: University of Massachusetts Press, 1990), 10.

10. Antonia Raeburn, *The Militant Suffragettes* (London: Joseph, 1973), 1.

11. Mackenzie, *Shoulder to Shoulder*, 6.

12. Ibid., 14–15.

13. David Mitchell, *The Fighting Pankhursts: A Study in Tenacity* (New York: Macmillan, 1967), 24.

14. Crow, *The Edwardian Woman*, 87.

15. Owen Peterson, "Boggart Hole Clough: A Nineteenth Century 'Speak-In,'" *Southern Speech Journal* 35 (Summer 1970): 288, 290, 293–94.

16. Holton, "In Sorrowful Wrath," 12–13.

17. Mackenzie, *Shoulder to Shoulder*, 21.

18. Roger Fulford, *Votes for Women: The Story of a Struggle* (London: Faber & Faber, 1957), 122.

19. Emmeline Pankhurst, *My Own Story*, 42–43.

20. Fulford, *Votes for Women*, 122–23.

21. Mackenzie, *Shoulder to Shoulder*, 28.

22. Ray Strachey, *The Cause: A Short History of the Women's Movement in Great Britain* (1928; reprint, New York: Kennikat Press, 1969), 294–95.

23. Fulford, *Votes for Women*, 129–30, 139.

24. Mackenzie, *Shoulder to Shoulder*, 58–59, 60.

25. Constance Rover, *Women's Suffrage and Party Politics in Britain, 1866–1914* (London: Routledge & Kegan Paul, 1967), 81.

26. Fulford, *Votes for Women*, 222.

27. Emmeline Pethick-Lawrence, *My Part in a Changing World* (London: Victor Gollancz, 1938), 249.

28. Emmeline Pankhurst, *My Own Story*, 180.

29. Pethick-Lawrence, *My Part in a Changing World*, 249.

30. Emmeline Pankhurst, *My Own Story*, 180.

31. Estelle Sylvia Pankhurst, *The Life of Emmeline Pankhurst: The Suffragette Struggle for Women's Citizenship* (London: T. Werner Laurie, 1935), 97.

32. Pethick-Lawrence, *My Part in a Changing World*, 250.

33. Ibid., 235.

34. Many accounts of forcible feeding may be found in autobiographies of individual suffragettes. A particularly harrowing account may be found in

Lady Constance Lytton's *Prisons and Prisoners: Some Personal Experiences by Constance Lytton and Jane Warton, Spinster* (London: William Heinemann, 1914). Other good sources for descriptions of forcible feeding and its symbolic meaning may be found in Roger Fulford's *Votes for Women*, Midge Mackenzie's *Shoulder to Shoulder*, and Lisa Tickner's *The Spectacle of Women: Imagery of the Suffrage Campaign, 1907–14* (Chicago: University of Chicago Press, 1988).

35. Estelle Sylvia Pankhurst, *Life of Emmeline Pankhurst*, 99.

36. Pethick-Lawrence, *My Part in a Changing World*, 257.

37. Lisa Tickner, *The Spectacle of Women*, 9.

38. Raeburn, *Militant Suffragettes*, 247.

39. Rosen, *Rise Up, Women!*, 154.

40. *The Suffragette*, December 26, 1913, 258.

41. Mackenzie, *Shoulder to Shoulder*, 216.

42. Ibid., 218.

43. Raeburn, *Militant Suffragettes*, 248–49.

44. Ibid., 187–90.

45. Fulford, *Votes for Women*, 282.

46. Estelle Sylvia Pankhurst, *Life of Emmeline Pankhurst*, 125.

47. Edward W. Gude, "Political Violence in Venezuela: 1958–1964," in *When Men Revolt and Why: A Reader in Political Violence and Revolution*, ed. James Chowning Davies (New York: Free Press, 1971), 264.

48. Raeburn, *Militant Suffragettes*, 158.

49. Roberta Kay Carson, "From Teacups to Terror: The Rhetorical Strategies of the Women's Social and Political Union, 1903–1915" (Ph.D. diss., University of Iowa, 1975), 9.

50. Chaim Perelman, *The New Rhetoric and the Humanities: Essays on Rhetoric and Its Applications* (London: Reidel, 1979), 128; Chaim Perelman, *Justice* (New York: Random House, 1967), 61–62.

51. Chaim Perelman and Lucie Olbrechts-Tyteca, *The New Rhetoric: A Treatise on Argumentation* (Notre Dame, Ind.: University of Notre Dame Press, 1969), 55.

Chapter 2. The Strategy of Forcing the Crisis

1. Eugene Garver, *Machiavelli and the History of Prudence* (Madison: University of Wisconsin Press, 1987), 84, 46.

2. Richard W. Leeman, *The Rhetoric of Terrorism and Counterterrorism* (Westport, Conn.: Greenwood Press, 1991), 56.

3. Peter Kropotkin, "On the Need for Individual Action," in *Revolutionaries on Revolution: Participants' Perspectives on the Strategies of Seizing Power*, ed. Phillip B. Springer and Marcello Truzzo (Pacific Palisades, Calif.: Goodyear Publishing, 1973), 61.

4. Quoted in Leeman, *Rhetoric of Terrorism*, 56.

5. Garver, *Machiavelli*, 82.

6. *Votes for Women*, July 19, 1912, 680.

7. Lisa Tickner, *The Spectacle of Women: Imagery of the Suffrage Campaign, 1907–1914* (Chicago: University of Chicago Press, 1988), 134.

8. Emmeline Pethick-Lawrence, "The Coping Stone to the Constitution," *Votes for Women,* April 18, 1913, 413.

9. Emmeline Pethick-Lawrence, *My Part in a Changing World* (London: Victor Gollancz, 1938), 180.

10. "Be Ready," *Votes for Women,* February 9, 1912, 292.

11. Emmeline Pankhurst, "Why We Are Militant," *The Suffragette,* November 14, 1913, 99.

12. Chaim Perelman, *The Realm of Rhetoric* (Notre Dame, Ind.: University of Notre Dame Press, 1982), 35.

13. Chaim Perelman and Lucie Olbrechts-Tyteca, *The New Rhetoric: A Treatise on Argumentation* (Notre Dame, Ind.: University of Notre Dame Press, 1969), 117.

14. Chaim Perelman, *The New Rhetoric and the Humanities: Essays on Rhetoric and the Humanities* (London: Reidel, 1979), 17.

15. See Leeman, *Rhetoric of Terrorism.*

16. Christabel Pankhurst, *Unshackled: The Story of How We Won the Vote* (London: Hutchinson, 1959), 256.

17. Emmeline Pankhurst, Verbatim report of Mrs. Pankhurst's speech, delivered Nov. 13, 1913 at Parson's Theatre, Hartford, Connecticut (Hartford: Connecticut Woman Suffrage Association, 1913), 16–17 (hereafter cited as "Hartford").

18. Christabel Pankhurst, "The Need for Action," *Votes for Women,* March 1, 1912, 340.

19. Christabel Pankhurst, "Women's Deeds and Men's Words," *The Suffragette,* August 1, 1913, 720.

20. Christabel Pankhurst, "Need for Action," 340.

21. Christabel Pankhurst, "The Present Situation," *The Suffragette,* April 18, 1913, 450.

22. Christabel Pankhurst, "Need for Action," 340.

23. Emmeline Pankhurst, "The Women's Insurrection," *The Suffragette,* February 28, 1913, 309.

24. Jane Marcus, ed., *Suffrage and the Pankhursts* (London: Routledge & Kegan Paul, 1987), 183–84.

25. Emmeline Pankhurst, "Hartford," 19.

26. Paul Wilkinson, *Terrorism and the Liberal State,* 2nd ed. (New York: New York University Press, 1986), 116.

27. *The Suffragette,* December 6, 1912, 116–17; December 20, 1912, 148–49; February 7, 1913, 260–61; February 21, 1913, 292–93; April 11, 1913, 428–29; September 5, 1913, 816–17.

28. *The Suffragette,* October 31, 1913, 58.

29. Alex P. Schmid and Janny de Graaf, *Violence as Communication: Insurgent Terrorism and the Western News Media* (London: Sage, 1982), 217.

30. Emmeline Pankhurst, "Hartford," 21–22.

31. *Votes for Women,* May 24, 1912, 547.

32. Annie Kenney, "Our Spirits Are Eternal," *The Suffragette,* July 18 1913, 675.

33. Emmeline Pankhurst, "Hartford," 22.

34. Christabel Pankhurst, "In Fear of Women," *The Suffragette*, December 19, 1913, 226.

35. *Votes for Women*, August 9, 1912, 738.

36. Mrs. Israel Zangwill, "The Burning Question," *The Suffragette*, May 23, 1913, 530.

37. Christabel Pankhurst, "How Many Dare You Kill?" *The Suffragette*, November 28, 1913, 150.

38. Flora Drummond, "The Great God Property," *The Suffragette*, March 27, 1914, 543.

39. *Votes for Women*, August 2, 1912, 709.

40. Christabel Pankhurst, "How Many Dare You Kill?" 150.

41. *Votes for Women*, August 2, 1912, 711.

42. Christabel Pankhurst, "In Fear of Women," 226.

43. David S. Kaufer and Christine M. Newwirth, "Foregrounding Norms and Ironic Communication," *Quarterly Journal of Speech* 68 (February 1982): 33.

44. Tickner, *The Spectacle of Women*, 27.

45. *Votes for Women*, July 12, 1912, 661.

46. See Tickner, *The Spectacle of Women*, particularly the chapter entitled "Representation," for an excellent study of the hegemonic effect of humor directed at the suffragettes.

47. Ibid., 163. Tickner shows how the tendentious joke was used against the suffragettes.

48. Tickner's book is invaluable on this subject.

49. Claims that their movement could and would succeed formed one of the first junctures WSPU rhetoric had with the traditional rhetoric of the just war. Suffragette emphasis upon their own success was necessary since traditionally the right to call for a just war (or a just revolution) only rests with "someone or some group capable of representing a better *pax-ordo*, and capable of bringing this to pass without letting worse befall" (Paul Ramsey, *War and the Christian Conscience: How Shall Modern War Be Conducted Justly?* [Durham, N.C.: Duke University Press, 1966], 124).

50. Emmeline Pankhurst, "Hartford," 14.

51. Ibid., 12.

52. Christabel Pankhurst, "Shall Women Fight?" *The Suffragette*, November 1, 1912, 36.

53. Christabel Pankhurst, "How to Stop Militancy," *The Suffragette*, February 28, 1913, 308.

54. George Bernard Shaw, "Bernard Shaw on Forcible Feeding," *The Suffragette*, April 18, 1913, 457.

55. Brian Harrison, *Separate Spheres* (London: Croom Helm, 1978), 73.

56. Tickner, *The Spectacle of Women*, 155.

57. Constance Rover, *Women's Suffrage and Party Politics in Britain, 1866–1914* (London: Routledge & Kegan Paul, 1967), 43–44.

58. Ibid., 44.

59. Harrison, *Separate Spheres*, 73.

60. Emmeline Pankhurst, "Women's Insurrection," 309.

61. Robert K. Massie, *Dreadnought: Britain, Germany, and the Coming of the Great War* (New York: Random House, 1991), 784.

62. *The Suffragette*, December 13, 1912, 125.

63. Emmeline Pankhurst, "Women's Insurrection," 309.

64. Antonia Raeburn, *The Militant Suffragettes* (London: Joseph, 1973), 231.

65. Annie Kenney, *Memories of a Militant* (London: Edward Arnold & Co., 1924), 237–38.

66. Emmeline Pankhurst, "Why We Are Militant," *The Suffragette*, November 21, 1913, 127.

67. Garver, *Machiavelli*, 95.

68. Emmeline Pankhurst, "I Have Kept My Promise In Spite of His Majesty's Government!" *The Suffragette*, March 13, 1914, 492.

69. Frederick Pethick-Lawrence, "The Real Conspiracy," *Votes for Women*, May 31, 1912, 541.

70. Emmeline Pankhurst, "Women's Insurrection," 309.

71. Emmeline Pankhurst, "Why We Are Militant," *The Suffragette*, November 14, 1913, 99.

72. Ibid.

73. Garver, *Machiavelli*, 54.

74. George Dangerfield, *The Strange Death of Liberal England* (New York: Capricorn Books, 1961), 116.

75. Donald Read, *Edwardian England* (London: The Historical Association, 1972), 40–41.

76. Ibid., 41.

77. Ibid., 31–33.

78. Dangerfield, *Strange Death*, 329.

79. Christabel Pankhurst, "Mr. Lloyd George on Militancy," *The Suffragette*, June 27, 1913, 615.

80. Christabel Pankhurst, "For the Sake of Peace," *The Suffragette*, February 13, 1914, 394.

81. "Mrs. Pankhurst at Bow Street," *Votes for Women*, March 8, 1912, 360.

82. Christabel Pankhurst, "Mr. Lloyd George on Militancy," 615.

83. Christabel Pankhurst, "For the Sake of Peace," 394.

84. Christabel Pankhurst, "Mr. Lloyd George on Militancy," 615.

85. Christabel Pankhurst, "Humbug and Hypocrisy," *The Suffragette*, March 20, 1914, 516.

86. *Chambers Biographical Dictionary*, ed. J. O. Thorne (New York: St. Martins Press, 1969), 142.

87. *Votes for Women*, June 28, 1912, 629.

88. Emmeline Pethick-Lawrence, "O Liberty, How Glorious Art Thou!" *Votes for Women*, May 31, 1912, 565.

89. Emmeline Pankhurst, "Kill Me, or Give Me My Freedom," *The Suffragette*, July 18, 1913, 677.

90. Drummond, "The Great God Property," 543.

91. Emmeline Pethick-Lawrence, "Men Do Not Argue with a Flood," *Votes for Women*, June 20, 1913, 557.

92. Samuel Hynes, *The Edwardian Turn of Mind* (Princeton, N.J.: Princeton University Press, 1968, 15–19, 24, 25, 22, 32, 40–53.

93. Tickner, *The Spectacle of Women*, 189.

94. Christabel Pankhurst, "The Strength of Women," *The Suffragette*, December 12, 1913, 200.

95. Emmeline Pethick-Lawrence, "Coping Stone," 413.

96. Roger Fulford, *Votes for Women: The Story of a Struggle* (London: Faber & Faber, 1957), 289.

97. Andrew Rosen, *Rise Up, Women! The Militant Campaign of the Women's Social and Political Union, 1903–1914* (London: Routledge & Kegan Paul, 1974), 207.

98. Susan Kingsley Kent, *Sex and Suffrage in Britain, 1860–1914* (Princeton, N.J.: Princeton University Press, 1987), 5, 6–7.

99. Hynes, *The Edwardian Turn of Mind*, 281, 282.

100. Emmeline Pankhurst, "I Defy Them to Make Me Submit," *The Suffragette*, February 27, 1914, 443.

101. Emmeline Pankhurst, "We Are Not Ordinary Citizens," *The Suffragette*, April 11, 1913, 422.

102. Emmeline Pankhurst, "I Defy," 443.

103. Emmeline Pankhurst, "Women's Insurrection," 309.

104. Ibid.

105. Emmeline Pankhurst, "I Defy," 443.

106. *The Suffragette*, October 17, 1913, 1.

107. Christabel Pankhurst, "Personal Violence," *Votes for Women*, September 13, 1912, 800.

108. Tickner, *The Spectacle of Women*, 223.

109. "Militancy," *Votes for Women*, May 31, 1912, 564.

Chapter 3. The Defensive Response to a Culpable Opponent

1. Midge Mackenzie, *Shoulder to Shoulder* (New York: Knopf, 1975), 210–15.

2. Emmeline Pethick-Lawrence, *My Part in a Changing World* (London: Victor Gollancz, 1938), 286.

3. Chaim Perelman, *Justice* (New York: Random House, 1967), 64.

4. Robert W. Tucker, *The Just War: A Study in Contemporary American Doctrine* (Baltimore: Johns Hopkins University Press, 1960), 11.

5. Robert L. Ivie, "Images of Savagery in American Justifications for War," *Communication Monographs* 47 (November 1980): 290.

6. Paul Ramsey, *War and the Christian Conscience: How Shall Modern War Be Conducted Justly?* (Durham, N.C.: Duke University Press, 1961), 81n.

7. Ivie, "Images of Savagery," 279.

8. Ibid., 283.

9. Frederick J. Hacker, *Crusaders, Criminals, and Crazies: Terror and Terrorism in Our Time* (New York: Norton, 1976), 80.

10. Ivie, "Images of Savagery," 283.

11. Maxwell Taylor, *The Terrorist* (London: Brassey's Defence Publishers, 1988), 100.

12. Ibid., 131, 161.

13. Hacker, *Crusaders, Criminals, and Crazies*, 43.

14. Paul Ramsey, *Speak Up for Just War or Pacifism: A Critique of the United Methodist Bishops' Pastoral Letter "In Defense of Creation"* (University Park: Pennsylvania State University Press, 1988), 54.

15. Taylor, *The Terrorist*, 99.

16. Maurice A. J. Tugwell, "Guilt Transfer," in *The Morality of Terrorism: Religious and Secular Justifications*, ed. David C. Rapoport and Yonah Alexander (New York: Pergamon Press, 1982), 275.

17. Taylor, *The Terrorist*, 100.

18. Ivie, "Images of Savagery," 279, 280.

19. Constance Rover, *Women's Suffrage and Party Politics in Britain, 1866–1914* (London: Routledge & Kegan Paul, 1967), 99–100.

20. "The Militant Movement in 1913," *The Suffragette*, January 2, 1914, 274.

21. Emmeline Pankhurst, Verbatim report of Mrs. Pankhurst's speech, delivered Nov. 13, 1913 at Parson's Theatre, Hartford, Connecticut (Hartford: Connecticut Woman Suffrage Association, 1913), 12 (hereafter cited as "Hartford").

22. Christabel Pankhurst, "Personal Violence," *Votes for Women*, September 13, 1912, 800.

23. Frederick Pethick-Lawrence, "The Real Conspiracy," *Votes for Women*, May 24, 1912, 542.

24. Emmeline Pankhurst, "The Women's Insurrection," *The Suffragette*, February 28, 1913, 309.

25. Mary R. Richardson, *Laugh a Defiance* (London: George Weidenfeld & Nicolson, 1953), 54, 12, 11–12.

26. Christabel Pankhurst, "Serious Violence," *The Suffragette*, May 16, 1913, 515.

27. Paul Wilkinson, *Terrorism and the Liberal State* (New York: Wiley, 1977), 44.

28. "Methods of Violence," *Votes for Women*, June 7, 1912, 584.

29. Richard E. Rubenstein, *Alchemists of Revolution: Terrorism in the Modern World* (New York: Basic Books, 1987), 13.

30. Emmeline Pethick-Lawrence, "The Coping Stone to the Constitution," *Votes for Women*, April 18, 1913, 413.

31. Ray Strachey, *The Cause: A Short History of the Women's Movement in Great Britain* (1928; reprint, New York: Kennikat Press, 1969), 314.

32. The Rev. E. H. Taylor, "Christian Atrocities," *The Suffragette*, September 5, 1913, 820.

33. "A Suffragette Alphabet," *Votes for Women*, August 2, 1912, 711.

34. Taylor, "Christian Atrocities," 820.

35. *Votes for Women*, December 8, 1911, 153.

36. "Militancy—A Spreading Fire," *The Suffragette*, December 6, 1912, 116.

37. Richardson, *Laugh a Defiance*, 103.

38. Emmeline Pankhurst, "Address to the Jury," *Votes for Women*, May 24, 1912, 533.

39. Mr. Healy, "A Great State Trial," *Votes for Women*, May 31, 1912, 558.

40. Emmeline Pankhurst, "Kill Me, or Give Me My Freedom!" *The Suffragette*, July 18, 1913, 677.

41. C. W. Mansell-Moullin, "Artificial vs. Forcible Feeding," *The Suffragette*, April 4, 1913, 405

42. Richardson, *Laugh a Defiance*, 84.

43. Mansell-Moullin, "Artificial vs. Forcible Feeding," 405.

44. Annie Kenney, "A Real Fraternity," *The Suffragette*, August 15, 1913, 763.

45. Mansell-Moullin, "Artificial vs. Forcible Feeding," 405.

46. George Bernard Shaw, "We Are Members One of Another," *The Suffragette*, March 28, 1913, 380.

47. See *The Suffragette*, September 5, 1913, February 13, 1914, March 27, 1914, or July 17, 1914.

48. Emmeline Pankhurst, "I Defy Them to Make Me Submit," *The Suffragette*, February 27, 1914, 443.

49. Emmeline Pankhurst, "Kill Me," 677.

50. Emmeline Pankhurst, "Address to the Jury," 533.

51. Kenneth Burke, "The Rhetorical Situation," in *Communication: Ethical and Moral Essays*, ed. Lee Thayer (London: Gordon & Bleach Science Publishers, 1973), 268.

52. Hacker, *Crusaders, Criminals, and Crazies*, 43.

53. Emmeline Pankhurst, "We Are Not Ordinary Citizens," *The Suffragette*, April 11, 1913, 421.

54. Emmeline Pankhurst, "Hartford," 29.

55. Ibid.

56. Emmeline Pankhurst, "Why We Are Militant," *The Suffragette*, November 14, 1913, 99.

57. Emmeline Pankhurst, "Not Ordinary Citizens," 421.

58. Emmeline Pankhurst, "Hartford," 28.

59. *Votes for Women*, January 5, 1912, 218.

60. Frederick Pethick-Lawrence, "For the Defense," *Votes for Women*, May 31, 1912, 557.

61. *Votes for Women*, December 22, 1911, 187.

62. Christabel Pankhurst, "How to Stop Militancy," *The Suffragette*, February 28, 1913, 308.

63. *The Suffragette*, April 18, 1913, 449.

64. Emmeline Pankhurst, "Great Speech at the Albert Hall," *The Suffragette*, October 25, 1912, 16.

65. Ibid.

66. Emmeline Pankhurst, "Kill Me," 677.

67. Emmeline Pankhurst, "Not Ordinary Citizens," 422, 421.

68. Annie Kenney, *The Suffragette*, July 4, 1913, 635.

69. Emmeline Pankhurst, "Not Ordinary Citizens," 422.

70. See Susan Kingsley Kent, *Sex and Suffrage in Britain, 1860–1914* (Princeton, N.J.: Princeton University Press, 1987).

71. Lisa Tickner, *The Spectacle of Women: Imagery of the Suffrage Campaign, 1907–1914* (Chicago: University of Chicago Press, 1988), 224.

72. *Votes for Women*, May 3, 1912, 481.

73. Emmeline Pankhurst, "Albert Hall," 16.

74. Flora Drummond, "The Great God Property," *The Suffragette*, March 27, 1914, 543.

75. Lady Constance Lytton, *Prisons and Prisoners: Some Personal Experiences by Constance Lytton and Jane Warton, Spinster* (London: William Heinemann, 1914), 221.

76. Hacker, *Crusaders, Criminals, and Crazies*, 43.

77. Emmeline Pankhurst, "Why We Are Militant," 99.

78. Emmeline Pankhurst, "Albert Hall," 16.

79. *Votes for Women*, July 19, 1912, 680.

80. Christabel Pankhurst, "The Martyr Spirit," *The Suffragette*, March 28, 1913, 384.

81. *The Suffragette*, November 14, 1913, 106–7; November 21, 1913, 132–33; December 12, 1913, 206–7; December 11, 1913, 222–23; January 2, 1914, 270–71; March 13, 1914, 491; March 20, 1914, 518–19.

82. *Votes for Women*, May 31, 1912, 555.

83. Frederick Pethick-Lawrence, "The Real Conspiracy," 541; Christabel Pankhurst, "Why We Did It," *Votes for Women*, November 24, 1911, 122.

84. Christabel Pankhurst, "The Need for Action," *Votes for Women*, March 1, 1912, 340; Annie Kenney, "The One Union," *The Suffragette*, July 24, 1914, 261.

85. Rubenstein, *Alchemists of Revolution*, 9.

86. Emmeline Pankhurst, "Address to the Jury," 534.

87. *Votes for Women*, January 19, 1912, 245.

88. *Votes for Women*, December 22, 1911, 185.

89. *The Suffragette*, January 31, 1913, 229.

90. Emmeline Pankhurst, "Albert Hall," 16.

91. *The Suffragette*, October 31, 1913, 45.

92. Christabel Pankhurst, "Why Women Should Support the W.S.P.U.," *The Suffragette*, November 7, 1913, 78.

93. Sandra Stanley Holton, "In Sorrowful Wrath: Suffrage Militancy and the Romantic Feminism of Emmeline Pankhurst," in *British Feminism in the Twentieth Century*, ed. Harold L. Smith (Amherst: University of Massachusetts Press, 1990), 14.

94. Emmeline Pankhurst, *My Own Story* (New York: Hearst's International Library, 1914), 214.

95. *Votes for Women*, May 31, 1912, 549.

96. *Votes for Women*, March 8, 1912, 349.

97. Emmeline Pankhurst, "Address to the Jury," 533.

98. Christabel Pankhurst, *Unshackled: The Story of How We Won the Vote* (London: Hutchinson, 1959), 229.

99. Christabel Pankhurst, "Things People Say," *The Suffragette*, November 14, 1913, 103.

100. Richard W. Leeman, *The Rhetoric of Terrorism and Counterterrorism* (Westport, Conn.: Greenwood Press, 1991), 54, 55.

101. Christabel Pankhurst, "Why We Did It," 122.

102. "Methods of Violence," *Votes for Women*, June 7, 1912, 584.

103. *The Suffragette*, October 18, 1912, 6.

104. Laurence Housman, "Proper Lessons," *Votes for Women*, April 5, 1912, 429.

105. Ibid.

106. Roger Fulford, *Votes for Women: The Story of a Struggle* (London: Faber & Faber, 1957), 284.

107. Christabel Pankhurst, "The Present Situation," *The Suffragette*, April 18, 1913, 450; Emmeline Pethick-Lawrence, "The Delegates at Bow Street," *Votes for Women*, August 1, 1913, 641.

108. *The Suffragette*, May 22, 1914, 109.

109. *The Suffragette*, July 25, 1913, 689.

110. Christabel Pankhurst, "Women at War," *The Suffragette*, October 25, 1912, 20.

111. Drummond, "The Great God Property," 517.

112. "War—Why We Are Militant," *The Suffragette*, November 15, 1912, 67.

113. Emmeline Pankhurst, "Albert Hall," 16.

114. Leeman, *Rhetoric of Terrorism*, 55.

115. See Kenneth Burke, "Definition of Man," in *Language as Symbolic Action* (Berkeley: University of California, 1966), 18.

116. Quoted in Robert L. Scott, "Justifying Violence—The Rhetoric of Militant Black Power," *Central States Speech Journal* 19 (Summer 1968): 103.

117. Ivie, "Images of Savagery," 292.

118. Emmeline Pethick-Lawrence, "Men Do Not Argue with a Flood," *Votes for Women*, June 20, 1913, 557.

119. *Votes for Women*, May 24, 1912, 526.

120. Ramsey, *Speak Up for Just War*, 53–54.

121. Robert L. Ivie, "Presidential Motives for War," *Quarterly Journal of Speech* 60 (October 1974): 344.

122. Emmeline Pankhurst, "Hartford," 30.

123. *Votes for Women*, March 15, 1912, 369.

124. Christabel Pankhurst, "How to Stop Militancy," 308.

125. Frederick Pethick-Lawrence, *Votes for Women*, May 31, 1912, 557.

126. Emmeline Pankhurst, "The Argument of the Broken Pane," *Votes for Women*, February 23, 1912, 319.

127. Emmeline Pankhurst, "Kill Me," 677.

128. Emmeline Pethick-Lawrence, "Do Ut Des," *Votes for Women*, January 5, 1912, 224.

Chapter 4. The Suffragette as Just Warrior

1. Robert L. Ivie, "Images of Savagery in American Justifications for War," *Communication Monographs* 47 (November 1980): 283.

2. Paul Ramsey, *War and the Christian Conscience: How Shall Modern War Be Conducted Justly?* (Durham, N.C.: Duke University Press, 1961), 114, 126.

3. Emmeline Pankhurst, "Victory Is Assured," *The Suffragette*, February 13, 1914, 397.

4. Eugene Garver, *Machiavelli and the History of Prudence* (Madison: University of Wisconsin Press, 1987), 70–71.

5. Richard E. Rubenstein, *Alchemists of Revolution: Terrorism in the Modern World* (New York: Basic Books, 1987), 17, 22, 25–26, 18, 23.

6. Lisa Tickner, *The Spectacle of Women: Imagery of the Suffrage Campaign, 1907–1914* (Chicago: University of Chicago Press, 1988), 9.

7. Emmeline Pankhurst, "The Argument of the Broken Pane," *Votes for Women*, February 23, 1912, 319.

8. Emmeline Pethick-Lawrence, "Albert Hall, Nov. 16, 1911," *Votes for Women*, November 24, 1911, 118.

9. Ibid., 118–19.

10. Emmeline Pankhurst, "Declarations of Policy," *The Suffragette*, January 31, 1913, 240.

11. Emmeline Pankhurst, "Speech at Albert Hall," *The Suffragette*, October 25, 1912, 16.

12. "Case for the Prosecution," *Votes for Women*, May 17, 1912, 525.

13. Emmeline Pankhurst, "Victory Is Assured," 397.

14. "The Outlook," *Votes for Women*, February 9, 1912, 285.

15. Emmeline Pankhurst, Verbatim report of Mrs. Pankhurst's speech, delivered Nov. 13, 1913 at Parson's Theatre, Hartford, Connecticut (Hartford: Connecticut Woman Suffrage Association, 1913), 5 (hereafter cited as "Hartford").

16. *Votes for Women*, March 1, 1912, 337.

17. *The Suffragette*, April 18, 1913, 445.

18. "War—Why We Are Militant," *The Suffragette*, November 15, 1912, 67.

19. *The Suffragette*, June 27, 1913, 609.

20. Christabel Pankhurst, "Women's Deeds and Men's Words," *The Suffragette*, August 1, 1913, 720.

21. Christabel Pankhurst, "The Martyr Spirit," *The Suffragette*, March 28, 1913, 384.

22. "Case for the Prosecution," 525.

23. Christabel Pankhurst, "The Policy of the W.S.P.U.," *The Suffragette*, October 18, 1912, 6.

24. Charles Kingsley, "The Day of the Lord," *The Suffragette*, December 27, 1912, 157.

25. Flora Drummond, "The Great God Property," *The Suffragette*, March 20, 1914, 517.

26. Christabel Pankhurst, "The Policy of the W.S.P.U.," 6.

27. Emmeline Pankhurst, "Why We Are Militant," *The Suffragette*, November 21, 1913, 127.

28. *Votes for Women*, May 24, 1912, 529.

29. George Lakey, "Technique and Ethos in Nonviolent Action: The Woman Suffrage Case," in *Dissent: Symbolic Behavior and Rhetorical Strategies*, ed. Haig A. Bosmajian (Westport, Conn.: Greenwood Press, 1980), 311.

30. See Mary R. Richardson, *Laugh a Defiance* (London: George Weidenfeld & Nicolson, 1953).

31. Christabel Pankhurst, "Why the Union Is Strong," *The Suffragette*, December 27, 1912, 160.

32. Christabel Pankhurst, "The Policy of the W.S.P.U.," 6.

33. Emmeline Pethick-Lawrence, "The Rune of Birth and Renewal," *Votes for Women*, December 20, 1912, 183.

34. Ibid.

35. Emmeline Pankhurst, "A Prisoner of War," *The Suffragette*, April 11, 1913, 423.

36. Emmeline Pankhurst, "Mrs. Pankhurst's Great Speech," *Votes for Women*, May 24, 1912, 531.

37. Dr. Louisa Garrett Anderson, "Prisoners of War," *Votes for Women*, April 26, 1912, 467.

38. "Political Prisoners," *Votes for Women*, May 17, 1912, 520.

39. Quoted in *The Suffragette*, October 18, 1912, 11.

40. *Votes for Women*, June 7, 1912, 577.

41. "Political Prisoners," *Votes for Women*, May 17, 1912, 520.

42. Tickner, *The Spectacle of Women*, 161.

43. Ibid., 161–73.

44. Ibid., 207, 201.

45. Ibid., 207. Anyone familiar with modern representations of terrorists can see the similarity of these views of the union militants and those of foreign (particularly Middle Eastern) terrorists. Images of these modern terrorists range from the portrayal of religious fanatics for whom human life (even their own) holds no value to incompetent "camel-jockeys" who carry inadequate weapons and can be tricked into surrender.

46. Ibid., 204.

47. Ibid., 205–7.

48. Ibid., 208, 205.

49. Ibid., 207.

50. Ibid., 209.

51. *The Suffragette*, May 16, 1913, 513.

52. Tickner, *The Spectacle of Women*, 211.

53. Christabel Pankhurst, "Joan of Arc," *The Suffragette*, May 9, 1913, 501.

54. John Masefield, "When They Had Joan of Arc among Them," *The Suffragette*, November 8, 1912, 45.

55. Tickner, *The Spectacle of Women*, 211; Christabel Pankhurst, "A Prisoner's Book II," *The Suffragette*, March 20, 1914, 509.

56. Tickner, *The Spectacle of Women*, 208.

57. Christabel Pankhurst, " 'An Invincible Repugnance to Disorder,' " *The Suffragette*, November 22, 1912, 82.

58. Emmeline Pankhurst, "Hartford," 11.

59. Christabel Pankhurst, "Things People Say," *The Suffragette*, November 14, 1913, 103.

60. Tickner, *The Spectacle of Women*, 226.

61. Frederick Pethick-Lawrence, "The Real Conspiracy," *Votes for Women*, May 24, 1912, 541.

62. Ibid.; Christabel Pankhurst, "The Present Situation," *The Suffragette*, April 18, 1913, 450.

63. Annie Besant, "Crowned with Honour," *Votes for Women*, April 5, 1912, 423.

64. *The Suffragette*, November 21, 1913, 132.

65. Annie Kenney, "To Help Humanity," *The Suffragette*, April 24, 1914, 37.

66. Christabel Pankhurst, "History Repeating Itself," *The Suffragette*, March 14, 1913, 348.

67. Christabel Pankhurst, "The Present Situation," *The Suffragette*, April 18, 1913, 450.

68. Tickner, *The Spectacle of Women*, 212.

69. "1913," *The Suffragette*, January 3, 1913, 169.

70. Christabel Pankhurst, "The Present Situation," *The Suffragette*, June 6, 1913, 558.

71. Christabel Pankhurst, "Militancy a Virtue," *The Suffragette*, January 10, 1913, 186.

72. "Methods of Violence," *Votes for Women*, June 7, 1912, 584.

73. Tickner, *The Spectacle of Women*, 34.

74. Joseph Clayton, "The Intolerable Tyranny That Provokes Rebellion," *The Suffragette*, November 8, 1912, 53.

75. Christabel Pankhurst, "How to Stop Militancy," *The Suffragette*, February 28, 1913, 308.

76. Emmeline Pethick-Lawrence, "The Coping Stone to the Constitution," *Votes for Women*, April 18, 1913, 413.

77. The Rev. E. H. Taylor, "Christian Atrocities," *The Suffragette*, September 5, 1913, 820.

78. Quoted in "Militancy," *Votes for Women*, May 31, 1912, 564.

79. Ibid.

80. Ibid.

81. J. J. F., "The Reformer," *Votes for Women*, January 5, 1912, 225.

82. Emmeline Pethick-Lawrence, "The Rune of Birth and Renewal," 183.

83. George Lansbury, "The Militant Movement: A New Birth for the Women of Our Land," *The Suffragette*, April 18, 1913, 449.

84. Chaim Perelman, *Justice* (New York: Random House, 1967), 10.

85. *Votes for Women*, December 22, 1911, 185; Kenney, "To Help Humanity," 37; Annie Kenney, "The One Union," *The Suffragette*, July 31, 1914, 281.

86. *The Suffragette*, October 18, 1912, 1.

87. *The Suffragette*, February 14, 1913, 269.

88. Ruth C. Bentinck, "An Impression," *Votes for Women*, December 1, 1911, 138.

89. "In Defence of Militancy," *Votes for Women*, September 6, 1912, 786.

90. *The Suffragette*, October 24, 1913, 26–27.

91. "Swift Retribution Follows Scotland's Betrayal," *The Suffragette*, March 6, 1914, 469.

92. *The Suffragette*, February 14, 1913, 276.

93. A. G., "Out of the House of Bondage," *Votes for Women*, January 5, 1912, 226.

94. *The Suffragette*, January 2, 1914, 277.

95. Tickner, *The Spectacle of Women*, 210, 38.

96. David Mitchell, *Queen Christabel* (London: MacDonald and Jane's, 1977), 213.

97. Antonia Raeburn, *The Militant Suffragettes* (London: Joseph, 1973), 63.

98. Richardson, *Laugh a Defiance*, 85.

99. Emmeline Pethick-Lawrence, *My Part in a Changing World* (London: Victor Gollancz, 1938), 264.

100. Raeburn, *Militant Suffragettes*, 63.

101. Richardson, *Laugh a Defiance*, 53.

102. Paul Ramsey, *Speak Up for Just War or Pacifism: A Critique of the United Methodist Bishops' Pastoral Letter "In Defense of Creation"* (University Park: Pennsylvania State University, 1988), 54.

103. Christabel Pankhurst, "Stoning the Prophets," *The Suffragette*, March 21, 1913, 366.

104. Tickner, *The Spectacle of Women*, 32.

105. Maxwell Taylor, *The Terrorist* (London: Brassey's Defence Publishers, 1988), 117.

106. Tickner, *The Spectacle of Women*, 107, 38.

107. *The Suffragette*, March 7, 1913, 321; Drummond, "The Great God Property," 543.

108. Christabel Pankhurst, "The Martyr Spirit," 384.

109. Tickner, *The Spectacle of Women*, 38.

110. Christabel Pankhurst, "Things People Say," 103.

111. Emmeline Pankhurst, "Why We Are Militant," *The Suffragette*, November 14, 1913, 99.

112. Emmeline Pankhurst, "Hartford," 27.

113. Christabel Pankhurst, "Why the Union Is Strong," 160.

114. Emmeline Pethick-Lawrence, "The Rune of Birth and Renewal," 183.

115. Kenney, "To Help Humanity," 37.

116. George Bernard Shaw, "We Are Members One of Another," *The Suffragette*, March 28, 1913, 380.

117. Christabel Pankhurst, "Stoning the Prophets," 366.

118. Emmeline Pethick-Lawrence, "Special Message," *Votes for Women*, November 24, 1911, 123.

119. *The Suffragette*, January 17, 1913, 197.

120. "Militancy," *Votes for Women*, May 31, 1912, 564.

121. Christabel Pankhurst, "Stoning the Prophets," 366.

122. Christabel Pankhurst, "The Appeal to God," *The Suffragette*, August 8, 1913, 740.

123. Tickner, *The Spectacle of Women*, 140.

124. Raeburn, *Militant Suffragettes*, 201.

125. Midge Mackenzie, *Shoulder to Shoulder* (New York: Knopf, 1975), 242.

126. Tickner, *The Spectacle of Women*, 140.

127. The Rev. Gertrude Von Petzold, "She Laid Down Her Life for Her Friends," *The Suffragette*, June 20, 1913, 602.

128. Christabel Pankhurst, "Emily Wilding Davison," *The Suffragette*, June 13, 1913, 576.

129. Von Petzold, "She Laid Down Her Life," 602.

Chapter 5. The Value of Violence

1. Paul Ramsey, *The Just War: Force and Political Responsibility* (New York: Scribner, 1968), 429.

2. Paul Ramsey, *War and the Christian Conscience: How Shall Modern War Be Conducted Justly?* (Durham, N.C.: Duke University Press, 1961), 135.

3. Ibid., 275.

4. Martha Crenshaw, *Terrorism, Legitimacy, and Power: The Consequences of Political Violence* (Middletown, Conn.: Wesleyan University Press, 1983), 4.

5. Maxwell Taylor, *The Terrorist* (London: Brassey's Defence Publishers, 1988), 99.

6. Ramsey, *War and the Christian Conscience*, 74.

7. Emmeline Pankhurst, "Declarations of Policy," *The Suffragette*, January 31, 1913, 240.

8. *The Suffragette*, December 13, 1912, 132.

9. Laurence Housman, "Proper Lessons," *Votes for Women*, April 5, 1912, 429.

10. Christabel Pankhurst, "How to Stop Militancy," *The Suffragette*, February 28, 1913, 308.

11. *The Suffragette*, December 6, 1912, 116.

12. Christabel Pankhurst, "Broken Windows," *Votes for Women*, December 1, 1911, 142.

13. "Window Breaking: To One Who Has Suffered," in Jane Marcus, ed., *Suffrage and the Pankhursts* (London: Routledge & Kegan Paul, 1987), 183–84.

14. Emmeline Pankhurst, Verbatim report of Mrs. Pankhurst's speech, delivered Nov. 13, 1913 at Parson's Theatre, Hartford, Connecticut (Connecticut: Connecticut Woman Suffrage Association, 1913), 17 (hereafter cited as "Hartford").

15. Franklyn S. Haiman, "The Rhetoric of the Streets: Some Legal and Ethical Considerations," in *Dissent: Symbolic Behavior and Rhetorical*

Strategies, ed. Haig A. Bosmajian (Westport, Conn.: Greenwood Press, 1972), 134, 139.

16. Emmeline Pankhurst, "The Women's Insurrection," *The Suffragette*, February 28, 1913, 309.

17. Emmeline Pankhurst, "Hartford," 16.

18. Sandra Stanley Holton, "In Sorrowful Wrath: Suffrage Militancy and the Romantic Feminism of Emmeline Pankhurst," in *British Feminism in the Twentieth Century*, ed. Harold L. Smith (Amherst: University of Massachusetts Press, 1990), 21, 20.

19. Emmeline Pankhurst, "Hartford," 16.

20. *The Suffragette*, December 13, 1912, 132.

21. Chaim Perelman and Lucie Olbrechts-Tyteca, *The New Rhetoric: A Treatise on Argumentation* (Notre Dame, Ind.: University of Notre Dame Press, 1969), 18.

22. Lisa Tickner, *The Spectacle of Women: Imagery of the Suffrage Campaign, 1907–14* (Chicago: University of Chicago Press), 136.

23. Flora Drummond, "The Great God Property," *The Suffragette*, March 20, 1914, 517.

24. *The Suffragette*, February 21, 1913, 285.

25. Emmeline Pankhurst, "Women's Insurrection," 309.

26. Emmeline Pankhurst, "Hartford," 20.

27. Ibid., 34.

28. Christabel Pankhurst, "Broken Windows," 142.

29. Mary R. Richardson, *Laugh a Defiance* (London: George Weidenfeld & Nicolson, 1953), 22.

30. Christabel Pankhurst, "Why the Union Is Strong," *The Suffragette*, December 27, 1912, 160.

31. Christabel Pankhurst, "The War against Slavery," *The Suffragette*, April 11, 1913, 426.

32. Christabel Pankhurst, "Why the Union Is Strong," 160.

33. Emmeline Pankhurst, "Hartford," 8.

34. Christabel Pankhurst, "Stoning the Prophets," *The Suffragette*, March 21, 1913, 366; Christabel Pankhurst, "Standards of Morality," *The Suffragette*, April 4, 1913, 404.

35. Christabel Pankhurst, "Why the Union Is Strong," 160.

36. William O'Brien, "The Challenge of War: A Christian Realist Perspective," in *Just War Theory*, ed. Jean Bethke Elshtain (New York: New York University Press, 1992), 260–64.

37. Christabel Pankhurst, "Why the Union Is Strong," 160.

38. Christabel Pankhurst, "Christmas Comes Again," *The Suffragette*, December 26, 1913, 250.

39. Laurence Housman, "Proper Lessons," *Votes for Women*, April 5, 1912, 429.

40. Emmeline Pankhurst, "Hartford," 21.

41. Christabel Pankhurst, "Burnt Letters," *The Suffragette*, December 6, 1912, 114.

42. Holton, "In Sorrowful Wrath," 13–14.

43. Ibid., 11–12.

44. Christabel Pankhurst, "Shall Women Fight?" *The Suffragette,* November 1, 1912, 36.

45. Mrs. Zangwill, "The Burning Question," *The Suffragette,* May 23, 1913, 530.

46. Christabel Pankhurst, "Militancy Wins," *The Suffragette,* November 21, 1913, 126; *The Suffragette,* February 27, 1914, 450.

47. Jean Bethke Elshtain, "Reflections on War and Political Discourse: Realism, Just War, and Feminism in the Nuclear Age," in *Just War Theory,* ed. Jean Bethke Elshtain (New York: New York University Press, 1992), 272

48. "War—Why We Are Militant," *The Suffragette,* November 15, 1912, 67.

49. "Militancy—A Spreading Fire," *The Suffragette,* December 6, 1912, 116.

50. Mrs. Zangwill, "The Burning Question," 530.

51. *The Suffragette,* January 3, 1913, 169.

52. "The Conspiracy Trial of the Old Bailey," *Votes for Women,* May 24, 1912, 547.

53. David Mitchell, *Queen Christabel* (London: MacDonald and Jane's, 1977), 238.

54. Quoted in ibid., 225.

55. *The Suffragette,* January 3, 1913, 169.

56. Quoted in Mitchell, *Queen Christabel,* 241.

57. Midge Mackenzie, *Shoulder to Shoulder* (New York: Knopf, 1975), 261.

58. Mitchell, *Queen Christabel,* 240.

59. *The Suffragette,* October 18, 1912, 4.

60. Perelman and Olbrechts-Tyteca, *The New Rhetoric,* 221.

61. Christabel Pankhurst, "Burnt Letters," 114.

62. "Militancy and Warfare," *Votes for Women,* August 2, 1912, 717.

63. Ibid.

64. *The Suffragette,* February 14, 1913, 270.

65. Christabel Pankhurst, "Burnt Letters," 114.

66. "Militancy and Warfare," 717.

67. Christabel Pankhurst, "Shall Women Fight?" *The Suffragette,* November 1, 1912, 36.

68. Christabel Pankhurst, "The War against Slavery," 426.

69. "Militancy and Warfare," 717.

70. Christabel Pankhurst, *Unshackled: The Story of How We Won the Vote* (London: Hutchinson, 1959), 263.

71. "The Methods of the Suffragettes," *The Suffragette,* February 14, 1913, 270.

72. Christabel Pankhurst, "History Repeating Itself," *The Suffragette,* March 14, 1913, 348.

73. *The Suffragette,* February 28, 1913, 301.

74. Annie Kenney, "A Real Fraternity," *The Suffragette,* August 15, 1913, 763.

75. Emmeline Pankhurst, "Mrs. Pankhurst's Great Speech," *Votes for Women,* May 24, 1912, 534.

76. Thomas E. Murray, *Nuclear Policy for War and Peace* (Cleveland and

New York: World Publishing Co., 1960), quoted in Ramsey, *War and the Christian Conscience*, 275–76.

77. Christabel Pankhurst, "The Martyr Spirit," *The Suffragette*, March 28, 1913, 384.

78. Emmeline Pankhurst, "Hartford," 10.

79. "Violent and Lawless Action," *Votes for Women*, July 26, 1912, 700.

80. "Feeding by Violence," *The Suffragette*, January 10, 1913, 181.

81. Emmeline Pankhurst, "Kill Me, or Give Me My Freedom!" *The Suffragette*, July 18, 1913, 677.

82. Drummond, "The Great God Property," 517.

83. *The Suffragette*, May 8, 1914, 77.

84. Emmeline Pankhurst, *My Own Story* (New York: Source Book Press, 1970), 268.

85. Quoted in "Standards of Morality," *The Suffragette*, April 4, 1913, 404.

86. Ibid.

87. Ibid.

88. Annie Kenney, "Our Spirits Are Eternal," *The Suffragette*, July 18, 1913, 675.

89. *The Suffragette*, November 1, 1912, 29.

90. Emmeline Pankhurst, "Hartford," 6.

91. Christabel Pankhurst, "Christmas Comes Again," 250.

92. The Rev. Edwin A. Mould, "The Suffrage Tangle," *The Suffragette*, May 30, 1913, 546.

93. Christabel Pankhurst, " 'An Invincible Repugnance to Disorder,' " *The Suffragette*, November 22, 1912, 82.

Chapter 6. Evil That Good May Come

1. Paul Ramsey, *War and the Christian Conscience: How Shall Modern War Be Conducted Justly?* (North Carolina, N.C.: Duke University Press, 1961), 43.

2. Robert L. Ivie, "Images of Savagery in American Justifications for War," *Communication Monographs* 47 (November 1980): 283n.

3. Ernest Ruede, *The Morality of War: The Just War Theory and the Problem of Nuclear Deterrence in R. Paul Ramsey* (Dublin: Cahill & Co., 1972), 72

4. Ramsey, *War and the Christian Conscience*, 80.

5. Paul Ramsey, *Speak Up for Just War or Pacifism: A Critique of the United Methodist Bishops' Pastoral Letter "In Defense of Creation"* (University Park: Pennsylvania State University Press, 1988), 89.

6. Paul Ramsey, *The Just War: Force and Political Responsibility* (New York: Scribner, 1968), 143, 142, 143.

7. Marie Naylor, "At the Steinway Hall," *The Suffragette*, October 18, 1912, 4.

8. *Votes for Women*, December 22, 1911, 185.

9. *The Suffragette*, December 27, 1912, 157.

10. Christabel Pankhurst, "Women at War," *The Suffragette*, October 25, 1912, 20.

11. Christabel Pankhurst, "Burnt Letters," *The Suffragette*, December 6, 1912, 114.

12. *The Suffragette*, December 20, 1912, 141.

13. Christabel Pankhurst, "Broken Windows," *Votes for Women*, December 1, 1911, 142.

14. "Political Prisoners," *Votes for Women*, May 17, 1912, 520.

15. Christabel Pankhurst, "Christmas Comes Again," *The Suffragette*, December 26, 1913, 250.

16. Emmeline Pankhurst, "Victory Is Assured," *The Suffragette*, February 13, 1914, 397.

17. *Votes for Women*, May 24, 1912, 545, 548; Emmeline Pethick-Lawrence, "Men Do Not Argue with a Flood," *Votes for Women*, June 20, 1913, 557; Emmeline Pethick-Lawrence, "In Women's Shoes," *Votes for Women*, June 13, 1913, 541.

18. *The Suffragette*, March 6, 1914, 462.

19. "The Deserters," *Votes for Women*, March 15, 1912, 376.

20. *The Suffragette*, February 28, 1913, 310.

21. Frederick Pethick-Lawrence, *Votes for Women*, May 31, 1912, 557.

22. *Votes for Women*, August 9, 1912, 738.

23. *Votes for Women*, April 5, 1912, 421.

24. Frederick Pethick-Lawrence, "Speech for the Defence," *Votes for Women*, May 31, 1912, 557–58.

25. Christabel Pankhurst, "Burnt Letters," 114.

26. Emmeline Pethick-Lawrence, *My Part in a Changing World* (London: Victor Gollancz, 1938), 263.

27. Christabel Pankhurst, "Militancy a Virtue," *The Suffragette*, January 10, 1913, 186.

28. Marie Naylor, "Evil That Good May Come," *The Suffragette*, March 27, 1914, 547.

29. Emmeline Pankhurst, "Victory," 397.

30. *Votes for Women*, August 2, 1912, 711.

31. *Votes for Women*, March 22, 1912, 385.

32. George Bernard Shaw, "We Are Members One of Another," *The Suffragette*, March 28, 1913, 380.

33. Christabel Pankhurst, "History Repeating Itself," *The Suffragette*, March 14, 1913, 348.

34. The Rev. E. H. Taylor, "Christian Atrocities," *The Suffragette*, September 5, 1913, 820.

35. Christabel Pankhurst, "Human Life in Danger," *The Suffragette*, April 25, 1913, 474.

36. James Russell Lowell, "The Present Crisis," *The Suffragette*, March 21, 1913, 361.

37. Joseph Clayton, "The Intolerable Tyranny That Provokes Rebellion," *The Suffragette*, November 8, 1912, 53.

38. Richard E. Rubenstein, *Alchemists of Revolution: Terrorism in the Modern World* (New York: Basic Books, 1987), 26–27, 22.

39. Emmeline Pankhurst, *My Own Story* (New York: Source Book Press, 1970), n.p.

40. Emmeline Pethick-Lawrence, *My Part in a Changing World*, 275.

41. *The Suffragette*, December 6, 1912, 116.

42. Jane Marcus, ed., *Suffrage and the Pankhursts* (London: Routledge & Kegan Paul), 184.

43. Mr. Healy, "A Great State Trial," *Votes for Women*, May 31, 1912, 559.

44. Annie Besant, "Crowned with Honour," *Votes for Women*, April 5, 1912, 423.

45. David Mitchell, *Queen Christabel* (London: MacDonald & Jane's, 1977), 212.

46. William O'Brien, *The Conduct of Just and Limited War* (New York: Praeger, 1981), 164.

47. Robert L. Ivie, "Presidential Motives for War," *Quarterly Journal of Speech* 60 (October 1974): 344.

48. George Lansbury, "Put Not Your Trust in Politicians," *The Suffragette*, October 25, 1912, 18.

49. "Methods of Violence," *Votes for Women*, June 7, 1912, 584.

50. Emmeline Pankhurst, "Victory Is Assured," 397.

51. Emmeline Pankhurst, "I Defy Them to Make Me Submit," *The Suffragette*, February 27, 1914, 446.

52. Lucius Grant, "Springtime," *Votes for Women*, March 8, 1912, 356.

53. On this point particularly see Samuel Hynes, *The Edwardian Turn of Mind* (Princeton, N.J.: Princeton University Press, 1968), 14.

54. Annie Kenney, "The One Union," *The Suffragette*, July 31, 1914, 281.

55. Flora Drummond, "The Great God Property," *The Suffragette*, March 27, 1914, 543.

56. Christabel Pankhurst, "The War against Slavery," *The Suffragette*, April 11, 1913, 426.

Conclusion

1. Christabel Pankhurst, "Stoning the Prophets," *The Suffragette*, March 21, 1913, 366.

2. Midge Mackenzie, *Shoulder To Shoulder* (New York: Knopf, 1975), 280.

3. Ibid., 283, 288.

4. Ibid., 283.

5. Ibid., 294.

6. Ibid., 318, 325.

7. Ibid., 326–28.

8. Ibid., 316–17.

9. Estelle Sylvia Pankhurst, *The Life of Emmeline Pankhurst: The Suffragette Struggle for Women's Citizenship* (London: T. Werner Laurie, 1935), 162.

10. Alex P. Schmid and Janny de Graaf, *Violence as Communication: Insurgent Terrorism and the Western News Media* (London: Sage, 1982), 217.

11. Lisa Tickner, *The Spectacle of Women: Imagery of the Suffrage Campaign, 1907–1914* (Chicago: University of Chicago Press, 1988), 230.

12. Quoted in Roberta Kay Carson, "From Teacups to Terror: The Rhetorical Strategies of the Women's Social and Political Union, 1903–1915" (Ph.D. diss., University of Iowa, 1975), 302–3.

13. Quoted in ibid., 303.

14. Tickner, *The Spectacle of Women*, 230.

15. Quoted in Carson, "From Teacups to Terror," 267.

16. Ibid., 233.

17. Eugene Garver, *Machiavelli and the History of Prudence* (Madison: University of Wisconsin Press, 1987), 110, 69, 133, 70.

18. *The Suffragette*, March 27, 1914, 541.

19. Emmeline Pethick-Lawrence, *My Part in a Changing World* (London: Victor Gollancz, 1938), 298.

20. *The Suffragette*, July 3, 1914, 194, 206, 212.

21. Constance Rover, *Women's Suffrage and Party Politics in Britain, 1866–1914* (London: Routledge & Kegan Paul, 1967), 92.

22. Brian Harrison, *Separate Spheres* (London: Croom Helm, 1978), 186–87. For Harrison's complete argument see his chapter "Scoring Off the Suffragettes," pp. 175–201.

23. Tickner, *The Spectacle of Women*, 201, 135.

24. Mary R. Richardson, *Laugh a Defiance* (London: George Weidenfeld & Nicolson, 1953), 192.

25. Annie Kenney, *Memories of a Militant* (London: Edward Arnold & Co., 1934), 190.

26. Brian Harrison, "The Act of Militancy: Violence and the Suffragettes, 1904–1914," in *Peaceable Kingdom: Stability and Change in Modern Britain* (Oxford: Clarendon Press, 1982), 26–81.

27. *The Suffragette*, December 20, 1912, 141.

28. Carson, "From Teacups to Terror," 59.

29. Mrs. Zangwill, "The Burning Question," *The Suffragette*, May 23, 1913, 530.

30. Rover, *Women's Suffrage*, 92.

31. Ibid., 91, 99.

32. Richard Leeman, *The Rhetoric of Terrorism and Counterterrorism* (Westport, Conn.: Greenwood Press, 1991), 46, 55, 50–51, 52.

33. Quoted in Leeman, *Rhetoric of Terrorism*, 53.

34. Emmeline Pethick-Lawrence, "Be Ready!" *Votes for Women*, February 9, 1912, 292.

35. Emmeline Pankhurst, "Speech at Albert Hall," *The Suffragette*, October 25, 1912, 16.

36. Leeman, *Rhetoric of Terrorism*, 64.

37. Ibid.

38. Garver, *Machiavelli*, 108.

39. "Militancy and Warfare," *Votes for Women*, August 2, 1912, 717.

Selected Bibliography

Andrew, James R. "The Passionate Negation: The Chartist Movement in Rhetorical Perspective." *Quarterly Journal of Speech* 59 (April 1973): 196–208.

Bailey, Harry A. "Confrontations as an Extension of Communication." In *Dissent: Symbolic Behavior and Rhetorical Strategies*, edited by Haig A. Bosmajian. Westport, Conn.: Greenwood Press, 1972.

Burke, Kenneth. "Definition of Man." In *Language as Symbolic Action*. Berkeley: University of California Press, 1966.

———. "The Rhetorical Situation." In *Communication: Ethical and Moral Essays*, edited by Lee Thayer. London: Gordon & Bleach Science Publishers, 1973.

Campbell, John Angus. "Scientific Revolution and the Grammar of Culture: The Case of Darwin's Origin." *Quarterly Journal of Speech* 72 (November 1986): 351–76.

Campbell, Karlyn Kohrs. *Man Cannot Speak for Her.* 2 vols. New York: Praeger, 1989.

———. "The Rhetoric of Women's Liberation: An Oxymoron." *Quarterly Journal of Speech* 59 (February 1973): 74–86.

Carson, Roberta Kay. "From Teacups to Terror: The Rhetorical Strategies of the Women's Social and Political Union, 1903–1918." Ph.D. diss., University of Iowa, 1975.

Chambers Biographical Dictionary. Edited by J. O. Thorne. New York: St. Martin's Press, 1969.

Coser, Lewis A. *The Functions of Social Conflict.* Glencoe, Ill.: Free Press, 1956.

Crenshaw, Martha. *Terrorism, Legitimacy, and Power: The Consequences of Political Violence*. Middletown, Conn.: Wesleyan University Press, 1983.

Crow, Duncan. *The Edwardian Woman*. London: George Allen & Unwin, 1978.

Dangerfield, George. *The Strange Death of Liberal England*. New York: Capricorn Books, 1961.

Davis, Grady Scott. *Warcraft and the Fragility of Virtue: An Essay in Aristotelian Ethics*. Moscow: University of Idaho Press, 1992.

Elshtain, Jean Bethke. "Reflections on War and Political Discourse: Realism, Just War, and Feminism in the Nuclear Age." In *Just War Theory*, edited by Jean Bethke Elshtain. New York: New York University Press, 1992.

Ferguson, Kathy. *The Feminist Case against Bureaucracy*. Philadelphia: Temple University Press, 1984.

Fulford, Roger. *Votes for Women: The Story of a Struggle*. London: Faber & Faber, 1957.

Garver, Eugene. *Machiavelli and the History of Prudence*. Madison: University of Wisconsin Press, 1987.

Gerrits, Robin P. J. M. "Terrorists' Perspectives: Memoirs." In *Terrorism and the Media*, edited by David L. Paletz and Alex P. Schmid. Newbury Park, Calif.: Sage, 1992.

Gude, Edward W. "Political Violence in Venezuela: 1958–1964." In *When Men Revolt and Why: A Reader in Political Violence and Revolution*, edited by James Chowning Davies. New York: Free Press, 1971.

Hacker, Frederick. *Crusaders, Criminals, and Crazies: Terror and Terrorism in Our Time*. New York: Norton, 1976.

Haiman, Franklyn S. "The Rhetoric of the Streets: Some Legal and Ethical Considerations." In *Dissent: Symbolic Behavior and Rhetorical Strategies*, edited by Haig A. Bosmajian. Westport, Conn.: Greenwood Press, 1972.

Harrison, Brian. "The Act of Militancy: Violence and the Suffragettes, 1904–1914." In *Peaceable Kingdom: Stability and Change in Modern Britain*. Oxford: Clarendon Press, 1982.

———. *Separate Spheres*. London: Croom Helm, 1978.

Holton, Sandra Stanley. "In Sorrowful Wrath: Suffrage Militancy and the Romantic Feminism of Emmeline Pankhurst." In *British Feminism in the Twentieth Century*, edited by Harold L. Smith. Amherst: University of Massachusetts Press, 1990.

Hynes, Samuel. *The Edwardian Turn of Mind*. Princeton, N.J.: Princeton University Press, 1968.

Ivie, Robert L. "Images of Savagery in American Justifications for War." *Communication Monographs* 47 (November 1980): 279–94.

———. "Presidential Motives for War." *Quarterly Journal of Speech* 60 (October 1974): 337–45.

Johnson, Chalmers. "Perspectives on Terrorism." In *The Terrorism Reader*, edited by Walter Laqueur. Philadelphia: Temple University Press, 1978.

Johnson, James Turner. *Ideology, Reason, and the Limitation of War: Religious and Secular Concepts, 1200–1740*. Princeton, N.J.: Princeton University Press, 1975.

Jorgensen-Earp, Cheryl R. "The Lady, the Whore, and the Spinster: The Rhetorical Use of Victorian Images of Women." *Western Journal of Speech Communication* 54 (Winter 1990): 82–98.

Kaufer, David S., and Christine M. Newwirth. "Foregrounding Norms and Ironic Communication." *Quarterly Journal of Speech* 68 (February 1982): 28–36.

Kenney, Annie. *Memories of a Militant.* London: Edward Arnold & Co., 1924.

Kent, Susan Kingsley. *Sex and Suffrage in Britain, 1860–1914.* Princeton, N.J.: Princeton University Press, 1987.

Kropotkin, Peter. "On the Need for Individual Action." In *Revolutionaries on Revolution: Participants' Perspectives on the Strategies of Seizing Power,* edited by Phillip B. Springer and Marcello Truzzo. Pacific Palisades, Calif.: Goodyear Publishing, 1973.

Lakey, George. "Technique and Ethos in Nonviolent Action: The Woman Suffrage Case." In *Dissent: Symbolic Behavior and Rhetorical Strategies,* edited by Haig A. Bosmajian. Westport, Conn.: Greenwood Press, 1980.

Leeman, Richard W. *The Rhetoric of Terrorism and Counterterrorism.* Westport, Conn.: Greenwood Press, 1991.

Lytton, Lady Constance. *Prisons and Prisoners: Some Personal Experiences by Constance Lytton and Jane Warton, Spinster.* London: William Heinemann, 1914.

Mackenzie, Midge. *Shoulder to Shoulder.* New York: Knopf, 1975.

Marcus, Jane, ed. *Suffrage and the Pankhursts.* London: Routledge & Kegan Paul, 1987.

Massie, Robert K. *Dreadnought: Britain, Germany, and the Coming of the Great War.* New York: Random House, 1991.

Miller, Richard B. *Interpretations of Conflict: Ethics, Pacifism, and the Just-War Tradition.* Chicago: University of Chicago Press, 1990.

Mitchell, David. *The Fighting Pankhursts: A Study in Tenacity.* New York: Macmillan, 1967.

———. *Queen Christabel.* London: MacDonald & Jane's, 1977.

Morgan, Robin. *The Demon Lover: On the Sexuality of Terrorism.* New York: Norton, 1989.

Murray, Thomas E. *Nuclear Policy for War and Peace.* Cleveland and New York: World Publishing Co., 1960.

O'Brien, William. "The Challenge of War: A Christian Realist Perspective." In *Just War Theory,* edited by Jean Bethke Elshtain. New York: New York University Press, 1992.

———. *The Conduct of Just and Limited War.* New York: Praeger, 1981.

Pankhurst, Christabel. *Unshackled: The Story of How We Won the Vote.* London: Hutchinson, 1959.

Pankhurst, Emmeline. *My Own Story.* New York: Hearst's International Library, 1914.

———. Verbatim report of Mrs. Pankhurst's speech, delivered Nov. 13, 1913 at Parson's Theatre, Hartford, Conn. Hartford: The Connecticut Woman Suffrage Association, 1913. General Research Division, The New York Public Library, Astor, Lenox and Tilden Foundations (SNS p.v. 14).

Pankhurst, Estelle Sylvia. *The Life of Emmeline Pankhurst: The Suffragette Struggle for Women's Citizenship.* London: T. Werner Laurie, 1935.

Perelman, Chaim. *Justice.* New York: Random House, 1967.

———. *The New Rhetoric and the Humanities: Essays on Rhetoric and Its Applications.* London: Reidel, 1979.

———. *The Realm of Rhetoric.* Notre Dame, Ind.: University of Notre Dame Press, 1982.

Perelman, Chaim, and Lucie Olbrechts-Tyteca. *The New Rhetoric: A Treatise on Argumentation.* Notre Dame, Ind.: University of Notre Dame Press, 1969.

Peterson, Owen. "Boggart Hole Clough: A Nineteenth Century 'Speak-In' " *Southern Speech Journal* 35 (Summer 1970): 287–94.

Pethick-Lawrence, Emmeline. *My Part in a Changing World.* London: Victor Gollancz, 1938.

Priestley, J. B. *The Edwardians.* New York: Harper & Row, 1970.

Raeburn, Antonia. *The Militant Suffragettes.* London: Joseph, 1973.

———. *The Suffragette View.* New York: St. Martin's Press, 1976.

Ramsey, Paul. *The Just War: Force and Political Responsibility.* New York: Scribner, 1968.

———. *Speak Up for Just War or Pacifism: A Critique of the United Methodist Bishops' Pastoral Letter "In Defense of Creation."* University Park: Pennsylvania State University Press, 1988.

———. *War and the Christian Conscience: How Shall Modern War Be Conducted Justly?* Durham, N.C.: Duke University Press, 1961.

Read, Donald. *Edwardian England.* London: The Historical Association, 1972.

Richardson, Mary R. *Laugh a Defiance.* London: George Weidenfeld & Nicolson, 1953.

Rosen, Andrew. *Rise Up, Women! The Militant Campaign of the Women's Social and Political Union, 1903–1914.* London: Routledge & Kegan Paul, 1974.

Rover, Constance. *Women's Suffrage and Party Politics in Britain, 1866–1914.* London: Routledge & Kegan Paul, 1967.

Rubenstein, Richard E. *Alchemists of Revolution: Terrorism in the Modern World.* New York: Basic Books, 1987.

Ruede, Ernest. *The Morality of War: The Just War Theory and the Problem of Nuclear Deterrence in R. Paul Ramsey.* Dublin: Cahill & Co., 1972.

Schmid, Alex P., and Janny de Graaf. *Violence as Communication: Insurgent Terrorism and the Western News Media.* London: Sage, 1982.

Scott, Robert L. "Justifying Violence—The Rhetoric of Militant Black Power." *Central States Speech Journal* 19 (Summer 1968): 96–104.

Simons, Herbert W. "Requirements, Problems, and Strategies: A Theory of Persuasion for Social Movements." *Quarterly Journal of Speech* 56 (February 1970): 1–11.

Skolnick, Jerome H. "The Politics of Protest." In *Dissent: Symbolic Behavior and Rhetorical Strategies,* edited by Haig A. Bosmajian. Westport, Conn.: Greenwood Press, 1972.

Strachey, Ray. *The Cause: A Short History of the Women's Movement in Great Britain*. 1928. Reprint, New York: Kennikat Press, 1969.

Taylor, Maxwell. *The Terrorist*. London: Brassey's Defence Publishers, 1988.

Tickner, Lisa. *The Spectacle of Women: Imagery of the Suffrage Campaign, 1907–14*. Chicago: University of Chicago Press, 1988.

Tucker, Robert W. *The Just War: A Study in Contemporary American Doctrine*. Baltimore: Johns Hopkins University Press, 1960.

Tugwell, Maurice A. J. "Guilt Transfer." In *The Morality of Terrorism: Religious and Secular Justifications*, edited by David C. Rapoport and Yonah Alexander. New York: Pergamon Press, 1982.

Vatz, Richard E. "The Myth of the Rhetorical Situation." *Philosophy and Rhetoric* 6 (Summer 1973): 154–61.

Vicinus, Martha, ed. *A Widening Sphere: Changing Roles of Victorian Women*. Bloomington: Indiana University Press, 1977.

Wilkinson, Paul. *Terrorism and the Liberal State*. 2nd ed. New York: New York University Press, 1986.

Index

About the Series

STUDIES IN RHETORIC AND COMMUNICATION
General Editors:
E. Culpepper Clark, Raymie E. McKerrow, and David Zarefsky

The University of Alabama Press has established this series to publish major new works in the general area of rhetoric and communication, including books treating the symbolic manifestations of political discourse, argument as social knowledge, the impact of machine technology on patterns of communication behavior, and other topics related to the nature or impact of symbolic communication. We actively solicit studies involving historical, critical, or theoretical analyses of human discourse.

About the Author

Cheryl R. Jorgensen-Earp is an Assistant Professor of Communication Studies, Lynchburg College. She has a bachelor's degree in Speech and Dramatic Art and a master's degree in Dramatic Art from the University of North Carolina, Chapel Hill. She obtained a master's degree and a doctorate in Speech Communication from the University of Washington.